Praise for *How You Can Profit from Credit Cards*

This book is a must-read for credit card holders of all ages. Curtis Arnold offers insights into how consumers can not only profit financially from credit cards, but importantly, how to avoid falling into debt.

—Thomas R. Evans
President and CEO of BankRate.com, Inc.

Finally, someone has written a guide for savvy consumers who want to make the most of the plastic in their wallets. Curtis Arnold explains exactly how to maximize your rewards so you're quite literally getting free money and also outlines winning strategies for negotiating the lowest interest rate and using balance transfers to your advantage. Anyone who wants to build credit, improve their credit, or profit from their credit cards should read this book.

—Liz Pulliam Weston
MSN Money Personal Finance Columnist and
Bestselling Author of *Your Credit Score* and *Easy Money*

Curtis Arnold is America's premier credit card expert. Whether you're trying to get your first card, compare credit offers, or figure out how to beat the credit card companies at their own game, Arnold's wisdom and insider tips will prove invaluable.

—Lynnette Khalfani-Cox
The "Money Coach" and Author of *The New York Times*
Bestseller *Zero Debt: The Ultimate Guide
to Financial Freedom*

If you have had enough of credit card tricks and traps, this book will show you how to turn the tables. Curtis Arnold knows the credit card business inside and out and offers proven ways to put plastic to work for you, rather than against you.

—Gerri Detweiler
Consumer Advocate and Author of four books
on personal finance including the
forthcoming book *Stop Debt Collectors*

For most Americans, credit cards are seen as a necessary evil. Curtis Arnold transforms that perception. Using his advice, people can get rebates, perks, better interest rates, and all kinds of benefits from their cards that they never knew were possible. This book helps you become the master of your credit cards instead of a victim.

—Jordan E. Goodman
"America's Money Answers Man" and Bestselling
Author of *Everyone's Money Book on Credit*

Curtis Arnold provides you with tips for protecting yourself from costly credit card traps, how to use credit to your advantage, and much more. This is a must-read book!

—Marcia Brixey
Author of *The Money Therapist*
and Founder and President of
Money Wise Women Educational Services

How You Can Profit from Credit Cards

HOW YOU CAN PROFIT FROM CREDIT CARDS

Using Credit to Improve Your Financial Life and Bottom Line

Curtis E. Arnold

Vice President, Publisher: Tim Moore
Associate Publisher and Director of Marketing: Amy Neidlinger
Executive Editor: Jim Boyd
Editorial Assistant: Pamela Boland
Development Editor: Russ Hall
Operations Manager: Gina Kanouse
Digital Marketing Manager: Julie Phifer
Assistant Marketing Manager: Megan Colvin
Cover Designer: John Barnett
Managing Editor: Kristy Hart
Project Editor: Jovana San Nicolas-Shirley
Copy Editor: Krista Hansing Editorial Services, Inc.
Proofreader: Heather Waye Arle
Indexer: Lisa Stumpf
Compositor: Nonie Ratcliff
Manufacturing Buyer: Dan Uhrig

© 2008 by Pearson Education, Inc.
Publishing as FT Press
Upper Saddle River, New Jersey 07458

FT Press offers excellent discounts on this book when ordered in quantity
for bulk purchases or special sales. For more information, please contact
U.S. Corporate and Government Sales, 1-800-382-3419,
corpsales@pearsontechgroup.com. For sales outside the U.S., please
contact International Sales at international@pearson.com.

Printed in the United States of America

First Printing: June 2008

ISBN-10: 0-13-235377-6
ISBN-13: 978-0-13-235377-9

Pearson Education LTD.
Pearson Education Australia PTY, Limited.
Pearson Education Singapore, Pte. Ltd.
Pearson Education North Asia, Ltd.
Pearson Education Canada, Ltd.
Pearson Educatión de Mexico, S.A. de C.V.
Pearson Education—Japan
Pearson Education Malaysia, Pte. Ltd.

Library of Congress Cataloging-in-Publication Data

Arnold, Curtis E.
    How you can profit from credit cards : using credit to improve your financial
life and bottom line / Curtis E Arnold.
        p. cm.
    ISBN 0-13-235377-6 (pbk. : alk. paper) 1. Credit cards. 2. Consumer credit.
3. Finance, Personal. I. Title.
    HG3755.7.A76 2008
    332.7'65—dc22

2008011159

To my wonderful wife, Nancy. Thank you for being my best friend and for the countless times you embraced me after a long day at the office. Together, we're teaching the next generation about credit and money issues—including our own kids, Dallas, Erin, Hunter, Avery, and Claire—which gives me hope that today's young people will be much savvier about credit and money issues than any previous generation.

CONTENTS

Chapter 1   **It's Not Just Plastic—It's Money** 1

The Power of Credit Cards 1

Choosing a Credit Card That Will
Benefit Your Bottom Line 3

Stricter Liability Laws 4

Consumer Protection 5

Establish or Build Your Credit 6

Which Card Should Be in
Your Wallet? 6

Chapter 2   **Show Me the Money! Credit Card
Rebates** 23

America's Love Affair with Card
Rebates 23

What You Need to Know to Make
the Most of Cash-Back Cards 30

You've Considered the Basics,
Now... 34

You Might Also Want to Consider... . . . 39

Cut Your Gas Bill by 5% with Gas
Rebate Credit Cards 41

Should You Get an Airline
Reward Card? 43

Have Fun 50

Chapter 3   **Unlock the Key to Huge Savings:**
Master Credit Card Rates
and Transfer Offers 51

Know Your Interest Rate 52

How Your Rate Is Determined 52

Is a Fixed Rate Truly Fixed? 57

Fees 65

The Three Keys to Using a Low-Rate
Card to Your Advantage 66

Low-Rate Introductory Offers
and Blank Checks 69

Use a Low-Rate Credit Card
to Pay Down Any Type of Loan 73

Chapter 4   **Avoid Problems That Hinder**
Maximum Profits 75

Avoid Card Debt: Preventive
Medicine for Your Pocketbook 77

1. Keep Some Perspective—Don't Fall
for the Hype 77

2. Actively Manage Your Finances 78

3. Reach Out to Get Support
and Save Money 80

4. Avoid Extra Expenses 81

5. Is a Card Right for You? 82

6. Pay the Balance in Full 82

7. Pay Before Your Due Date 83

8. Treat Your Credit Cards like Cash . . . 84

9. Limit the Plastic in Your Pocket 85

10. Cash Advances = Financial
Suicide? 85

11. Say "No!" to Extra Products
and Services 86

12. Benefit from Planning
and Saving 86

Chapter 5   How to Slash Your Debt and Keep Your
Hard-Earned Money for Yourself 89

Is It Time to Get Serious about
Your Debts? 90

Diagnose the Problem 91

Planning a Debt-Defying Strategy:
The Basics 92

Create a Repayment Plan:
The Do-It-Yourself Strategy 98

More Proven Techniques to Pay
Down Debt 102

Is It Time for Professional Help? 109

Debt Settlement and/or Negotiation . . . 114

Bankruptcy 115

Chapter 6 **Watch Out: Traps and Scams
Can Cost You Big Bucks!** 119

Grace Periods Are Shrinking 120

Confusing Cash Advance Fees 122

Small Cash Advances Have
Sky-High Interest Rates 123

Trailing Interest: A Phantom Interest
Charge 124

Credit Discrimination: Retirees
and Race 127

Where to Turn for Help 129

Credit Card Fraud and
Credit-Related Scams 130

Elder Fraud 133

Life after ID Theft: A Step-by-Step
Plan of Action 139

Is ID Theft Insurance the Answer? 147

Protecting Yourself from Fraud 149

Virtual Account Numbers Offer
Extra Online Security 151

Virtual Numbers: What's the Point? .. 152

Some Final Tips 153

Chapter 7   **Start Out on the Right Foot: Credit Cards for Students and Saving for College** 155

Why Do Credit Card Companies Court College Students? 156

Mixed Marketing Messages 157

The New College Order 159

Remembering Sean Moyer 160

How Students, Their Families, and the Industry Can All Win 160

You Have to Start Somewhere: Money Management 101 162

Should My Teenager Get a Credit Card? 164

Foundations for Good Credit: Tips for College Students 166

Keeping It Good 168

Developing a New View about Credit 168

Advice to Grow On 169

Saving for College Tuition 172

You Are in the Driver's Seat 177

Chapter 8   **Use Targeted Cards to Your Financial Advantage** 179

Need to Rebuild or Build Credit? Get a Secured Card 180

How Your Business Can Profit
from Cards 186

Retail and Department Store Cards:
Worth a Look? 193

Affinity Cards: Using a Card
to Help Others 199

Credit Cards for the Rich and
Famous 203

Final Thoughts 207

Chapter 9 **Your Credit Report and Score: The Better
You Look, the More You Profit 209**

Improve Your Credit Report 210

Protecting Your Credit Reports
during Bankruptcy 223

Improve Your Credit Score 227

Where Should I Get My Credit
Score? 234

Final Tips 235

Chapter 10 **Maximize the Benefits of Your Cards
by Taking Advantage of Additional
Free Perks 237**

Purchase Protection 238

Purchase Protection for All 239

Extended Warranties 240

Special Merchandise Discounts 242

Travel Insurance 243

Rental Car Insurance 244

Price Protection 247

Lost Luggage Help 249

International Travel Discounts 249

Card Registration Services 251

Credit Card Protection Insurance
(aka Credit Insurance) 254

Final Thoughts 256

Chapter 11 **Master Advanced Card Techniques to
Save and Make Money** 259

Reallocating Credit Lines 259

Making Biweekly Credit Card
Payments 262

Using Credit Cards to Make
Money 264

Paying Your Taxes with a
Credit Card 272

Steering Clear of Universal Default . . . 274

Chapter 12 **Capitalize on Future Card Trends** 283

Trend 1: Cards Will Be Accepted
in New Places 283

Trend 2: Cards Will Be Even
Smarter and Safer 285

Trend 3: Issuers Will Keep Finding
New Markets 288

Trend 4: Seniors and Debt—
a Disturbing Trend 291

Credit Cards for Seniors 292

Trend 5: New Enticements Will
Be Trendy, Targeted, and Even
Practical 293

Watch For New Incentive Programs . . . 296

The Rest Is Up to You 297

Glossary 301

Index 315

ACKNOWLEDGMENTS

I'm living the American dream, and I have a lot of people to thank for it. Back in the mid-90s, when I was $45,000 in debt and stressed out to the max, I never would have believed that just a few years later, I'd be the proud owner of an award-winning website that helps people find the best credit cards and get out of debt. I certainly never expected to be in a position to write a book about how to profit from credit cards!

Special thanks to my younger brother, Major Johnpaul Arnold, for his endless encouragement, especially at times when I lacked motivation. I pray for his safe return from his second tour of duty in Iraq.

Special thanks to Mom and Dad as well, for believing in me and instilling a love of learning, which stems from the 40-plus years each has spent teaching in public schools.

These family members and many friends encouraged me to rise above and out of backbreaking debt. I soon wanted to make sure what happened to me wouldn't happen to others. I also began to think about new ways to play my cards, so to speak, putting my plastic to work *for* me—making me money instead of overwhelming me with bills I couldn't pay.

After working for several years in the financial industry, I started CardRatings.com to share what I had learned about credit cards. Never in my wildest dreams did I think we could be responsive to the needs of so many people! But we began hearing from cardholders around the country right away, who have helped to make CardRatings.com even more useful.

I'm especially grateful for the input of the thousands of members of the CardRatings.com forum as well as the many other people who have sent us emails, posted card-holder reviews on the website, and subscribed to our newsletter. Thanks to them the site is truly consumer-powered and consumer-driven!

CardRatings.com freelancers—including Lucy Lazarony, Pammila Allen, Rebecca Lindsey, Amy Arnold, Mike Killian, and Nancy Castleman—were also extremely helpful with *How You Can Profit from Credit Cards*. I will especially be eternally grateful to Nancy for the active role she played—she was my rock and a constant source of wisdom and encouragement. Thanks Nancy!

Heshan Demel, Amber Stubbs, Shane Tripcony, Larry Jameson, Angelica Gooley, and Jessica Austin—the staff at CardRatings.com—deserve my special appreciation for great teamwork, support, research, and a willingness to go the extra mile to make this book a reality. The entire CardRatings.com team has really become an extension of my own family, and I feel very fortunate to have them working on the cause with me.

Thanks also go to the folks at Pearson. I very much appreciate the time and energy that Executive Editor Jim Boyd and Development Editor Russ Hall gave to this project. If you profit from your credit cards, these two men will have had a lot to do with making that possible. Project Editor Jovana San Nicolas-Shirley and Krista Hansing from Editorial Services, Inc. deserve credit for their efforts in polishing the text. And I'm counting on Tim Moore, Amy Neidlinger, Julie Phifer, Megan Colvin, Nonie Ratcliff, Lisa Stumpf, and Dan Uhrig, who also see the potential of this book and will do everything they can to make it fly off the shelves.

MSN Personal Finance Columnist Liz Weston helped me get my foot in the door in the publishing business. Liz was also extremely generous with her expert advice on credit, as was Gerri Detweiler, author of *Invest in Yourself: Six Secrets to a Rich Life*—both taught me a lot about the ins and outs of the industry and helped me ferret out card benefits just sitting there, waiting for us to take advantage of them. Liz and Gerri's dedication to consumers is truly awe-inspiring!

Mary Ann Campbell, who recently got her Ph.D. in personal finance from Iowa State University, deserves special appreciation for her guidance. Mary Ann inspired me to become passionate about personal finance during the early years of CardRatings.com.

I also want to thank the many reporters and editors who have asked me tough questions and helped me educate cardholders about credit. Similarly, the public relations departments in the industry, particularly at Discover, American Express, Citibank, and Chase, deserve thanks for their help with my endless queries about their products and services!

There are wonderful consumer advocates who also deserve all our praise for their passionate work on behalf of consumers. In particular, Dr. Robert Manning, author of *The Credit Card Nation*, Linda Sherry from Consumer Action, Bill Cheeks of the Jump$tart Coalition for Financial Literacy, Scott Bilker, author of *Talk Your Way Out of Credit Card Debt*, and James Walden of Crown Financial Ministries have offered me invaluable guidance over the years. It is truly an honor to have become acquainted with so many folks who care so much about the financial plight of others.

Finally, I want to thank God for the strength He has given me throughout this endeavor. And, if any good comes of this book, He deserves the praise.

ABOUT THE AUTHOR

Curtis E. Arnold, a well-known consumer educator and advocate, is the founder of CardRatings.com, an award-winning website that has been providing objective, current information about credit cards free of charge since 1998. His website has made it easy for millions of cardholders to find more attractive credit cards and lower their card debt.

Some 1,000 unique credit card offerings are rated by both experts and cardholders on CardRatings.com, and new reviews are added daily. Cards are categorized for people with no credit or poor, fair, good, or excellent credit— and by whether they offer a low-interest rate, cash back, miles, or other rewards. CardRatings.com also provides a free forum (containing over 115,000 posts)—where Curtis interacts regularly with participants—to discuss credit issues such as sharing ideas on how to make the most of credit cards, get out of debt, and solve credit issues.

Sharing detailed information with consumers has three important additional benefits from Curtis's point of view: It encourages stronger competition among card issuers, helps create a more consumer-friendly credit card industry, and keeps CardRatings.com in touch with the needs of cardholders.

Curtis knows firsthand the devastating effects of credit card debt. By the time he was finished with his graduate studies at the University of Texas at Dallas, his credit card debt reached $45,000. The stress it created in his life was "unbelievable," as Curtis puts it, and has a lot to do with why he wrote this book. His goal is to spare you the experience of what he went through and to show you the best ways to benefit from your credit cards.

Over the years, Curtis and CardRatings.com have received an enormous amount of national publicity and praise, thanks to interviews Curtis has given to *The Wall Street Journal*, *The New York Times*, *The Washington Post*, *USA Today*, *Money Magazine*, NPR (National Public Radio), CNN, ABC News Radio, AARP, Dow Jones Newswire, *Bottom Line/ Personal*, PBS, *SmartMoney Magazine*, *Reader's Digest*, MSN Money, MSNBC TV, The Associated Press, CNBC, *TIME Magazine*, and more.

Since its founding, Curtis has expanded CardRatings. com's role and online offerings. For example, the site now provides all the data (card terms and conditions) for the credit card and ATM/debit survey published by the New York State Banking Department, the oldest bank regulatory agency in the nation. The site also includes credit card news and advice on everything from getting a line of credit to getting a copy of your credit report to getting a better rate or rebate. It's also a good place to turn if you're looking for business or student cards.

Arkansas Business, a weekly journal, selected Curtis as a "Top 40 Under 40" business leader in 2005, recognizing him as an intriguing business and political leader who bears watching. He was selected as a National Council of La Raza panelist in 2006 to discuss Hispanic credit card issues, and he was a guest speaker in 2007 at The Responsible Credit Roundtable, which provides a forum for leaders of the credit card industry and nonprofit organizations to devise, test, and implement ways to improve communication and account practices to build value for both companies and customers.

Curtis has a particular passion for educating students about credit. He serves on the Advisory Board for the Center for Consumer Financial Services at Rochester Institute of Technology, which provides national leadership and research on student credit issues. Curtis also regularly speaks on college campuses about the ins and outs of credit. Finally, he currently serves as co-chair of the Arkansas chapter of the Jump$tart Coalition for Financial Literacy, which seeks to educate students about personal finance issues.

Curtis participates in other consumer advocacy groups with various missions. For example, he contributes on a weekly basis to CreditBloggers.com, a blog where leading financial experts discuss credit, loan, debt, and identity theft topics. Curtis is also a member of Arkansans Against Abusive Payday Lending, a coalition of Arkansans dedicated to combating abusive payday-lending practices. Finally, he's a member of the Financial Literacy Education Consortium, a community of professionals concerned with "best practices" in the delivery of financial education to their constituents.

Before founding CardRatings.com, Curtis worked in various capacities in the financial industry, for example, at Advancial Federal Credit Union, Regions Bank, and Metropolitan National Bank. In addition, Curtis gained some valuable "eBusiness" experience by working for Intelemedia Communications in the high-tech corridor of North Dallas.

Curtis enjoys being involved in community organizations in the Little Rock area, where he has served on the Board of Directors for Arkansas Festival Ballet. He has been a member of Toastmaster's International, the West Little Rock Rotary Club, Techpreneur, a nonprofit organization that encourages technological entrepreneurship, and the Little Rock Bop Club. Curtis is also an active member of The Summit Church in North Little Rock.

Last but not least, Curtis cherishes his family life. His wife Nancy serves as the accounting supervisor for CardRatings.com. Curtis and Nancy currently reside in North Little Rock, Arkansas with their five children— Dallas, Erin, Hunter, Avery, and Claire.

CHAPTER 1

It's Not Just Plastic—It's Money

What would we do without **credit cards**?[1] Most of us have at least one in our wallet. From purchasing airline tickets and shopping online to filling up the grocery cart and topping off the gas tank, we use credit cards as a convenient, quick way to pay.

But they can be far more than just fast and easy. Although it sounds counterintuitive and even an oxymoron, *you can actually profit from credit cards* if you apply the insider tips I share in the following chapters:

- Your cards will pay you between 1% and 5% in cash just for charging things you would have bought anyway.

- You can use cards as creative financing tools to buy virtually anything, at **rates** as low as 0%.

These ideas have helped countless consumers, including me, get hundreds and even thousands of dollars from their credit cards. It's my sincere hope and expectation that this book will do the same for you.

The Power of Credit Cards

With more than a billion cards out there—around five cards for every American—it's a safe bet that you've got at least one handy. Take a good look at it. What does it

---

[1] This term and others that you see in bold are defined in the Glossary.

1

represent to you—a financial management tool or a burden? Do you receive many benefits from your cards, or is the lender the one receiving all the benefits, in the form of interest payments and fees from you?

Credit makes it easy to buy what we need and want, but in this society obsessed with obtaining all kinds of things, credit can become a crutch instead of a convenience. Still, credit cards have become virtual necessities in our capitalistic, technology-driven society. Try to rent a car without a card, and you'll see what I mean!

With credit cards, shopping online is a breeze. What about reserving airline tickets? Ordering from a catalog? And mailing a check is almost a thing of the past. Using a credit card is faster, easier, and generally a more secure way of doing business.

What's more, if you follow my advice and strategically use the right cards, you'll get many other benefits from them, including generous gift certificates, airline tickets, and cash rebates. If you're wondering how that can be possible, it's largely because of competition. At any given time, typically thousands of competing credit card offers are targeting you. Card **issuers** want your business so badly that they're willing to dangle all sorts of juicy carrots in front of you, chock full of tempting rewards and rebates.

Industry research indicates U.S. card issuers will spend $18.4 billion on rewards in 2010. In 2006, they "only" spent $10.3 billion. If they're giving away that much to get and keep our business, imagine how much money they're making! Still, isn't it great that competition is so tough for them, they have to offer generous perks just to woo and keep us?[2] If you "play your cards right," you'll become what lenders call a *deadbeat,* meaning you reap the rewards of your cards without paying any interest or fees. Or maybe you're a cardholder with *revolving debt,* which

---

[2] Bézard, Gwenn. (2007, January 18). Loyalty & Rewards: A Market Overview. Aite Group. Statistic retrieved from aitegroup.com/reports/200701181.php

means you don't pay off your balance in full each month—and you do pay interest. If you fall into this category, you're the credit card issuers' ideal customer.

Whichever type of card user you happen to be, you can learn a lot about using credit wisely, getting out of debt, avoiding a high-debt lifestyle, *and* taking advantage of the benefits and rewards of card usage. That's just the kind of valuable information we focus on in this book.

In fact, a very unique value proposition of this book is that credit cards can significantly enhance your financial well-being. Stick around, and I'll empower you to become a savvy credit card user who wisely manages your plastic for personal profit!

Choosing a Credit Card That Will Benefit Your Bottom Line

Comparison shopping is the best way to find a card with the right perks for you. Before we get to fun subjects like deciphering the fine print in credit card offers, let's quickly go over the basic characteristics of a credit card.

One of the easiest ways to understand how a credit card works is to compare it to a **debit card**. Even though a debit and credit card look the same, their functions are very different.

Credit Card Basics

Every time you use a credit card, you're actually borrowing money from a bank or other financial institution. When you charge something, the card-issuing bank pays what you owe to the merchant that accepted your card for payment. In turn, you pay the money back to the bank.

By signing up for a credit card, you agree to pay back the money that you borrow, plus any **interest** or **finance charges** that accrue on the amount you owe until you've paid it all back. Put simply, credit cards are a type of loan.

Debit Card Basics

Most banks now give you the option of using a debit or check card to get instant access to the money in your checking account. When you use one, your bank takes the funds directly from your bank account on the same day or soon thereafter.

With a debit card, you don't have to carry cash or checks, and you don't have to pay interest or finance charges. Now that they're accepted at a variety of places, including gas stations, grocery stores, restaurants, and retail stores worldwide, it's no surprise that debit cards are becoming more popular. In fact, for the first time, debit card usage actually surpassed credit card usage in 2006.

Debit or Credit—Which Is Better?

The answer is, it depends. How careful are you? How do you actually use your card? Can you trust yourself not to rack up a pile of debts?

The features that make debit cards convenient—instant access to your money, plus the ease of not having to write a check and often not having to drag out your photo ID— also make fraud much easier. Unless reported quickly, theft of your debit card can quickly deplete your bank account.

A thief can spend all the money in your checking account in a matter of minutes, leading to bounced checks, overdraft fees, and a major headache! This is where there's a big difference between credit and debit cards.

Stricter Liability Laws

Credit cards are subject to strict **liability** laws that limit a consumer's cost for credit card fraud to $50. Even better, almost all credit cards now come with zero liability policies, meaning you generally don't have to pay a cent for any unauthorized charges. Of course, restrictions apply, but most consumer feedback regarding this benefit has been quite positive.

With debit card fraud, your liability is $50 *if* you notify the bank within two days. After two days, your liability increases to $500

> **TIP**
>
> No matter what your liability, report fraud as soon as possible. It will often save you time, grief, and money.

for purchases and charges you didn't make—and up to your entire account balance after 60 days.

Although many banks have implemented voluntary plans that limit debit card liability to $50, there's no federal requirement. And although Visa and MasterCard do extend limited zero liability protection to debit cards branded with a Visa or MasterCard logo, there are restrictions.

Even if you're fortunate enough to recover all your money and get all the associated fees reversed, once your checking account is exposed to fraudsters, you might face **identity theft** issues. Many fraud victims spend countless hours straightening it all out. And, as the wise old saying goes, time is money!

Consumer Protection

Credit cards also offer more consumer protection. On purchases, for example, if items are stolen within a limited time frame (typically, 90 days), you usually get your money back. Unfortunately, I can personally attest to this: When my family's brand new lawn mower was stolen, I got a check in the mail for the full purchase price of the mower a few weeks later. The theft was very upsetting, but that check definitely helped ease our pain!

Similarly, chargeback privileges, which are standard benefits protected by law, come in handy when we have disputes with merchants over goods or services bought with a credit card. Some cards also come with extra insurance, which can be a real benefit—for example, in case there's damage to something that's shipped to you. Chapter 10, "Maximize the Benefits of Your Cards by Taking Advantage of Additional Free Perks" contains a detailed listing of such benefits.

Establish or Build Your Credit

One final but very significant advantage of credit cards is that they're a great tool if you need to establish or build a good credit history. Credit cards typically report account activity to at least one of the three major national **credit reporting companies** (Equifax, Experian, and TransUnion) on a monthly basis. Their report of your responsible credit card use helps improve your credit rating, also known as your **credit score**.

The better your credit, the more likely it is that you'll get the most favorable terms (low **interest rates**, low fees, and so on) on all types of credit, including credit cards, car loans, and mortgages. That could easily translate into thousands of dollars in savings. Good credit can also lead to big savings on your insurance premiums year after year, and it can even help you land your dream job. (For more on **credit reports** and credit scoring, see Chapter 9, "Your Credit Report and Score: The Better You Look, the More You Profit.")

Which Card Should Be in Your Wallet?

Follow these three simple tips to decide which card or cards are best for you:

1. Put yourself in the driver's seat.
2. Understand the *terms and conditions*.
3. Learn about credit card features and how they can benefit you.

Put Yourself in the Driver's Seat

Be proactive instead of reactive. The goal is to find a card that will work *for you*—by offering low interest rates, incentives, services, and so on. There's no benefit in allowing a bank to profit excessively from you, raking in **annual fees, late fees,** high interest charges, and more, right?!?

Many consumers that I talk with assume the offers they get in the mail are the best offers that they can get. Did you know that those "**preapproved**" offers you're probably inundated with aren't guarantees of credit at all? Your name was simply retrieved from a mailing list, and the offers are the result of expensive marketing campaigns.

More Than Meets Your Eye

Ira Stoller, a senior member of the CardRatings. com forum, says,

Preapproved offers can hit your mailbox from any and every card issuer. They are not what you might think they are. If you read the fine print you will see that all a 'preapproved' offer means is that you fit into a series of gross [marketing] parameters that the card issuer gives to the credit bureaus *or agencies. The credit bureaus send a list of potential clients to the card issuer who then sends out a solicitation piece trying to interest folks like you and me in actually applying for the card. There is no guarantee that we will be approved.*

The industry loves to bait us with tempting offers that frequently include very generous **credit lines** and rock-bottom rates. The odds that you'll actually qualify for that much credit are small unless you have a high credit score and above-average income. Otherwise, you'll probably get a card with a lower **credit limit** and a higher annual interest rate (also known as the *APR*).

Look for the phrases "as low as" and "up to" in the sales pitches. They're usually associated with many card offers and should alert you to carefully review the terms of the offer.

Definitely review mail solicitations where you can find some great direct-mail offers. However, if you consider only the offers that show up in your mailbox, you're probably missing out on some great opportunities. It pays to explore every available avenue when you're on the hunt for a great card, including websites, personal finance magazines, and newspapers. Picking up the phone to call your bank or other card issuers directly is another good idea. (Visit CardRatings.com/Book for the phone numbers of the major card issuers as well as for more information on many of the resources mentioned in this book.) Each avenue might yield unique card offers that you won't find anywhere else.

In comparing several different cards, I strongly advise that you rely on unbiased, up-to-date resources. A great place to start is our website, CardRatings.com, which is now the most comprehensive free source for comparing cards. We strive to give an accurate picture of the best (and worst) of the *current* crop of cards out there. Issuers frequently change their offers, so it's advantageous to check out the latest opportunities.

Perhaps the most unique feature of the site is the "Consumer Reviews" section, where some 20,000 cardholders rank cards based on various criteria, like fees, rewards, and customer service. What could be a more valuable measure of how good or bad a particular card is than the word of many real, live users?

Understand the Terms and Conditions

When you apply for a credit card, the company assumes that you agree to the terms and conditions—whether or not you really understand them. Most people do quickly glance at the fine print. But let's be honest: When the words start sounding too legal and the print is too small, isn't that when we lose interest and tell ourselves that we know enough to use the card wisely? All those pesky details don't really apply to us, right?!?

Wrong. The terms and conditions apply directly to us! Knowing our intolerance for legalese, the card industry is notorious for slipping some very important clauses into the terms and conditions, making them extra hard to decipher, even for many attorneys. Historically, many issuers have taken advantage of fine print technicalities, and critics claim that a significant share of the industry's revenues comes from "deceptive tactics" hidden in the fine print.

Some clauses do seem sneaky or unfair, but as long as the card issuer discloses certain information in the terms and conditions, they're perfectly legal. No one said we had to like it, though!

Regulating the Card Industry

So many cardholders and consumer advocates have been complaining about controversial industry practices. Both houses of Congress—as well as key federal agencies—are considering legislation and regulations that, if implemented, would represent the most far-reaching crackdown on the card industry in decades. Hopefully, by the time you read this, the system will be fairer. The powerful banking industry is claiming that more regulation would lead to higher prices and less consumer credit. While I do have fears that too much regulation might backfire, we're a long way from too much regulation. As an added benefit, lenders may find that more reasonable terms and conditions might actually help lower credit card delinquency and bankruptcy rates.

While I'm optimistic that some improvements are in the offing, there will likely always be details buried in card agreements that can cost you big bucks. My goal is to explain the system as it exists today and give you the heads-up on what might be changing in the near future.

What's in that fine print determines how you can profit from a card. You've been forewarned! Now it's time to forearm you with tools that make it easy to take advantage of the financial benefits that come with clever credit card use.

The Schumer Box

Card offers have to include a handy table known as a *Schumer Box* that clearly shows key card info. Named after Senator Chuck Schumer of New York and first introduced in 1988, a Schumer Box includes these important terms:

- Annual fee (if applicable).
- Annual percentage rate for purchases (APR)— Although a rate will be shown, the actual rate you'll

get will be based on the lender's evaluation of your creditworthiness.

- Other APRs:
  - Balance transfers—In this situation, you pay off a credit card balance with another credit card. A typical balance transfer offer is 0% for 6 to 12 months, with the rate applying only to balances transferred from another card. (More about this and all the other Schumer Box details later.)
  - Cash advances—This is the rate you must pay when you use your card to get cash, for example, from an ATM.
  - Default and penalty rate—This is the rate you must pay if you make a late payment, go over your credit line, and so on.
- Grace period for purchases—This is the amount of time you have, after the billing period ends to pay off your credit card balance before you're charged interest. It's typically 20 to 25 days and applies when you are not carrying a balance.
- Interest or finance charge calculation method—This is how the issuer determines how much interest you owe if you don't pay the balance in full.
- Other transaction fees—These could be for cash advances, balance transfers, late payments, and so on.

Because this information is included in all offers in the same basic format, Schumer Boxes let us do "apples to apples" comparisons to find a card to use to our best advantage. Table 1.1 illustrates a sample Schumer Box as seen on the following page.

Table 1.1   Sample Schumer Box

Annual percentage rate (APR) for purchases	9.99%–23.99%
Other APRs	**Balance transfers:** 0% until the last day of the billing period ending during April 2009; then the standard APR for purchases.
	Default or penalty rate: Up to 32.24%
	Cash advances: 22.99%
Variable rate information	The standard **purchase APR** may vary monthly and equals the prime rate plus an amount between 2.74% and 9.74%. (The prime rate used is the highest prime rate listed in *The Wall Street Journal* on the last business day of the month. The **prime** rate as of the printing of this book is 5.25%. Visit CardRatings.com/Book for the current prime rate.)
Grace period for repayment	At least 20 days when you pay your balance of the balance of purchases in full each month.
Method of computing the balance for purchases	Two-cycle average daily balance, including new purchases.
Annual fee	$0
Minimum finance charge	50¢
Cash advance transaction fee	3% for each cash advance, with a minimum of $5 and no maximum.
Late fee	$15 on balances up to $500, and $39 on balances over $500.
Over-the-limit fee	$15 on balances up to $500, and $39 on balances over $500.

Billing Cycles

Interest is calculated in two common ways: **two-cycle billing** and **average daily balance** methods. Be wary of cards that use two-cycle billing, aka double-cycle billing. They calculate interest on your average daily balance over the current *and* the previous billing periods instead of on the average daily balance for just the current billing period.

With two-cycle billing, you usually end up paying much more in interest, especially if you occasionally carry a balance. The good news is that, because of political and media pressure, Chase abandoned this practice in early 2007 and now most major issuers don't use this billing method. New legislation or regulations may outlaw it entirely. (Visit CardRatings.com/Book for a list of the major card issuers that do and don't use two-cycle billing.)

Fees

Fees, fees, and more fees! Card issuers have become increasingly dependent on fee income in the last few years. Some surveys claim that fees are now almost as important to their bottom lines as interest income. In 2007, card issuers raked in some $160 billion industry-wide, according to industry expert R. K. Hammer, who estimates that 39% of that amount (some $63 billion) comes from fees. For comparison, in 2000, fees amounted to only 28%. In 2006, penalty fees alone generated $17.1 billion, according to Hammer.

Although fees are usually defined in the Schumer Box, they can be hard to comprehend. Fortunately, in May 2007, the Federal Reserve began an initiative to require lenders to provide additional disclosures regarding fees in an easy-to-read format. And even better, they're considering a ban on exorbitant fees in Washington, and lenders may be prohibited from charging interest on certain fees.

The most common fees are levied for paying late and charging over the credit limit. Late fees have risen much faster than inflation, from an average of $12.83 in 1995 to $33.64 in 2005. They're currently as high as $39 and will probably continue to spiral upward.

Balance transfer fees are also increasingly prevalent, and they're on the rise. Most balance transfer offers, designed to entice us to take advantage of super-low **introductory (aka teaser) rates,** now have fees attached. Alas, the days of virtually unlimited no-fee balance transfer offers are becoming a thing of the past.

Some transfer fees increased as much as 300% to 400% just in the first few months of 2008. Despite such dramatic increases, you can still find good transfer offers and save a lot of money in the process. Chapter 3, "Unlock the Key to Huge Savings: Master Credit Card Rates and Transfer Offers," shows you how.

On a positive note, annual fees, which were prevalent 15 years ago, are now few and far between. When they do exist, it's usually for cards that offer generous airline reward points. (More on cards that will be a boon to all you travelers in Chapter 2, "Show Me the Money! Credit Card Rebates.")

Figure 1.1 shows the amount of money card issuers received in 2007 from these various fees.

The Notorious Fine Print

Everything in the Schumer Box is must-know information, and it pays (literally!) to understand other details as well. If you become familiar with common fine-print phrases, such as the following four examples, you won't end up being sucker-punched by the bank, and you'll be in a position to take maximum advantage of your cards:

- *...if the cardholder is reported as delinquent on an account with any other creditor, we may increase the APRs on your account up to the maximum default APR.*

   This controversial clause, commonly known as *universal default,* means that if you're late paying another bill, the interest rate on your credit card

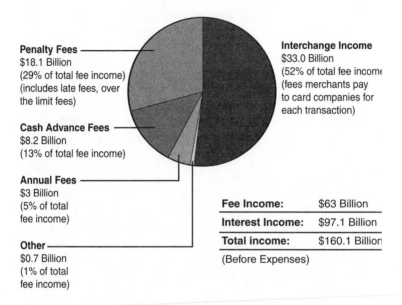

2007 Card "Fee Income"

Penalty Fees
$18.1 Billion
(29% of total fee income)
(includes late fees, over
the limit fees)

Cash Advance Fees
$8.2 Billion
(13% of total fee income)

Annual Fees
$3 Billion
(5% of total
fee income)

Other
$0.7 Billion
(1% of total
fee income)

Interchange Income
$33.0 Billion
(52% of total fee income
(fees merchants pay
to card companies for
each transaction)

Fee Income:	$63 Billion
Interest Income:	$97.1 Billion
Total income:	$160.1 Billion

(Before Expenses)

Source: R.K. Hammer Investment Bankers, Thousand Oaks, CA

Figure 1.1   *Various sources of fee income in 2007*

could be raised. In fact, if your credit score is lowered for any reason (late payments, high debts on loans, and so on), the universal default clause can be activated. Yes, that's true even if you have a perfect bill-paying record with the card issuer.

Unfortunately, many card issuers now practice universal default, raising the rate on new and existing balances, even when they don't call it that. On a positive note, some issuers are starting to distance themselves from universal default, and soon, new laws may require any interest rate increases apply only to future card debts. It's a fairly complicated topic, so we delve into it in more detail in Chapter 11, "Master Advanced Card Techniques to Save and Make Money."

Universal Default in Action

Courtney, a frequent poster on the CardRatings.com forum, was surprised to find that the APR on her card had been raised from 8.99% to 18.49%. When she called the lender, she was informed her credit record revealed a "high **debt-to-income** ratio" that made the issuer decide her risk as a borrower had risen.

"I consider myself to be very capable with my finances," says Courtney. "But I've had a few years when I ran up more debt than usual, including a home equity loan. I made all of my payments on time, but evidently, my new debt affected what used to be a stellar credit record. It's frustrating."

Soon after, another credit card bill arrived from another company with a new interest rate of 27.4%—up from 8.9%. This was yet another unpleasant surprise for Courtney who said, "In all the years that I held this card, I never made a late payment."

- *Disputes relating to the account are subject to binding arbitration.*

  This clause protects the card issuer from lawsuits and class action suits. If you have any problem or dispute regarding your account, you're limited to a *binding arbitration* hearing. The arbitrator is generally hand-picked and hired by the bank, and your legal options are normally severely limited.

According to Paul Bland, an attorney with Public Justice, a public-interest law firm, once an arbitrator has made a decision, it's next to impossible to get a court to overturn the decision.

"Few consumers read and understand all of the terms and conditions of the credit cards that they use," Bland explains. "Therefore, not enough consumers know about binding arbitration to produce a public outcry."

Unfortunately, cards without mandatory arbitration clauses are getting harder to come by. Some organizations, such as Union Privilege and AARP, have enough muscle to insist that the mandatory arbitration clause not be applied to cards issued with their name. (The same banks typically include the clause in other cards they distribute.) Additionally, credit unions and smaller banks are usually more consumer-friendly than the big card issuers and generally don't include such clauses.

Mandatory Arbitration Clauses Are Everywhere

According to GiveMeBackMyRights.com, mandatory arbitration clauses can also be found in health insurance contracts, telephone contracts, car contracts, rental clauses, bank loans, house repairs, and so on. Most consumers are in at least one binding arbitration contract...and don't even know it!

- *We apply payments and credits to balances with low introductory/special APRs (such as special balance transfer and purchase APRs) prior to balances with standard APRs. Therefore, your savings will be reduced by making additional transactions or having balances that are subject to standard APRs.*

This is certainly quintessentially confusing credit card jargon! It means that any payment you send in will be applied to the balance with the lowest interest rate. In other words, if you have more than one interest rate being applied to the balance on your account, the company charges the highest interest rate for as long as it can. I sincerely hope this practice will be outlawed, and payments will have to be credited against the balance with the highest rate. But as of now, lenders are free to credit payments against our lowest rate debt.

This can really burn you if you're taking advantage of a low-rate balance transfer offer and are also charging new purchases to the same card. This is a violation of cardinal rule #1 when it comes to the smart use of balance transfers. See Chapter 3 for details.

- *The Introductory APR does not apply to bank and ATM cash advances.*

A very high APR of 20% to 30% is typical for cash advances. To maximize profit from your credit cards, never use those pricey cash advances. Keep away from the ATM at all costs. (More on cash advances in Chapter 5, "How to Slash Your Debt and Keep Your Hard-Earned Money for Yourself.")

Many other phrases included in the terms and conditions can be confusing. Consult the Glossary if you need help understanding any credit terms. Although spending time analyzing credit card terms is no fun, it's definitely time well spent because it can save you much stress and money down the road. And who among us wants more stress and less money, especially when the goal is to get more money and perks from our cards?

> **TIP**
>
> If you still have questions about an offer after you've looked it over, don't hesitate to call the issuer for further clarification—before you apply. Merely applying for credit can negatively affect your credit report, so if the customer service rep doesn't answer your questions to your satisfaction, then don't apply!

Learn About Card Features

Ask yourself these questions to decide which card is the best choice for you.

Which Type of Card Can I Get?

Several kinds of cards exist, including **secured**, platinum, business, student, and reward or **rebate** cards. The cards you'll qualify for depend largely on your credit history. If you're in the process of trying to rebuild your credit, for example, a secured card is best. See Chapter 8, "Use Targeted Cards to Your Financial Advantage Use."

Each type of card offers unique pros and cons. For example, although reward cards generally have great perks, they normally charge higher interest rates. That can end up being very, very costly if you don't pay your balance in full every month. See Chapter 2.

How Will I Use the Card?

Will you carry a balance or pay the entire bill each month? Your answer to this question should carry a great deal of weight in choosing a card. If you pay your bill in full every month, you'll never have to pay interest. You can take advantage of cards with attractive reward programs because you don't have to be as concerned about the interest rate.

If you'll be carrying a balance, pick the card with the lowest interest rate you can get. That will keep your cost of borrowing as low as possible. Usually perks won't be worth it until you no longer carry a balance. For the lowest rates, your credit score has to be very good. It's important to find out what your credit score is before you apply for a new credit card. See Chapter 3 to find out why.

What Rewards Will Benefit Me the Most?

Consider your lifestyle when you're reviewing card benefits and incentive programs. If you rarely travel, air miles won't prove very useful to you; you'd do better with a cash-back card.

So many reward cards are out there—take your pick! For example, you can get a card that rewards you with the following:

- Cash
- Air miles or frequent-flyer miles good for free tickets
- Generous rebates on future purchases of gasoline
- Gift certificates
- Contributions to your retirement or college savings plans
- Partial mortgage payments

By using these tips and the ones that follow, you'll find a credit card that comes with the right payoffs for you. As your situation changes—when you no longer carry a balance, for example—take a fresh look and adapt the tips to your current situation. Finding a card that fits you to a T and gives you bonuses for charging things you'd use anyway can be a very fun, profitable experience.

Credit cards, fun? Profitable? Who'd have "thunk" it? And we're just getting started! Now let's take a closer look at some of those great fringe benefits to smart charging.

Show Me the Money!
Credit Card Rebates

There's gold in them thar hills, and I'm going to show you how to mine it. This is no gimmick. Not only can you use credit cards to conveniently buy things, but you can easily make money from them, get free airline tickets, cut the cost of gasoline, and more! In this chapter, I show you how.

America's Love Affair with Card Rebates

Ahhh, love! Romantic escapes, red roses, chocolate, and...credit cards. What? Granted, we don't typically associate those little pieces of plastic with romance, but our love affair with reward and rebate cards seems to grow stronger every year. About 85% of U.S. households had at least one reward card in 2007, and 80% of cardholders received some type of reward from their cards.

Let's take a look at reward card basics. Then I share specific tips on how to get the most bang for your buck with each kind of reward. Believe it or not, you can receive hundreds of dollars in cash, **gift cards**, or airline tickets every year just for using a reward card for your everyday purchases. My wife and I typically get $700 to $1,000 back annually simply by being smart about how we use our cards.

If you're not currently getting your slice of this tasty pie, I have a treat in store for you. A reward card is one of the best freebies available to consumers. When you discover the joys of taking advantage of one, I assure you that you will never use a card that gives you nothing back again. Why do business with a company that doesn't make it as lucrative for you as its competitors do?

If you're already getting a piece of the pie, then let's aim to get you an ever-bigger slice going forward. Cash-back reward cards, airline reward cards, gas rebate cards, and any other reward cards they dream up can all boost your bottom line with remarkably little effort on your part.

Important!

This chapter is for people who pay off their balance in full each and every month. If you carry a balance—even on occasion—then move on to the next chapter. Reward cards usually carry a higher interest rate than non-reward cards, and the interest you'll be charged will more than wipe out any rewards you might earn. (Of course, there are a few exceptions to this rule, which we'll discuss in Chapter 11, "Master Advanced Card Techniques to Save and Make Money.")

If seeing how much more you can get from your cards will motivate you to get out from under the burden of your debt, by all means keep reading! Just don't start charging on a reward card until you've paid off what you owe. ☺

When Did the Reward Card Craze Begin?

Discover, which deserves much credit for transforming the card industry, introduced the first cash-back, no-fee card in a catchy commercial during the 1986 Super Bowl. The card offered a cash rebate of up to 1% on every purchase made using it. At a time when many cards had annual fees and when cash rewards were unheard of, Discover's new card certainly stood out in a big way. No one had ever offered a no-fee card that gave cash back to boot.

Airline reward cards, which typically offer frequent-flyer miles for every purchase you make on the card, began to grow in popularity as well back then. When the popular Citi/AAdvantage card debuted in 1987, this co-branded card (meaning it was affiliated with both American Airlines and Citibank) was among the first to offer miles that could be redeemed for free airline tickets.

What Accounts for the Growing Popularity of Reward Cards?

One of the primary reasons for their increasing appeal is the stiff competition among card issuers, who have to work hard to make their cards stand out in the deluge of offers we receive every year. Tempting us with rewards is one of their best bets for getting us to apply for *and* use their cards. That's why their direct-mail campaigns consistently include more sales pitches for reward cards than nonreward cards. For example, according to Mintel Comperemedia, a Chicago-based market research firm, 55% of all credit card direct-mail promos had a reward component in 2007.

These programs have become so popular in the last few years that it's hard for card issuers to compete in today's market without a rebate program. Even better from our perspective as cardholders, their competition means increasingly generous rewards for us. I've been amazed over the years at how issuers are constantly trying to one-up each other with ever more enticing cards.

A good illustration of how competition has made reward cards more appealing involves rebate percentages. Until a few years ago, reward cards typically offered a 1% cash rebate or 1 reward point for each dollar spent. Now it's not uncommon to see reward cards offering rebates up to 3% and even up to 5% on certain purchases.

Imagine getting 3% to 5% back just for using a particular piece of plastic. That's more than we often earn on our savings at the bank! Moreover, we have to pay taxes on the money we earn in our savings account. Not so with card rebates, which are generally tax-free. (Consult your tax advisor for more info.)

This competition is working to our benefit in another way: Issuers are tempting us with more flexible redemption options. Historically, reward cards allowed cardholders to earn only cash rebates, airline tickets, a narrow selection of merchandise, or gift cards. Lenders are now trying to woo us by presenting many more choices in how we can capitalize on our rewards.

Chase's Freedom Card, introduced in 2007, is a good example. Marketed aggressively through flashy TV ads featuring the hit song "I'm Free" by The Rolling Stones, it gives cardholders a lot of control over their reward choices. They can choose cash rebates, gift certificates, hotel stays, car rentals, travel on most airlines with no blackout dates, and/or a wide array of merchandise.

In their quest to get us to use their cards, lenders will no doubt introduce other reward cards and modify their existing programs to increase flexibility and customer control. And their popularity will likely grow even more as programs become increasingly specialized and targeted to tempt very specific markets. As Comperemedia puts it:

> *Credit card reward programs have become more sophisticated and tailored for particular consumers based on their lifestyles, needs, and desires. Thus, affluent cardholders may be offered elite lifestyle experiences such as a Tiffany's engagement ring or even a trip into space....*

Finally, the growth of the Internet has also helped spur Americans' seemingly insatiable appetite for card rewards. Case in point: On a whim back in 1996, Peter Flur, a research engineer from Charlotte, North Carolina, started an online community called the Grapevine, devoted to card rewards. The Grapevine was simply an expression of Flur's personal interest in the subject, but it has since morphed into a popular online community where people discuss reward cards every day. Similarly, the active CardRatings.com forum has thousands of user tips on making the most of reward cards.

Although our love of reward cards is a great thing, as with any love affair, there are some potential pitfalls. Follow these tips to avoid them and maximize your benefits from reward cards.

The Dark Side of Reward Cards

Perhaps the greatest trap you can fall into is overspending. Studies show that most consumers spend more on a reward card than a nonreward card. So even if you pay off your balance in full each month, if you routinely spend more on a reward card than you can afford, you'll quickly find yourself in financial quicksand.

Another reason why you might feel a strong temptation to overspend is that reward cards can become quite addictive. The more you spend, the greater the rebate. Watch out for that, especially if your card company tries to egg you on to spend more with what economists call "purchase acceleration."

When you near a reward threshold, the lender sends you a letter or an email trying to get you to spend more. "It's a way for issuers to remind their customers that they're getting close to cashing in," explains Lars Holmquist, president of TSYS Loyalty, which helps financial institutions develop loyalty programs.

Issuers also know that consumers tend to spend more after getting a reward. If you get a free airline ticket as a reward, for example, you're likely to spend more on the trip itself (hotel room, meals, souvenirs, and so on).

To avoid temptation, strictly adhere to your monthly budget. If you don't have a budget, create one. Homemoneyhelp.com, operated by my endearing friend Terry Rigg (aka Grandpa Terry), is a great resource for free budgeting tools and advice. Similarly, *The Budget Kit* (Kaplan Publishing, 2008) by Judy Lawrence, is chock full of worksheets that make it easy to plan.

Spending and Point Levels

When shopping for and using a reward card, be mindful of your average annual spending levels (that is, the average amount you charge on a card during a year). Some reward cards offer reduced rebates if cardholders don't reach annual spending thresholds.

When estimating your annual spending level, pull out last year's card statements and total what you spent, or at least look at your average monthly spending for the past three months and multiply by four. If you've never used a credit card, you can get a good picture of your spending level by determining what items in your monthly budget can be charged on a card. If checks have been your main form of payment, take a look at your check register.

Similarly, most cards require that you accumulate a certain number of points before you can redeem them. And a few cards offer more generous rebates if you let your reward points grow and don't cash in your points at the lowest point redemption level.

A good real-life example of this is the Chase Freedom Card, which I mentioned earlier. It allows you to earn a "$50 check once you've earned $50 in rewards." However, as an added incentive, if you save up $200 in rewards, you can redeem them for $250 cash back. That's right. You can earn a 25% cash-back bonus just by choosing a higher point redemption level—and of course, continuing to charge on that card!

Knowing how many points are required for the rewards you're most interested in—and how much you have to spend to reach a desired point level—is crucial if you want to get the max from your reward card.

TIP

Keep your eyes out for offers that come in the mail. My wife and I are currently taking advantage of an exclusive postal offer we received on one of our existing Chase cards. It's designed for people like us who routinely charge quite a bit—in our case, we have five kids and tend to charge more than the average family. Once we charge $24,000 on the card during 2008, $500 will be credited to our account. We automatically get another $500 if our annual spending reaches $48,000. The total will be $1,000 cash-back (which translates into an amazing overall rebate of 2.08%)—easy money don't you think?

Watch closely for offers like this that come in the mail because this was a mail solicitation only. It's also proof of how badly issuers want to keep our business. In this case, we hadn't used the card in a long time. Needless to say, I was delighted to do business with Chase again!

What You Need to Know to Make the Most of Cash-Back Cards

A little extra cash in your pocket sounds great, doesn't it? Maybe you could use it for a nice dinner out on your birthday, a movie night with that special someone, a rainy-day shopping spree, college savings for you or your child, or even a way to pay down your debt. For all these reasons, and the thousands of others you can dream up, a cash-back credit card might be the perfect fit for your wallet.

Cash-back cards are fairly straightforward, and, in my opinion, they're the simplest type of reward card to use. You usually get a credit to your account, ranging from 1% to 5% of your spending. Some cash-back cards, like the one in my wallet, give automatic credits on a regular basis. A few cards send you an actual check in the mail.

I love simplicity. So as you might have guessed, because of this and several other reasons that we discuss in this chapter, cash-back cards are my favorite type of reward card.

What Type of Reward Card Do You Prefer?

Based on a 2007 online poll conducted by CardTrak LLC, 56% of Americans prefer cash-back cards while 23% said they favored air miles. Approximately 12% preferred points while only 9% selected automatic rebates or discounts as their favorite rewards.

Cash-Back Credit Cards Are Great *If...*

...you don't carry a balance from month to month. Credit cards that offer cash rebates tend to have a higher interest rate, which usually wipes out any reward you might receive if you carry a balance. If you don't pay off your bill every month, use a credit card with the lowest interest rate you can get.

Dr. Mary Ann Campbell (CFP), president of Money Magic, Inc., and a money educator, sums it up best: "Cash-back is a good option if you are truly managing your credit cards so you are literally earning that cash, and not turning around and paying it back in any other form."

Use your rebate card wisely and pay off the balance in full every month. Then the cash you receive is a reward, pure and simple, for all the hard work you've done in managing your card responsibly.

Wonder How Credit Card Companies Can Afford It?

They can afford to send us cash rebates because lots of people mess up by carrying balances and paying late. Aside from all the interest they earn and the fees they collect, card issuers charge merchants a fee on every credit card transaction, typically between 2% to 3%. So. even if you pay your balance in full each month (and are therefore a "deadbeat" in the industry's jargon), your card company is still generating fee income from your spending!

You Don't Carry a Monthly Balance But...

...not all cards are created equal, either. As with any other type of card, you should definitely shop around. Ideally, pull out your calculator to determine the best reward card, given your spending habits and lifestyle. Consider it a wise investment of your time, with the payoff being more money. You'll also get peace of mind from knowing that you've done some profitable decision making. (The "Consumer Reviews" section of CardRatings.com is a good place to start because the site enables you to conveniently search for cards by reward types.)

Here are some things to keep in mind when reviewing offers:

Is There an Annual Fee?

Paying an annual fee is a pet peeve of mine, particularly when it comes to cash-back cards. But because only a few cards out of the hundreds and hundreds available charge an annual fee, you shouldn't have to settle for one that does. If a card with an annual fee seems too good to resist, it's time to crunch the numbers and compare the benefits to those offered by other cards that don't have an annual fee.

When comparing benefits, be realistic about which ones you'll actually use. If a card with a $200 annual fee offers a generous perk, such as a free international companion airline ticket every year, but you'd never use it, then that perk isn't worth a dime to you! Rarely does the math add up. The one notable exception, which we discus in Chapter 8, "Use Targeted Cards to Your Financial Advantage," is a relatively new breed of cards that targets affluent card members.

Does the Card Require You to Carry a Balance?

A few cards offer you a greater rebate percentage or some other freebie if you carry a balance. A typical example here is a card that offers a 1% rebate on all purchases but increases that rebate to 2% in any month when you carry a balance.

This scenario should be a big red flag. Any interest that you pay to get a more generous rebate will invariably cost you *much* more than the amount of cash you get back. Paying 15% in interest on your balance for the privilege of earning an extra 1% rebate is a good way to end up in a pauper's prison.

If you're considering such an offer, start with your annual spending level (how much you'll charge during the year). Figure out how much you'll pay in interest and fees, and note how much cash you'll get back. I'd be shocked if you actually ended up receiving more cash than you'd pay in interest and fees. (Please let me know if you do!) Be sure to compare your findings to other offers to determine which one gives you the most back.

Five Tips for Making Cash-Back Cards Work for You

1. Carefully review reward program rules.

2. Never carry a balance.

3. Charge everything, but don't blow your budget.

4. Keep up with your rebate on a monthly or quarterly basis.

5. Maximize your rebate based on your spending patterns.

You've Considered the Basics, Now...

... it's time to consider the particulars.

What's an Everyday Purchase?

Some cash-back cards offer a higher rebate when you shop at such places as supermarkets, gas stations, and drug stores. The precise definition of these "everyday purchases" (as the issuers often call them) should be defined in a card's fine print, its "terms and conditions." Read them! The extra money you can earn will be worth a few minutes of your time.

For example, the Citi Dividend Platinum Select MasterCard offers up to a 5% rebate at supermarkets, drugstores, and gas stations:

> *Supermarkets are defined as stand-alone merchants that primarily sell a complete line of food merchandise for home consumption. Drugstores are stand-alone merchants that sell prescription and proprietary drugs and nonprescription medicines. Gas stations are stand-alone merchants that sell vehicle fuel for consumer use.*

In other words, supermarkets aren't departments of superstores (such as Wal-Mart) or warehouse clubs (such as Costco).

Typically, it's up to the merchant to make sure a purchase is coded correctly to qualify for an enhanced rebate. But you need to read the fine print to know exactly which merchants qualify and who is responsible for making sure transactions are coded properly.

Here's a great way to find out if the store where you shop currently qualifies for an enhanced rebate and to get the real 411 from people who are maximizing their rebates: Browse through the messages on the CardRatings.com forum or post a question.

Other Qualifying Merchants It Pays to Know

Sometimes lenders send out a list of specific merchants where you can earn a higher rebate and/or where there won't be a "cap" (a limit) on the amount you can earn. If you shop often with the merchants on this list, your earnings will quickly mount up. For the most part, they're usually online retailers, so if you often shop online, definitely consider this option.

Bullet875, an active member of the CardRatings.com forum, takes advantage of this benefit with his Discover card: "When I purchase things online using the Shopdiscover feature, I can rack up at least another 5–20% in rewards, depending upon where I shop."

Do You Have to Reach a Threshold Before Receiving Any Cash?

As a general rule of thumb, if you charge less than $10,000 a year, the best deal in cash-back cards is usually one that pays you a flat rebate percentage with every purchase. A flat 1% rebate on all purchases is the industry standard.

Other cards are "tiered"— the more you spend, the higher your rebate percentage. For the greatest returns, be sure you read the fine print and understand how much you have to charge to earn more generous rebates. Tiered cards normally favor cardholders who charge a lot on their card.

> **TIP**
>
> Tiered cards can be confusing, but it's definitely in your best interest to take the time to understand tier levels to maximize your profits.

One of the primary ways to identify a tiered card is to look for the "up to" clause. For example, with the Blue Cash card from American Express that my wife and I often use, you can earn "up to" 5% cash-back on your purchases. But if you read the fine print, you'll find that you earn that 5% rebate only after you charge more than $6,500 annually on "everyday purchases." You'll receive a 1% rebate on "everyday purchases" below $6,500, while all other purchases start at 0.5% and go "up to" 1.5%, after you spend more than $6,500. So if you spent less than $6,500 on this card in a year, you would be much better off going with another card that offered you a 1% flat rebate on all purchases (and that didn't require you to meet any spending levels).

You Get Great Rewards for 90 Days, but Then What?

You might come across a card that offers an amazing rebate, but when you read the fine print, it applies only to purchases made within a set time frame: the first 30, 60, or 90 days, for example. Pay close attention to what happens to the terms when the set time expires.

Does the rebate drastically decrease, as is typical? Does an annual fee kick in? Will the interest rate increase? (Although you always want to pay your balance in full each month, financial problems do occur. If you end up carrying a balance at some point, you're much better off with the lowest rate possible.)

> **TIP**
>
> Use a reward card with a generous introductory period when you're planning to make a large purchase. You can earn a hefty, quick return by doing so. The Citibank Cash Returns Card, for example, offers a 20% bonus cash rebate on all purchases made during the first 12 months. Do keep in mind

your ability to pay off such purchases—but for goods or services you would have paid for anyway, you can cut your costs considerably and keep more money in your pocket!

Is There a Limit to How Much You Can Earn?

There's usually an annual limit on your rewards, known as a "cap," but it depends on the card. Some cards enable you to earn cash at a high rate, but they have a relatively low annual cap, meaning that you might not end up with very much. Other cards offer a lower percent back or have rate tiers (the more you spend, the more you earn), but there is no limit to how much you earn. To see which card will benefit you most, figure out how much you plan to charge and how quickly you can get to the higher tiers.

Ira Stoller, a sharp, savvy consumer and frequent contributor to the CardRatings.com forum, likes to have more than one cash-back card so if he does reach the rebate cap on one, he can start earning cash with another. The key is figuring out what strategies will work best for you as you strive to make the most of reward cards. Get your fair share of this free money, people!

How Is the Cash Issued?

Occasionally, lenders mail a check, but more often than not, a credit appears on your statement. With some cash-back cards, you have to request a check or credit while others send you the reward automatically. In some cases, you have to earn a set amount (usually around $25 to $50) before you can receive a check.

Know the details before getting any card. If you're saving up for a trip, for example, you might rather get an actual check in the mail that you can deposit in your savings account rather than a credit on your statement.

The Secret to Foolproof Rewards

All other things equal: Always go with a card that automatically gives you your reward—that way you don't have to worry about calling the issuer or going online to redeem your rewards on a regular basis. Your goal is to make the redemption process as hassle-free as possible. I love putting my reward cards on autopilot as much as I can!

What Is Meant by a "Year"?

A year is a year is a year, right? Not necessarily. It could be a calendar year or an anniversary year that starts when you're approved for the card. Knowing how the lender defines the year can mean money in your pocket. If you don't reach the required yearly thresholds, you'll be out of luck. At the beginning of the next year, you might be back to zero. Timing, as they say, is everything. (Please remember that I'm not encouraging overspending—just strategic spending!)

The Terms Can Change at the Drop of a Hat

Credit card issuers generally reserve the right to change the terms at any time for any reason. This can include the rebate rate itself, the list of merchants where you can earn a higher rebate, and any other detail of the card. It's vital to read all those fine-print notices you get in the mail (the ones we normally throw in our garbage bin). Bottom line is you should keep your eyes out so that what the lender gives you with one hand isn't taken back with the other.

You Might Also Want to Consider...

Also consider a card that directly applies your rebate to your mortgage, deposits it into a brokerage or high-yield savings account, or deposits it into a college savings account or other tax-advantaged account.

Paying Down Your Mortgage

Would you like to save money on your mortgage? Who wouldn't? Citibank says you can save $15,640.37 and shave off 10 months from a $250,000, 30-year mortgage at 6.25%—if you use the Citi Home Rebate card. Rebates are automatically applied to the outstanding balance on your mortgage.

Imagine that—increasing your net worth by $15,000 just by using a particular credit card! Bear in mind, though, that a return like this takes many years and the continued use of the reward card to achieve. This particular example assumes monthly charges of $1,500 on the card for the entire life of the mortgage.

This category includes a few other cards. For example, Wells Fargo introduced a similar card in 2007. This sort of reward—offered in conjunction with other banking products—seems to be a growing trend.

On the surface, using a credit card to pay down debt seems so counterintuitive. But if there's a hitch, I haven't found it. You can truly use these unconventional reward cards to your great advantage ($15,000, great!) *if* you use them wisely. Also, there's a lot of value in the automated, forced savings principle associated with these cards, especially for homeowners who have a hard time saving.

The main drawback that I see is that these cards typically offer only a 1% rebate on all purchases. Frankly, you can earn a higher return with a lot of regular cash-back cards. Then, if you want to pay down your mortgage, you can simply apply your cash rebate to your mortgage yourself.

Setting Aside a Little

We all know it's important to save for emergencies and retirement. But when it comes right down to it, at the end of the month, not much might be left over. A relatively new breed of reward cards offers a convenient way to help jumpstart or supplement your savings.

These cards have great appeal because your rebate can automatically be deposited in brokerage accounts or high-yield savings accounts—or even in tax-deferred retirement accounts like traditional IRAs and Roth IRAs.

I particularly like the concept of putting rebates in tax-advantaged accounts and having that free money grow for the future. Keep in mind that if you choose to contribute to a tax-deferred account, the rebate normally counts against annual contribution limits set by the IRS. At the same time, if the account is a tax-deductible IRA, you might be able to deduct the rebate as a contribution to the account. (Consult your tax advisor for more info.)

Increasing Your College Savings

Are college expenses in your future? Reward cards that apply your rebate to a 529 college savings plan might be a good option. Significant tax advantages accompany making deposits into these accounts. Although you probably won't earn near enough for full tuition, every little bit helps! The rebate and contribution limits vary from program to program, but all rebates you earn go toward the maximum allowed contributions to the 529 savings plan associated with the card. For detailed information on this topic, see Chapter 7, "Start Out on the Right Foot— Credit Cards for Students and Saving for College."

Cut Your Gas Bill by 5% with Gas Rebate Credit Cards

Are you feeling a little light in the wallet? Suddenly regretting the decision to go for that V-8 engine? Vowing to look into one of those hybrid cars? Chances are you've just been to the gas station. ☺

With gasoline prices so high, many people are searching for ways to cut costs at the pump. If you're one of them, you might be interested in credit cards that offer rebates on gas purchases.

Traditionally, gas cards have been affiliated with a particular oil company—Shell, Exxon Mobil, Phillips 66, and so on. These cards are great if you habitually purchase your gas from a specific company, but they're not so handy if you're not particular about where you fill up, or if you might find it aggravating to have to search for a certain gas station.

Thanks, Shell!

Shell is credited by many with launching the gas-rebate card craze with its first MasterCard in 1992, which came with a 3% rebate. A year later, Shell increased the rebate to 5% cash-back on gas bought at its stations, and it remains at the 5% level to this day.

Carolyn Yapp, Shell's payments and loyalty manager, told the *L.A. Times,* "We know that if we can get our card in a customer's wallet, they'll buy more frequently from us." She went on to say that customers have earned $100 million in rebates under the 5% rebate program. Now that's some serious savings!

Newer gas cards are more versatile and offer rebates regardless of where you fill your tank. As Ira Stoller explains on the CardRatings.com forum:

Ten years ago, credit cards charged consumers a premium for using their credit cards at the pump. Now these same companies have recognized that the pay-at-the-pump business is huge, and they're engaging in a 'semibattle' competing for that business by offering increasingly better rewards and rebates.

Here's how to take the maximum advantage of the available gas cards:

- Most gas rebate cards don't charge an annual fee. Most that do charge a fee will waive it if you make a minimum number of purchases. Ask!
- Plan to pay off your gas card every month. Gas rebate cards generally offer higher APRs than other rebate cards, thus you'll end up losing most of your reward if you carry a monthly balance and pay interest.
- Pick a card that gives rewards in the way you prefer. Usually, the gas rebate is given as a monthly credit on your statement. Sometimes, however, a gift card for a particular vendor is issued.
- Some offers come with incredible introductory rebate rates that will decrease in just a few months. Find out when the starting rebate expires and what the new rebate rate will be.
- Most cards have rebate restrictions on gas purchases made at wholesale clubs, grocery stores and discount stores. As always, read the fine print carefully!

With skyrocketing gasoline prices, there has never been a better time to check into a credit card that gives cash rebates for your gasoline purchases. You'll certainly remember this tip the next time you hit the pump for a fill-up.

Visit the "Card Reports" section at CardRatings.com to find out about the current offerings and ratings of different rebate cards, and to look over the applications.

Should You Get an Airline Reward Card?

Frequent-flyer programs (FFPs) have become an integral part of the modern travel world. According to FrequentFlier.com, American's AAdvantage, United's Mileage Plus, and Delta's SkyMiles each has more than 20 million members.

With all the travel options and programs where you can earn free miles, it might seem natural to jump on board with your own mileage-earning credit card. But before you jump, take a step back and carefully evaluate the situation. Earning free miles with an airline credit card might or might not be the best course of action.

Is a Mileage Reward Card for Me?

- Am I a frequent flyer, a frequent buyer, or both?
- Am I loyal to a particular airline, or do I choose the airline with the lowest ticket price?
- Based on my spending habits, how long will it take me to earn a free ticket? Consider how much you typically charge, annual fees, the number of points needed for a free ticket, and your rate of accumulating points.
- Am I willing to deal with possible black-out dates and seating restrictions? Airline reward cards invariably have restrictions when it comes to redeeming miles, and many consumers complain about such restrictions.

Frequent Flyers and Frequent Buyers

Tim Winship, publisher of FrequentFlier.com, divides the world into two categories: frequent flyers and frequent buyers. He says the quickest way to earn miles is to fly and use an airline FFP. If you travel often, you might want to supplement an FFP with a credit card affiliated or branded with that airline. Such branded cards let you to combine points earned on the card with the FFP points you've earned from flying. (Note there are a few exceptions to this rule. For example, cards issued by Diners Club International and some American Express [AmEx] reward cards that aren't affiliated with a particular airline allow you to combine points with existing FFP points.)

On the other hand, if you're a bigger spender than flyer, think about using a generic bank card that isn't linked to a particular airline. These cards generally offer annual fees of around $20, compared to the fees on branded cards, which are usually between $60 and $80. The other big benefit is that you can choose to redeem your miles with any major airline. As you might expect, branded cards allow you to redeem your miles with only that one airline.

Gary Foreman, a former Certified Financial Planner (CFP) and the founder of the frugal Stretcher.com website, recommends that not-so-frequent flyers keep in mind the times of year they're most likely to fly. Will it be over the holidays, when there's a higher chance of blackout dates and seating restrictions? Do you travel as a family? If you're trying to earn free tickets for everyone, it will probably take much longer and require much more spending.

Which Mileage Reward Card Is Best for Me?

- What major airlines fly in and out of the airport I use most frequently?

- Where do I travel most often?

- Can I combine the points earned on the card with points earned through my frequent-flyer program?

- What's the cost of carrying one particular card over another? To find out, compare the value of the rewards they offer minus the fees.

- What other merchants are associated with the card? Would I earn bonus points or want to redeem points with any of them?

Do the Fees Outweigh the Rewards?

Fees tend to be considerably higher for airline reward cards than for other types of reward cards. If you don't charge fairly aggressively on your card, the high fees might cancel out any reward benefit.

When talking to folks, I like to use following scenario to explain this important concept: Let's say you spend $8,000 a year on your card, earning 1 mile for every dollar spent (which is typical) and paying an $80 annual fee. It'll take you a little more than three years to earn a free domestic roundtrip ticket on most airlines, assuming the usual 25,000 miles for a free ticket.

But given the $80 annual fee, that ticket won't be free. At $80 a year for more than three years, it will really cost you $240 in cold, hard cash. We're talking money right out of your pocket, not rewards. You can fly on a discount carrier to a lot of destinations for $240!

Now let's see what happens if, instead, you use a typical cash-back reward card with no annual fee. Assuming you charge the same $8,000 a year and earn 1% cash back, you'd get $250 back in a little over three years. At that point, you could just pay for the ticket yourself—without having spent an extra penny on fees.

Of course, a fee might be justifiable, given your lifestyle, especially if you charge more each year and combine your miles with a FFP, making it easier to earn a free ticket in a shorter amount of time. As with any reward card, consider charging routine expenses such as groceries, gas, and utilities to increase your rewards each year.

Expiration Dates

Unfortunately, many programs do have expiration dates for earned miles. Some require accounts to show activity during a certain time frame to avoid expiration dates. Other cards, particularly bank cards, have firm expiration dates (usually within three years) that can't be extended for any reason. Read the fine print and make sure you understand the exact requirements of a program.

Doing the Math

1. To figure out how long it will take you to earn a free ticket, divide 25,000 (the standard level required for a ticket) by the amount you typically charge on a credit card each year. For example, 25,000 ÷ $8,000 is 3.125 years.

2. To determine the true cost of the ticket, multiply the annual fee by the number of years it will take to earn the reward. Then add any interest you had to pay on outstanding balances, as well as ticket redemption fees, which are usually charged when you convert your miles to a ticket.

3. To see if you'll save or spend more money for the ticket, subtract the cost for the reward from the price of buying a ticket outright.

4. Some experts suggest that you use a monetary value of 2¢ per mile on frequent-flyer miles if you assume a round-trip ticket price of $500, or 1¢ per mile for a ticket price of $250.

Using and Losing Rewards

FrequentFlier.com's Tim Winship says that, in today's market, it is important to use earned miles as soon as the threshold for a free ticket is reached because if an airline fails, it's unlikely that another airline will step in and allow you to still use your accrued miles. With so many airlines competing and experiencing financial difficulties, absorbing all those miles is too high a cost.

On top of the danger of losing miles to failed airlines, which is a cyclical situation, Winship points out that there's a long-term loss in the value of frequent-flyer miles. That might be due to declining ticket prices, higher award levels, and/or fewer available award seats. For example, a program could up the ante, making the price of a free ticket 35,000 miles instead of 25,000. That erosion in value, which is expected to continue, creates a compelling reason to use miles sooner rather than later. So instead of saving all those miles for retirement, go ahead and take that dream vacation now!

Racking Up Bonus Miles

Despite all the negative factors associated with airline cards (you can probably tell that I'm not a big fan), there's a unique advantage to signing up for one—if it gives very generous bonus miles just for getting the card, like many of them do. Branded cards tend to be the most generous with several offering anywhere from 15,000 to 25,000 bonus miles.

So if you play your cards right (pun intended), you can earn enough for a free airline ticket in a very short amount of time. Consider the experience of a coworker of mine, Heshan Demel, who got 25,000 miles for signing up for his American Express Delta Card and received 15,000 miles soon after his first purchase.

He recently flew with his wife from Arkansas to New York City for free, thanks to this card. "It was a pretty easy process for me, with no complications," Heshan reports. All he had to do was go to Delta's website and make the reservation. He had a little more than 50,000 miles in his SkyMiles account (he already had some miles in his account before he got the card) and cashed in 25,000 miles for each ticket. The only possible catch was that he would have to spend double the amount of miles if he flew during the weekend. This didn't matter to him because he flew to

New York on a Monday and came back a week later. A small processing fee of around $10 per ticket was charged, but apart from this, Heshan and his wife got two free airplane rides to New York and back.

Needless to say, Heshan's wife was quite impressed with his savvy card usage. ☺

Other Important Tips for Frequent Flyers

Here are a few other tips that will help you make the most of your reward cards:

- Watch your spending levels with an airline reward card. Avoid the trap of spending more just to earn the reward.
- Free reward tickets might be taxable if you earned them during business travel and then used them for personal, leisure travel.
- Consolidate, consolidate, consolidate! Miles spread out over various airlines, cards, and FFPs will not likely get you your desired reward.
- If you won't be able to use all your earned miles, consider getting a cash-back card instead.

Finding the right card takes a little research and use of your math skills, but the payoff in the end is worth it, whether or not you choose to apply for an airline reward card. CardRatings.com makes it easy to evaluate and compare the different airline reward cards available. Good luck and bon voyage!

Table 2.1 shows a handy way to compare cash-back, airline, and gas reward cards, highlighting the pros and cons of each type of card:

Table 2.1 Cash-Back versus Airline versus Gas Reward Cards

	Cash-Back	**Airline**	**Gas**
Annual fees	None (usually)	Usually	Not usually—if so, you can usually get it waived.
Restrictions	Few	Blackout dates, airline capacities, expiration dates	Some require you to redeem rewards for a particular brand of gas.
Sign-up bonus	Usually none	Usually	Rarely.
Uses	For anything	Usually only for airline tickets or travel-related expenses	Generally gas and merchandise.

Have Fun

Finally, have fun with reward cards! Peter Flur, founder of the Grapevine, views the pursuit of credit card rewards as a game—albeit, a potentially profitable one—where cardholders can rack up considerable rewards on a regular basis. If you don't like one card after trying it out for a while, simply switch to another. As I've often said, you aren't married to the current credit card in your wallet or purse.

Reward cards are expanding and evolving so fast that it's worth making sure your current card is still the best fit for you. New cards come out all the time, so keep your eyes peeled and go to CardRatings.com regularly to learn about new choices.

The good news is that reward cards already offer a plethora of ways for you to get freebies, and more offers are on the way. Go forth and enjoy the fruit of the competition among card issuers!

CHAPTER 3

Unlock the Key to Huge Savings: Master Credit Card Rates and Transfer Offers

Want to save yourself hundreds or even thousands of dollars on your credit card bills? When you understand how card issuers set interest rates, you'll be able to spot the good, better, and even exceptional card offers that can significantly improve your financial picture.

I have routinely used low-rate offers to creatively finance all sorts of purchases, including real estate, wedding-related expenses, and a minivan (to accommodate our five kiddos). I've saved thousands and have improved my cash flow in the process.

Many people also use credit cards to get out of other types of debt, as strange as that may sound. There's no good reason to pay 10%, 15%, or more in interest when card issuers are eager to sign you up for a card at 0% or a very low rate.

Maximizing the benefits of low card rates does require a little bit of knowledge, though. I explain in this chapter how to locate attractive low-rate offers, and I tell you what else you need to know so you too can realize incredible savings.

Know Your Interest Rate

Rates change from time to time, so it's smart to stay aware of the current rate on your credit card, especially if you carry a balance and pay interest based on that rate. Knowing your rate will help you decide when it's time to shop for a better deal because you'll be able to compare your rate to new offers. If you have more than one credit card, knowing each one's rate will keep you from accidentally using a card with a high rate when a lower rate card would have been more advantageous.

Even if you pay your balance in full each month, it's important to know your interest rate. Cars break down, jobs are lost, and unfortunately, marriages end. In short, life happens! Although it's always a good idea to have an emergency fund, that isn't always an option. Sometimes the job search takes longer than expected or you might have a costly auto repair, leaving you with no other choice but to put some expenses on a card. If you're not up-to-date on your rates, you could end up paying more in interest than you would with a different card.

How Your Rate Is Determined

> **TIP**
>
> Remember the Schumer Box from Chapter 1, "It's Not Just Plastic—It's Money"? It said, "The Prime Rate used is the highest prime rate listed in *The Wall Street Journal* on the last business day of the month." Most issuers turn to *The Wall Street Journal* when setting the rates on variable rate cards.

Finding attractive rates can result in big savings, so understanding how they work—and, more important, how you can work them to your advantage—is key.

How exactly is a rate configured? It normally starts with

the short-term interest rates set by the main bank of the federal government, the Federal Reserve Bank (aka the Fed). When the Fed raises or lowers short-term rates (to control inflation, spur economic growth, and so on), banks typically pass on such changes to their customers by raising or lowering their prime rate, which is the lowest interest rate banks charge their best customers. The prime rate has varied greatly over the past decade or so, from as low as 4.00% in 2003 to as high as 8.25% in 2007. (Visit CardRatings.com/Book to see the current prime rate as well as how it has fluctuated over time.)

Variable versus Fixed-Rate Credit Cards

All cards can be classified as either **fixed** or **variable** rate. Fixed rate means the interest rate never changes—at least, in theory (more on this later). The rate on variable-rate cards, however, can go up or down, depending on the prime rate. Variable rate cards have become much more prevalent in recent years. In 2006, 86% of all credit cards were variable rate, while five years earlier, fixed-rate cards were more widespread than variable rate cards.

The rates of most variable cards mirror the prime rate. If the prime rate increases .25%, the rate on the card also increases .25%, typically by the next billing cycle.

Almost all variable-rate cards in the United States are tied to the prime rate, but it's only one **index** issuers use to decide on rates. A few cards are tied to the London Interbank Offered Rate (**LIBOR**), the rate banks pay when they borrow money from each other in England. (The LIBOR is usually lower than the prime rate.) A few cards are tied to other indices, such as Treasury Bills. The index should be disclosed in the Schumer Box, but because it's usually the prime rate, we will use that going forward.

Although lenders start with the prime rate, very few cards have rates at or below prime. Lenders determine the actual rate of a variable rate card by adding the **spread**, a certain number of percentage points or "basis points," to the prime rate. For example, under "Variable Rate Information," a Schumer Box might say "Prime + 6%," meaning that the rate is determined by adding the prime rate plus a spread of 6%. Add the prime rate of 5.25% (at the printing of this book) to the spread, and you'll find out that the effective interest rate is 11.25% (5.25% + 6%). It's simple math.

Exceptions to the Rule

Early on in tracking the card industry, I discovered there are invariably exceptions to every rule, particularly with regard to interest rates.

One notable exception is called a **floor**, which is a minimum rate that goes into effect if the prime rate drops below a certain level. For example, let's assume the rate on your card is "Prime + 4%," with a floor of 10%. If prime drops to 5%, your card would still have a 10% APR. No 9% (5% + 4%) for you because of the card's 10% floor.

Until recently, only a few cards had rate floors, particularly cards targeted to consumers with bad or no credit. Now, more cards are using rate floors to avoid having to pass on all of the Fed interest rate cuts that we've recently witnessed. According to Linda Sherry, Director of National Priorities for Consumer Action, a national nonprofit education and advocacy organization, rate floors can also be associated with default and cash advance APRs (more on these APRs shortly). Sherry points out that the "never lower than" rates for penalty and cash advance APRs are always very high.

Some card issuers reserve the right to change the terms and conditions, including the APR, for virtually any reason...at any time. The controversial universal default clause referenced in Chapter 1 is one way card issuers justify such changes.

Good News!

Citibank announced in early 2007 that it will no longer increase the rates and fees of its customers' accounts at "any time for any reason." Chase instituted a similar policy on March 1st, 2008, and, hopefully, other issuers will follow suit. Along with many consumer advocates, I believe these policy changes are mainly in response to consumer and political pressure, including recent Senate hearings to examine the card industry. Whatever the motivation, the end result is definitely a step in the right direction.

To make matters worse, depending on the circumstances, card issuers might not be required to even give you advance written notice of rate hikes. Even if advance notice is required, it's typically as little as 15 days, and consumers often mistake such notices as being junk mail. ☹

As a safeguard, carefully check your statement every month to see if any changes have been made to your interest rate. As Consumer Action's Linda Sherry points out, if your card company raises your rate and you overlook this change, the mere act of charging something can constitute your agreement to the increase.

The worst part of such rate hikes is that in every instance, the increase affects not only current and future purchases, but also your outstanding balance. *Translation:* The increase is retroactive. Your past purchases are subject to the new rate, even though your card had a lower rate when you made them.

If this practice seems unfair, it is! If you're a victim of such a rate hike, I urge you to complain to the issuer, your legislators, and your favorite consumer protection groups. For a list of my favorite groups, visit CardRatings.com/ Book. Also take a few minutes and write about your experience in the popular "Consumer Reviews" section of my site. You'll give a heads-up to other cardholders and create some negative publicity.

Fortunately, many issuers allow you to opt out of rate increases. You normally have to respond in writing, stating that you want to retain your current interest rate. One major drawback of opting out, though, is that your account is normally closed immediately or soon after you write to opt out. You won't be able to use the card for any future purchases, but you won't have to pay the higher rate on what you owed. Unfortunately, as of this writing, no federal law guarantees that a card issuer must give you the right to opt out.

If opting out doesn't appeal to you, your other recourse is to transfer your card balance to a lower-rate card. This is often a much better option. You'll pay a lower rate, which will save you money, and you won't have to worry about losing your charging privileges.

The wife of Hdporter, a senior member of the CardRatings.com forum, benefited from paying attention to a change of terms notice:

> *My wife's least attractive Visa (which has a Prime + 5.99% rate) issued a hike notice of 2%—interestingly, there was an "opt out," one that didn't involve closing the account. You just had to say no, and that was the end of the story.*

> *So she called and the rep confirmed this...and opted her card out (not that we carry a balance on it). It would seem that on their "less than premier cards," they simply decided to see if anyone was paying attention.*

Although the likelihood that a card issuer would attempt such a stunt might seem a little far-fetched, I have no reason to doubt such a claim. Exceptions to the rules always arise. Be vigilant, folks—power to the people!

Is a Fixed Rate Truly Fixed?

To further complicate things, card issuers can change a fixed-rate card to a variable-rate card, and vice versa, with little notice. The phrase "fixed rate" is mostly marketing jargon because even the rate on a fixed-rate card will normally change over time. As I often tell college students in my frequent lectures, there "ain't no such thing as a truly fixed-rate card."

The rate on fixed-rate cards doesn't change as often as it does on variable cards, however. This can be a real advantage in a time of rising rates. For example, between June 2004 and June 2006, there were 17 consecutive prime rate increases of .25%. That's a total rate increase of a whopping 4.25%. Rest assured, though, that when numerous rate increases occur, fixed rated cards will eventually follow suit.

On the flip side, a fixed-rate card can actually be a disadvantage in a decreasing-rate environment such as the one we witnessed in the last few months of 2007 and early 2008. The bottom line is that the issuers aren't in a hurry to charge you less.

When a Fixed-Rate Card Truly Has a Fixed Rate

Most balance transfers have fixed rates that actually stay fixed—as long as you pay on time and don't exceed your credit line. If you move a credit card balance from, say, a 13% card to one that offers 0% balance transfers, you don't have to pay a penny in interest, usually as long as you're never late or you don't exceed your credit limit.

Over the many years that I've been taking advantage of balance transfers, I've never experienced a rate increase. A few members of the CardRatings.com credit forum haven't been as lucky as me, but the vast majority of consumers I come into contact with report very favorable experiences with balance transfer rates. More on this money-saving topic soon.

Table 3.1 explains the various interest rates that might appear on your credit card bill.

Table 3.1　Key Rate Terms

Purchase annual percentage rate (APR)	Annual percentage rate charged when you carry a balance month to month on any purchases made with your card.
Balance transfer APR	APR for balance transfers, which is typically different than the purchase APR.
Default/penalty APR	APR charged if you default on the account. For example, you might make a late payment, exceed your credit limit, or make a payment that is not honored (for example, write a bounced check).
Variable rate	Interest rate that changes according to the index rate (prime or LIBOR) it is tied to.
Fixed rate	Interest rate that isn't tied to a rate index and is not truly fixed.
Daily periodic rate	The annual percentage rate expressed as a daily rate (divided by 365 because there are 365 days in a year).
Finance or interest charge	Interest charge based on the APR on the outstanding credit card balance.

Get a Lower Rate for Unbelievable Savings

Now that you know some of the nuances of credit card rates, let's focus on what you're most concerned about: how to pay as little interest as possible. According to the Federal Reserve, only about 40% of cardholders said they paid their credit card balance in full every month in 2004 (the most recent year for which figures are available). If you carry a balance, the best way for you to get the most from your credit cards is to find one(s) with as low a rate as possible. The money you save will be your own.

The current average interest rate is around 13%. That might sound like a high rate, but bear in mind that the average interest rate 15 years ago was around 20%. The good news is that several card offers advertise rates below 10%—any rate below 10% is generally considered an attractive rate.

But are the savings really all that much if you have a low-rate card? Absolutely! Take a look at this example of how much you can save by lowering your interest rate:

Let's say you have a $2,500 balance on your card, and although you make only the required 2.5% **minimum payments**, you don't add any new charges to the card. With an 18% APR, you'd shell out $3,366 in interest by the time you pay off the card—some 20 years from now!

Lower that interest rate to 13%, and you'd pay $1,733 in interest—a 48.5% savings over the 18% APR offer—and you'd reduce the term to a little more than 15 years. Where else can you save 48.5%? Certainly not at the bank or on Wall Street.

But wait: If you can qualify for a 9% APR, you'd pay only $977 in interest over 12.6 years. That's an incredible 71% savings over the 18% card. Wall Street tycoons would be thrilled with such a return on an investment. But in this case, nothing is invested and no risk is involved. You don't have capital gains or other taxes to worry about. Your savings are tax-free and guaranteed. ☺

For an even better return, send in the first month's required payment of $62.50 every month until the entire balance is paid off. You'd save another $494 and shave off almost nine years of payments. Your total interest savings over the 18% card would be $2,882—more than you owed in the first place!

Table 3.2 shows how much you would save in these different scenarios.

Table 3.2   Big Savings from Credit Cards

Balance	APR	Payment	Total Interest	Savings
$2,500	18%	Min. 2.5%	$3,365	$0
$2,500	13%	Min. 2.5%	$1,733	$1,632
$2,500	9%	Min. 2.5%	$977	$2,388
$2,500	9%	$62.50	$483	$2,882

Set a Goal, Save a Fortune

Let's say you owe $10,000 on an 18% card with a 2% minimum payment, and you'd love to be out of debt in five years when you expect to retire or start paying college bills. Only sending in the required minimums is certainly out because it would take 57 years. Your total costs would be $38,931. (The lower the minimum, the higher your potential costs. We'll talk more about this in Chapter 5, "How to Slash Your Debt and Keep Your Hard-Earned Money for Yourself.")

Now look what happens if you get a lower-rate card and then consistently send in the same amount every month to pay off that $10,000 in five years. If you qualify for a 13% card, send in $228 a month—you'll save $25,279, which is enough to pay for a year at many colleges. With a 9% card, it would take $208

> **TIP**
>
> Seeing how much time and money you can save will motivate you to get a lower rate and pay down your debt. The user-friendly calculators on CardRatings.com make it a snap to crunch credit card numbers.

a month to be debt-free at the end of five years. Addition to your nest egg: $26,476.

Comparison-Shop to Get a Lower Rate

Although low rates can be incredibly beneficial, getting credit cards with rock-bottom rates can be a challenge. The people who get the lowest rates have solid credit scores, generally in the 720 range. (See Chapter 9, "Your Credit Report and Score: The Better You Look, the More You Profit," for more about credit scores, including ways to improve your credit score.)

If you do have good to excellent credit, then you're in the driver's seat, but most cardholders can find great deals. According to credit expert Gerri Detweiler, author of *Invest in Yourself: Six Secrets to a Rich Life* (Wiley, 2001), you can use several different avenues of approach to obtain a lower rate, and it's worth trying them all:

- Don't put it off: The money you save will be your own. The longer it takes you to get going, the more money you'll give to your lender. "There are many banks that want your business and are willing to give you good rates and terms," explains Scott Bilker, author of several best-selling books on consumer debt, including *Talk Your Way Out of Credit Card Debt* (Press One Publishing, 2003). "You just need to start looking for these credit options."

- Write down the rate information for the first card that seems appealing, and compare that offer to others as you collect the pertinent information on each card. You can also compare the Schumer Boxes. Just be sure to read the offers very carefully to make sure you know the deal. Is there a low introductory "teaser" rate or an ongoing (nonintroductory) rate? Any great freebies to be had?

- Don't be so quick to trash those envelopes from issuers. Some real gems can get buried among the junk, including some offers that are exclusively marketed by mail. You might even find a balance transfer offer with no expiration date, meaning that the rate remains in effect until you pay the balance in full (more on these offers later).

- Find some of the best offers online. Either visit each individual card issuer's site or use CardRatings.com to quickly search a comprehensive, current listing of low-rate offers from various lenders.

- Pick up your phone and call issuers directly. You might hear about some offers that aren't being advertised online or through direct mail. It makes the most sense to call when you're familiar with the online and mail offers, because some customer service representatives don't seem to know many of the details of their card offers.

- Check with local or regional banks. These smaller institutions often have some of the best rates in the country—you might save the most right there on Main Street. Talk about keeping money in a community!

  One potential drawback is that although you might find the customer service more personal and appealing, smaller issuers usually apply very selective approval criteria in deciding who gets their super-low-rate cards (at or slightly above the prime rate), and their credit lines tend to be less than $10,000. (Larger banks usually give more generous lines.)

- Consider credit unions, which are also known for offering attractive rates. Plus, their fees are usually more modest. Credit unions tend not to push low introductory rate offers, but they have a reputation for marketing lower ongoing rates than banks typically offer.

If you belong to a credit union, find out if the credit union offers a card. If so, get the rate details and compare.

Not a member of a credit union? Visit joinacu.org to see if you're eligible to join one. Many have recently expanded their membership criteria.

- Be sure to investigate credit card offers from associations and nonprofit organizations. Whether it's an alumni group, a labor union, or a cause you support, you might find a really great deal.

The larger groups often have more muscle and can negotiate special terms for their members. As I mentioned in Chapter 1, AARP got the anti-consumer binding arbitration clause removed from the terms and conditions of credit cards using its name. Cards offered through such other organizations, which are also called **affinity credit cards**, are definitely worth taking a look at.

Negotiate a Better Rate

When you've taken a gander at the current rates being offered, you can use them as a negotiating tool with your card issuer. Trying to bargain down your rate might sound like an intimidating, complex process, but it's actually quite simple and can be very empowering as it saves you money. Believe it or not, many consumers have saved hundreds and even thousands of dollars by simply making a five minute phone call and asking their issuer for a lower rate.

Unless you already have a great rate, it's definitely worth calling your lender to see if you can get a better deal. I've done this myself many times over the years, so I know that it works. However, your chances of succeeding are significantly diminished if you have a poor credit rating or you haven't used your card responsibly (for example, you've had more than one late payment in the past year or you exceed your credit line on a regular basis).

Here are five tips to increase your chances of getting a lower rate when you talk to a customer service rep:

1. Always be courteous and professional.
2. Say that you're keenly aware that there are better offers available to you. Mention specific low-rate offers from other card issuers.
3. Point out your good track record and your good credit score.
4. Explain that you'd like to continue using the card—and plan on doing so—if your rate is lowered.
5. If the answer is "No," politely ask to speak to a supervisor, and repeat steps 1 through 4.

Talking to a supervisor is often worth it because the customer service reps are more limited in their ability to make account changes. If the supervisor can't help, your next step should be to threaten to stop using the card and to transfer your balance elsewhere. When you call their bluff, you'll probably be transferred to the *account retention department*. Its sole purpose is to keep customers (hence the name), so this department can often give significant concessions to make you happy.

> **TIP**
>
> When you're on the phone, remember that your card issuer really wants to keep you around. Otherwise, given the amount of competition out there, it'd cost up to $300 in marketing expenses to replace you. Use this insider information to your advantage when you negotiate for a better rate!

Although the lender isn't totally at your mercy, you have a good chance of achieving positive results if you follow these tips. Just be realistic about your expectations. If your current rate is 21%, for example, don't expect your issuer to instantly lower you to 6.9%. ☺

It's fairly common for an issuer to lower a rate by a few percentage points, but some members of the CardRatings.com forum have achieved dramatic results. Jevon McAlister, a regular poster from Brooklyn, New York, was able to lower the rate on his Chase MasterCard from 21.99% to 11.45%. That's more than 10% from one phone call. Where can you earn that guaranteed rate of return today?

This was McAlister's first credit card, and he'd made on-time payments for 21 months before he made the call. His approach was very straightforward:

> *I just called and asked the customer service rep, 'So...what can you do to help me with my rate today?' Actually, she told me that I can call every three months and should be eligible for a rate decrease. So I called three months later and they lowered my rate yet again to 8.99%!*

I hope that McAlister's two toll-free calls, which together saved him a whopping 13%, inspire you to take the initiative.

Expect a positive outcome, but if your efforts don't result in even a small rate decrease, I suggest you follow through with the threat you made to the supervisor. Look for an attractive balance transfer offer from another card.

Fees

Annual fees on low-rate card offers are rare, but a few cards with very low ongoing rates do come with annual price tags. These cards, sometimes referred to as "super-prime" cards, typically have rates that are close to or even below the prime rate. As you might expect, they're targeted to people with excellent credit scores (around 720 or above). If your score is that high and you're considering a card that falls into this category, compare the cost savings to a card without an annual fee that probably has a slightly higher APR.

Paying a nominal annual fee of $25 to $75 often results in significant interest savings, particularly if you have a balance of a few thousand dollars or more. On the other hand, if you never carry a balance and have a cash reserve to deal with financial emergencies, I see no reason to pay an annual fee of any amount.

The Three Keys to Using a Low-Rate Card to Your Advantage

1. Make your payments early

If your card issuer uses the average daily balance method to calculate interest (most do), make your payments before the due date to reduce the interest bite. According to Nancy Castleman, cofounder of GoodAdvicePress.com, lenders are *required* to credit payments when they're received, so the earlier you pay your credit card bills, the lower the average daily balance will be. The less you owe, the more you'll save in interest. Bottom line: To save the most, pay as early as you can—and as often as you can, for that matter.

2. Avoid the Dreaded Default Rate

With any card, particularly a low-rate card, make sure you always do the following:

- Make your payments on time.
- Never exceed your credit limit.
- Don't write a check for payment that is dishonored.

Otherwise, you might end up getting hit with a default (aka penalty) rate, which is normally much higher and can be over 30%. Ouch!

You should know the default rate of your current cards and any cards that you're considering. (Check the Schumer Box.) Perhaps more important, pay attention to what can trigger the default rate.

Especially if you can't trust yourself to follow my tips to avoid a rate hike, look for the lowest default rate you can find. Some smaller card issuers, such as Simmons First National Bank in Arkansas, offer default rates in the midteens, while the average default rate in 2007 was 24.51% according to Consumer Action.

> **TIP**
>
> Simmons First National Bank has historically offered one of the lowest rate cards in the country. The current purchase rate is 7.25% fixed.

Finding out what triggers the default rate can be a challenging proposition because this information is not normally adequately disclosed. Fortunately, you can easily research default rate triggers by perusing the New York Banking Department's quarterly online credit card survey. (I'm proud to say that CardRatings.com compiles the data for this survey. Visit CardRatings.com/Book for the direct link.)

One worst-case scenario should encourage everyone to pay their bills on time: Some lenders charge a default rate if you're one day late making one payment. Other issuers institute a penalty rate if your monthly minimum payments are late twice during any portion of a 12-month period. Exceeding your credit limit is also a common default pricing trigger.

Finally, those late payments with other creditors or even late payments to utility companies can result in default pricing. That controversial universal default clause can cost you money here, too, as can that lovely phrase, "anytime for any reason." That's where issuers can raise your rate strictly based on information in your credit report or a change in your credit score (more on this practice later).

Hoping to Restore Your Original Rate?

Don't expect the lender to automatically lower your rate on its own. Be smart, and call your bank to request a reduction in your interest rate as soon as you've lived up to the bank's requirements for resetting your rate.

Already paying a default rate? Find out what you have to do to get your account changed to a lower rate. Some lenders require you to make 6 or 12 consecutive on-time payments before the rate returns to the normal purchase APR. But the policies vary greatly.

3. Consider Credit Score Implications

Every time you apply for a new account, your credit score usually drops a few points. As a general rule, I recommend that you don't apply for more than one new account every 6 to 12 months.

A similar question that I'm frequently asked is, "How does taking advantage of multiple balance transfers affect my credit rating?" Viewpoints on this vary from "Risky" because of all the open credit accounts that it produces, to "It really doesn't change things much." The general consensus among experts is that your credit rating will not be adversely affected...as long as you do not do so excessively. In fact, some experts, including myself, maintain that "balance transferring" can actually improve your credit rating, at least in some instances.

More important, be careful not to use most of the credit limit on any of your cards (commonly called maxing out a card). Doing so really causes your credit rating to suffer. Ideally, you want to use only 10% or less of your credit limit. The higher your utilization, the more your score will suffer.

Finally, never make a late payment—never! Not only will this affect your credit score (generally when you are 30 days or more late), but as I've already showed, just one late payment could raise your low rate to exorbitant levels. And if you have more than one card, that single late payment can have a domino effect, with your other cards hiking up your rates. More details on credit scoring come in Chapter 9.

> **TIP**
> For the best payoffs from your credit cards, manage your credit responsibly, monitor your statements for rate changes, and keep your eyes out for better deals.

Low-Rate Introductory Offers and Blank Checks

Have you received a credit card offer recently that contains blank checks? I know I have. They often come with a letter that says, "Simply fill out these checks to pay off your loans, bills and other higher-rate credit card accounts. Or use them to improve your home, take a dream vacation, or...."

Piques your interest, doesn't it?

> **WARNING**
> Once you use some convenience checks, you may be billed at the pricey cash advance interest rate. Make sure you know the exact rate before you sign the check! If the check is treated as a cash advance, avoid it like the plague!

The key word to look for in these offers is *introductory.*

The offer has a great teaser rate for new purchases and balance transfers, typically for 6 to 12 months. Then the rate shoots up. Don't make the mistake of letting your debt ride at the higher rate when the introductory rate expires. You might as well throw money out the window.

If you're like most folks, you find these offers annoying and immediately toss them in the junk mail pile. Scott Bilker thinks this might be a costly mistake:

> *People don't want to be bothered with transferring their balances, but if it takes you 10 hours over the course of a year to save $1,000 by doing [balance] transfers, that's $100 per hour for your time, which isn't a bad hourly wage.*

Amen! Transferring balances from one card to another to take advantage of low introductory rate cards can result in *huge* interest savings. Likewise, financing purchases with low introductory rate cards can result in big savings.

As I write this, CardRatings.com is showing several cards touting a 0% introductory rate for 12 months. Tempting, I know, but proceed with caution and a little wisdom, or you could wind up paying so much in interest and fees that you actually end up losing money on the deal.

Let's look at how to make these offers work for you.

Don't Skip the Fine Print

Marketing departments are in the business of making the most enticing details jump out at you, distracting your attention from the less attractive parts of the offer: the details usually listed in the fine print. Educate yourself about all the terms before you sign on. If the fine print seems too daunting to comb through, give the bank a call and ask about the terms. The "Card Reports" section of CardRatings.com also tries to translate hard-to-understand terms into simple English.

So what should you look for? For starters, see what the introductory rate is, how long it lasts, and what the rate will be after the introductory period. Is there a balance transfer fee? (There usually is.) If so, what's the fee and how is it calculated?

Always find out if new purchases have a different rate than balance transfers. On cards being marketed to entice us to move our debts around, new purchases usually have a much higher rate. If so, follow this cardinal rule of balance transferring: Don't use this card for new purchases.

Getting the Best of Both Worlds!

Keep your eyes peeled for low intro rate offers that apply to both new purchases and balance transfers as these offers really can help you maximize your savings. Although most offers apply to balance transfers only or new purchases only, a few offers give you the best of both worlds. ☺

Lenders typically apply your payments first to the lower-interest debt—that is, to your transferred balance. This means that, until the balance transfer has been paid off, none of your payments are applied to your new purchases, which are being billed at a much higher rate. That can quickly wipe out any potential interest savings. As I write, Congress is considering legislation that will require card issuers to credit payments against the highest interest rate. Here's hoping!

If you use cards only for the reason you chose to have them in your wallet, you'll be in great shape. Simply put, use low-rate balance transfer offers strictly for balance transfers, and use cards that have as low a rate as possible for new purchases. Pay them off as quickly as you can, and you'll get to keep a lot more of your hard-earned dollars.

Do the Math

To get the most from the current crop of balance transfer offers, there's no avoiding it—you have to do the math. The good news is that the math is pretty simple. With transfer fees on the rise, it's important to take them into account. Here's how: Let's say you're considering a 12-month 3.99% transfer offer with a balance transfer fee of 4% (no cap on the fee). Add the rates, and you'll see that this is really the equivalent of a 7.99% purchase rate (3.99% + 4%), assuming that you pay off the transfer in one year. You'd want to take advantage of the offer only to transfer balances at rates that are greater than 7.99%.

Paying a fee for a balance transfer might be a good financial decision if it will result in interest savings. Of course, try to avoid fees, if at all possible. The bad news is that no-fee offers are becoming increasingly harder to find.

If you're considering an offer with fees, try to always find one that has a maximum fee (aka a fee cap). Issuers are required to disclose whether an offer has a maximum fee. It's usually located in or just below the Schumer Box. Maximum fees are generally in the range of $75 to $200. Obviously, the lower the cap, the greater your potential savings. Sometimes banks will eliminate or reduce the fees if you ask. It certainly doesn't hurt to try.

Watch the Dates

Scott Bilker says consumers make a "major mistake" by not tracking when a low-rate offer ends and then letting their debt ride at a much higher interest rate. Mark your calendar with the beginning and ending dates of teaser rates. Then you can guard against a higher interest rate either by paying off your debt before the intro period ends or by transferring the balance again.

Although they might not be as attractive on the surface as a 0% piece of plastic, don't rule out cards where the rate, usually in the 3.99%–6.99% range, remains in effect for the life of the transfer. This would mean that even if it takes you ten years or more to pay off your balance, your rate would not increase. These offers aren't nearly as widespread as introductory rate offers, but they're out there and are definitely worth considering.

For example, I was able to take advantage of a great offer from Capital One that was 1.99% for the life of the transfer. I used the proceeds to partially finance the purchase of a condo that my wife and I are using for investment purposes. (Right now, we're renting it out.) We were offered a mortgage of around 7%, but graciously declined. Compared to a mortgage, we will likely have saved thousands of dollars by the time we finish paying off the balance—even despite the fact that we won't get a tax deduction on our credit card interest like we would have gotten had we opted for a mortgage.

Pursue this type of offer if it will take you more than 6 to 12 months to pay down your debt—and if you don't want the risk associated with looking for another transfer offer after the current teaser rate expires. Bear in mind that although attractive transfer offers have been plentiful for many years, there's no guarantee that an attractive offer will present itself 12 months down the road. The beauty of these "life of the transfer" offers is that they allow you to lock in at a great rate for the long haul.

Use a Low-Rate Credit Card to Pay Down Any Type of Loan

Is a loan making a dent in your wallet? To save big bucks, follow the lead of my coworker Heshan Demel, who wanted to take advantage of his new Advanta card to pay down his auto loan. He learned that the bank will transfer balances from credit card companies, but not from creditors that hold installment loans, such as a car loan. However, Advanta was more than happy to deposit any amount, up to his credit line, into Heshan's bank account. Here's what Heshan had to say:

> *That was good enough for me...I told Advanta to transfer $8,000 to my checking account. The balance transfer fee was the maximum amount—of only $50. And as soon as I received the money, I paid off my car loan. Now $8,000 of my car loan is at 0% interest for 15 months! I'm saving a lot of interest doing this.*

Heshan's car loan was at 7.25%, which means that during those 15 months, he'll save around $700 in interest. Now, that's some creative financing and some serious savings! He's really practicing what we at CardRatings.com preach.

Be inspired by Heshan's success and his out-of-the-box thinking. I hope that you will carefully consider low-rate as well as low introductory rate offers. Play your cards right with a little organization and discipline, and you, too, can financially benefit in a big way.

CHAPTER 4

Avoid Problems That Hinder Maximum Profits

Credit cards can be great financial tools, rewarding us with low rates and nice perks when we use them wisely. But they can wreak tremendous financial and emotional havoc when used irresponsibly. There's just no profit in paying a pile of bank interest or having your credit score lowered—or your confidence shaken—because of too many credit card bills.

I've had first-hand experience with the incredible stress that card debt can cause. By the time I finished my graduate studies at the University of Texas at Dallas, I owed about $45,000 on my credit cards. So this is a topic that's near and dear to my heart.

Assuming that the interest rate was 18% and I sent in only the minimums, I'd have paid $67,115 in interest by the time I was out of debt, some 44 years later! Needless to say, card debt can quickly lead to financial devastation.

What makes it even worse is that we pay credit card interest with "after-tax dollars," the money that's left after we pay income taxes. Assuming that I'm in the 28% tax bracket, I'd have had to earn $93,215 to pay that $67,115 in interest—plus another $62,500 to pay back the $45,000 balance. My total cost would be $155,715. Ouch!

Fortunately, I found ways to get out from under my debt and turn the tables on the card issuers. Now, instead of paying them 18% (which is the equivalent of 25%

before taxes), I have them paying me. If I can do it, you can, too—I show you how in Chapter 5, "How to Slash Your Debt and Keep Your Hard-Earned Money for Yourself."

Certainly, it's a lot easier to profit from your credit cards when you don't start with a $45,000 balance. Hopefully I've gotten to you before you have a bill like that, and this chapter will help you avoid credit card debt so you can immediately profit from your cards. If you're carrying a balance, this chapter will give you some insight into how you accumulated that debt load, and the next chapter will help you winnow it down.

Debt and Depression

According to a 2007 study by Charles Schwab, more than a third of 30-something Americans (commonly called Generation X) are buried so deep in debt that they'll never be able to dig themselves out. Twenty percent say they are in such dire straits financially that they've had serious bouts of depression.

Jonathan Craig, a vice president at Charles Schwab, told the *New York Post,* "We expected [the 50 million Generation-X members] to be saddled with debt but didn't expect the anxiety related to debt."

Avoid Card Debt: Preventive Medicine for Your Pocketbook

The key to good health begins with a dose of prevention—eat right, exercise regularly, and get a good night's sleep. Do this, experts say, and you'll stop disease before it has a chance to strike. You'll get more out of life and be able to do what you want—scuba-dive in the Caribbean, hike up a mountain, or take a bike ride with your kids.

Your financial health is no different. With a dose of prevention, your future finances will get a clean bill of health, freeing you to live a life of choice and opportunity instead of one of difficulty and demands. You'll be able to afford a family vacation, sleep well at night, and derive maximum benefit from your credit cards.

As with preventive health measures, the following 12 simple strategies (some well known, some not) can help you prevent a debt problem or begin to solve one. When you no longer have a problem with debt, credit cards can ironically become wealth-building tools.

1. Keep Some Perspective— Don't Fall for the Hype

With television, billboards, radio, print publications, and the Internet, we're often exposed to hundreds of advertisements every day. Wherever we go, we're encouraged to buy, buy, buy—and to use our credit cards when we do.

The use of credit cards is ubiquitous and heavily marketed. Think about those commercials that show someone paying with cash slowing everyone down. Other people might have to wait a little, but your finances will benefit a lot from you not carrying a balance, especially on a high-rate card. Don't let yourself be rushed into spending money.

Some card issuers, particularly those that target consumers with bad credit, have lowered their standards over the past several years. This "subprime" market is huge, and if you're a member of it, watch out. Subprime cards often come with exorbitant fees and rates.

As a result, today nearly everyone has access to a credit card. And "buy now, be happy, pay later" sales pitches are targeted to every income and age group.

At the same time, we're moving further away from the values that led to our country's prosperity following the Great Depression. For the first time since then, Americans spent more than they earned in 2005. Instead of buying only what we can afford and saving for the future, we want it bigger, faster, and better—and we want it *now*.

Attitudes such as these, coupled with the increased purchasing power that credit cards offer, are a recipe for financial disaster. But it doesn't have to be that way. If there's one thing I want you to take away from this book, it's that you don't have to be a slave to your card company or to the seduction of advertising. Adopt my mantra: Credit cards should enhance your financial life, not some banker's.

2. Actively Manage Your Finances

It might seem obvious, but the most foolproof method for avoiding debt is to consistently spend less than you make. Before you spend another dime, make sure you have a strategy to manage your finances that will help you build your net worth.

You might dread the B-word, but a budget is a crucial tool in managing your finances wisely. Your budget can give you better control of your spending and also get you to start saving. The first step is determining your monthly income and expenses. As part of your monthly expenses, set aside 5% to 10% of your income for emergencies, long-range savings (such as a retirement account), and short-term savings.

No Need to Do It Alone

For hands-on help setting up your budget, some **consumer credit counseling** agencies offer free budget counseling. Go to NFCC.org or call 800-388-2227 for an office near you. Mint.com is another unique and helpful money management site. According to the site, Mint connects to over 5,000 U.S. banks and credit unions, credit card, brokerage, and mutual fund companies to keep your transactions and account balances automatically up-to-date. Mint even auto-balances your checkbook and auto-categorizes your transactions. Prefer a book? I recommend *The Budget Kit,* by Judy Lawrence (Kaplan Publishing, 2008).

Creating a budget is just the first step. Sticking to it is the next and, as you might expect, often more difficult task. To help motivate you, set some goals, starting with a modest objective that has a deadline. For example, you might choose to save for a long weekend getaway. Savings goals can be for an emergency fund, a vacation, or a car—and don't forget long-range goals, such as retirement.

Giving yourself a reward for accomplishing a savings goal can be a great motivator. For example, take a friend out to celebrate—or cook a special meal at your place, and save some money toward your next goal at the same time. Whatever you choose as a reward, don't let it compromise the hard work you've done in managing your finances.

3. Reach Out to Get Support and Save Money

Sticking to a budget and resisting temptation isn't easy. A little help from friends—and even strangers—can make a big difference. Tell your friends and family that you are doing everything you can to avoid debt, and ask them to help. Post to the CardRatings.com forum. People generally *want* to help.

Do you know someone who would make a good "budget buddy" for you? Ideally, you want a person you can turn to for moral support and who would volunteer constructive suggestions if you start spending more than you should.

Find ways to make cost-cutting a benefit. For example:

- Picnics rock. A standing brown-bag lunch with a friend at a park will make bringing your own lunch seem like a treat instead of a deprivation.

- Carpooling can save you a bundle, bring you together with like-minded folks, and help our planet.

- Making a few phone calls to comparison-shop for car and home insurance, as well as other goods and services, doesn't take much time but could easily save hundreds of dollars. Also, BillSaver.com makes comparison shopping convenient.

Cutting expenses isn't the only way to go. Consider how you can bring in more income as well. Can you get overtime at work? You also might find a part-time job or career. Check out Craigslist.org for possibilities near you. Discuss alternatives with friends, do some research at the library and online, and find low-risk ways to grow your family's income. Be sure to check out every financial opportunity thoroughly as get-rich-quick scams abound.

4. Avoid Extra Expenses

At the end of the month, do you ever find yourself asking, "Now where did all my money go?" A little bit here and a little bit there…inexpensive items can add up to be big budget-busters. A magazine. Gum. A Danish, donut, or power bar. A latte at Starbucks or Diet Coke at 7/11.

These little purchases quickly add up, and if you don't pay attention, you'll never realize the impact they have on your finances. To get a handle on them, budgeting experts urge us to closely track our daily spending—even the most trivial expenses—for a month.

You can use a little notebook, or if you're more high-tech than me, use your Blackberry. Just be sure to write down every single purchase. At the end of the month, compare your daily spending to your budget.

Putting as many of your purchases on a credit card can help you conveniently track your expenses. However, please exercise prudence if you choose to do so. Before you know it, you might find yourself carrying a balance, and there's no money to be made off a card if it takes years to pay off your pizza habit.

On a related note, smaller purchases can add up quickly. Increasingly, card issuers are targeting smaller purchases, and they're doing it in places where cash had historically been the preferred payment method. So there has been huge growth in card purchases under $25. One example of this trend is that many fast food restaurants are now accepting plastic. It

> **TIP**
>
> If you don't carry a credit card balance, follow my leads on getting and using a cash-back or reward card. Then charging even very small purchases that fit in your budget makes sense—and will lead to more freebies or cash for you.

pays to be especially careful and not let $10 here, $15 there get you into trouble.

5. Is a Card Right for You?

If you're someone who can be easily swayed to spend, there's a real benefit in avoiding the temptations that will land you in debt. For example, if impulse buying is your weakness, stay out of the malls.

I give plenty of card shopping tips in Chapters 1 to 3, but here I want to stress that reward and cash-back cards can be a source of too much temptation for some people. Studies show that, on average, people will spend more on a card when they get perks.

Even if you're able to pay your balance in full every month, don't use a reward card if it's likely to encourage you to exceed your monthly budget. One thing will lead to another, and you might soon find yourself carrying a balance, which will probably end up costing you much more than you'd get in rewards. Even if you don't end up carrying a balance, blowing your budget can lead to serious financial problems.

Finally, having helped thousands of consumers over the years, I firmly believe that not everyone can handle having a credit card. If you know that a card has been or will be your financial downfall (please be honest with yourself), I strongly urge you to use a debit card or cash. Although there are drawbacks to debit cards and cash, no drawback outweighs the negative impact of debt.

6. Pay the Balance in Full

Before you buy something, ask yourself, "Do I have the cash in the bank right now to pay for this?" If you can honestly answer yes, you should be able to avoid racking up debts and to pay your bills in full, each and every month. To do otherwise is very costly: The lenders get to make money off you instead of you earning some really nice perks from them.

However, as we all know, emergencies happen. If your rainy-day savings fund won't cover the whole amount you need to charge, pay it off as soon as you possibly can. The ideas I share in Chapter 5 will help.

7. Pay Before Your Due Date

Never, ever make a late payment. Even if your payment is only a few hours late, you run the risk of a late fee and an increased interest rate on that card as well as your other cards, thanks to universal default. To avoid this, credit expert Mike Killian, founder of LearnCreditManagement. com, recommends paying as early as possible, in case there's a problem with the mail and to allow processing time by the credit card company.

If you ever carry a balance, there's an added bonus to paying early: You're guaranteed to save money. Interest is typically based on your average daily balance, and when your payment arrives early, you lower that average daily balance. The lower your average daily balance, the less you pay in interest. So whenever you can swing it, get that check in the mail as soon as you receive the bill.

One way to make sure you pay bills as early as possible is with online bill payment. Online payments post quickly to your account with some issuers even crediting payments on the same day.

I've made hundreds of online bill payments over many years and have never had any problems. I always make my payments directly at the website of each individual card issuer. Many banks offer free online bill payment services as well.

Get "Drafted"

Another very convenient payment option to consider is automatic bill payments, where the funds are "drafted" from your checking account every month. Several issuers offer this free service, and I have a few of my personal cards set up on auto-draft. You can typically draft your full balance every month, your minimum payment, or a set amount that you specify. This is definitely an idiot-proof method that eliminates any possibility of making a late payment—as long as you have enough money in your bank account, of course!

---

8. Treat Your Credit Cards like Cash

An effective way to avoid debt is to psychologically use your credit cards just like cash. Why? Imagine the feel of that sleek plastic card in your hand. It seems to effortlessly slide right out of your wallet at the check-out counter. Each time you pull it out, it looks and feels the same. You don't feel like you're actually handing over your hard-earned money to someone, and you cannot physically see your charges climbing higher.

Now imagine a wad of $20 bills. The first time you pull it out of your wallet, it's thick—you feel rich! But with each purchase you make, the wad gets a little smaller, until eventually it's gone and you can't afford to buy anything else.

Howard Dvorkin, author of *Credit Hell: How to Dig out of Debt* (Wiley & Sons, 2005) and founder of Consolidated Credit Counseling Services, calls this the "green factor": With cash, you can feel the money, how much or how little you have. It's much easier to spend more if you use a credit card for all your purchases.

Treat your credit card like it's the actual green stuff, and you'll be less likely to get into debt.

9. Limit the Plastic in Your Pocket

Every credit card comes with its own set of terms and conditions, including varying interest rates, penalties, fees, grace periods, and due dates. Keeping track of only one or two cards makes it much easier to do the following:

- Get those payments in on time
- Remember which card has the lowest rate
- Limit your exposure to fraud
- Simplify your finances

Multiple cards might tempt you to spend more—or, even worse, borrow from Peter to pay Paul. Moving debt from one card to another (attractive balance transfer offers excluded) is often aptly compared to moving the deck chairs around on the *Titanic:* It'll drown you!

10. Cash Advances = Financial Suicide?

Cash advances are very costly and can quickly lead to a "financial freefall" that spirals out of control. They typically have a 3% fee (with no cap), a sky-high interest rate (normally in the 20%–25% range), and no grace period. That's right. You're charged a fee and then a higher interest rate than you would be on purchases, from the moment you take a cash advance.

Even worse, credit card companies normally apply your payments to the balance with the lowest interest rate first, which is usually the rate for purchases. So your $200 cash advance continues growing at more than 20% a year until your $2,000 purchase balance is completely paid off.

A frightening example of just how much things can get of control comes from an anonymous poster on the CardRatings.com forum:

> *I had perfect credit, and thus I had a lot of available credit. I maxed out my cash advance limits on my cards, and now I owe $118,000. I lost this cash in Atlantic City betting the tables. Any advice? Can I file for bankruptcy for this? Can they garnish my wages?*

Although this is certainly an extreme example from someone whose money problems can probably be best solved at GamblersAnonymous.org, I hope it makes you think twice about getting a cash advance.

11. Say "No!" to Extra Products and Services

Credit card companies often try to get you to purchase additional products or services, such as credit-monitoring and various insurance products (more on this topic in Chapter 10, "Maximize the Benefits of Your Cards by Taking Advantage of Additional Free Perks"). The truth of the matter is, you usually don't need any of these products. The money you save by just saying, "No!" can be better applied to paying down your debt or, if you're not in debt, adding to your retirement account.

12. Benefit from Planning and Saving

Many folks have debts because of a lack of financial planning. For those predictable major life events, such as a future college education or even a baby, start saving today.

If life turns out differently, at the very worst, you'll have a nice nest egg for retirement or emergencies.

Speaking of emergencies, I've never met a person who hasn't had some type of financial emergency. Unfortunately, bad—sometimes even tragic—circumstances invade our lives, putting us under unexpected financial pressure.

No one can be 100% prepared for such events, but setting aside a little extra money each month can definitely help you cope when life throws you a curve ball. It's a good idea to have three to six months' worth of living expenses set aside in a savings account, just in case of a job loss or other emergency. With some money in the bank, you won't have to go into credit card debt during times of a crisis.

Although it could take several years to reach your emergency fund goal by saving just 5% to 10% of your income each month, as the old saying goes, half the battle is just getting started. So what are you waiting for?

Chances are, no matter how stretched you are financially, you can quickly discover ways to put aside some money. For example, as you receive raises or bonuses, instead of spending the extra money, continue living on the same budget and put the difference toward your savings. Similarly, save all tax refunds and bank all gifts of cash.

There you have it, a dozen practical tactics to help you avoid the trap of card debt. Start practicing them today. If you've already started, keep up the good work, stay debt-free, and make the most of your credit cards.

CHAPTER 5

How to Slash Your Debt and Keep Your Hard-Earned Money for Yourself

Preventive measures are great, but if you're burdened by debt, you need more than preventive medicine to conquer it. I won't sugar-coat it: Getting debts under control can be a bitter pill—but the alternatives are even less appetizing. The rewards, though, are delicious. Imagine getting actual cash from your credit card issuer instead of paying the company all the interest and fees. Imagine a time when no more bill collectors are calling.

I know how hard it is to imagine those scenes when you're worried about how you'll get through the next month. If it's any consolation, you're not alone. With these difficult economic times, the subprime mortgage crisis, and the credit crunch, far too many hard-working American families are one paycheck away from financial ruin.

Foreclosures filings are on the rise, up 75% in 2007, and bankruptcies are surging as well, up 27% nationwide in the first quarter of 2008, compared with the first quarter of 2007, according to the American Bankruptcy Institute. Credit card debt has more than quadrupled during the last two decades. All it takes is a job loss or a serious illness, and a middle-class family can find itself living below the poverty level.

Too many people don't fully grasp the gravity of their debts until it's too late. As credit expert Gerri Detweiler explains:

> *Americans are pretty optimistic, so it often takes a long time for a consumer to realize that debts are a problem. Most of us are counting on something to help us get rid of the debt quickly—a raise, business income, even an inheritance or lottery ticket.*

It's too costly to hope for fate to bail us out of debt trouble. Instead, let's roll up our sleeves and get to work.

Is It Time to Get Serious about Your Debts?

You don't want to be one of those statistics, but it's not always easy to tell when it's time to get serious. Detweiler says the following warning signs should serve as a "you're-over-your-head-in-debt" wake-up call:

- You have no clear plan for paying back the debt.
- You have no idea know how long it will take or how much it will cost.
- Your credit card balances continue to go up instead of down, even though you make monthly payments.
- You're juggling, using one credit card to help pay the balance on a different credit card.

Just moving debt around to other cards with similar or higher rates (low rate balance transfer offers excluded), which I call "credit card Russian Roulette," is a very dangerous, expensive game to play. Credit cards often charge the highest rates around, so you'll pay plenty of interest, and often, you'll add even more to your balance through various fees and rate hikes.

Does any of this hit home for you? If so, keep reading—I show you how you can master your credit card debt, keep more of your money, and start living debt-free.

Diagnose the Problem

Diagnosing the underlying problem is the first step in a successful debt-busting strategy. Too often, people decide to pursue debt relief without facing the underlying reason for their debt, which is usually overspending or poor money management.

Then within a couple of years, the person is often right back where he or she started, only this time, trying to pay off a **debt consolidation** loan while also figuring out what to do with new card charges. This can result in a vicious cycle, adding layer upon layer of debt.

> **TIP**
>
> Admitting that you have a problem is half the battle. So, the fact that you're reading this chapter implies that you're well on your way to becoming debt free!

Diagnosing the underlying problem(s) can be challenging. In some instances, it might require the intervention of an objective third party, such as a credit counselor, to help you figure out what's going on and to get you on the right track.

Many financial counselors advise that you choose a company affiliated with the nonprofit National Foundation for Credit Counseling (NFCC), which provides services in more than 1,300 locations. More than a third of people who consult with an NFCC counselor are soon able to manage their debts on their own. Go to CardRatings.com/Book to locate an office near you. More on credit counseling comes later in the chapter.

If your problem is a serious overspending issue, therapy or DebtorsAnonymous.org might help you overcome the habit—or addiction.

On the other hand, the diagnosis might be very simple. For many people, large credit card balances are caused by medical bills, not overspending. Believe it or not, doctors and hospitals have been known to lower their fees and offer more lenient repayment terms. I know this is true from personal experience. Ask and you just might receive.

For other people, debt can often be traced to one significant life event, such as a wedding. Many couples charge tens of thousands of dollars to pay for dream weddings. Caught up in the excitement and emotions of the event, it can be difficult, although not impossible, to remain level-headed. Unfortunately, the honeymoon soon ends, and the reality of large bills can be a source of major stress for newly married couples, according to Cindy Morus, a certified Divorce Financial Analyst and the founder of MendYourMoney.com.

Planning a Debt-Defying Strategy: The Basics

After you diagnose the problem, it's time to set in motion a strategic plan of attack to defeat your debts. I know how stressful and overwhelming this can be, so remember, if I can do this, you can too. It might not be simple and it won't happen overnight, but with a little persistence, you can do it.

Go Cold Turkey

If you want to really get serious about controlling your debts, decide right now, at this very moment, to stop using your cards. Going cold turkey could be one of the hardest things you've ever done, but I'm convinced that it will be a very significant turning point in your life.

No need to close the accounts—just take those cards out of your wallet and put them somewhere where you can't easily retrieve them. I recommend cutting them up into little pieces because if you're tempted to start charging again, it'll take days for a replacement card to come. Freezing them in a cup of water at the back of the freezer or locking them in a safe buried five feet underground will also work—whatever it takes to get rid of easy access!

> **TIP**
>
> If you're an online shopper, chances are, you've typed your card number into online forms so many times that you've committed it to memory or your number is saved on your computer. You'll have to delete those digits from your mind and computer, or figure out a way to exert extra self-control. Otherwise, you might have to stay offline, and I know you don't want to do that. ☺

It's not easy, but forget about your credit cards and don't apply for any more, especially at retail stores. Even if they promise to give you 50% off all purchases for the next 60 days (they normally offer only 10% to 20% off one purchase), remember that half of $500 is still $250 more than you would have spent if you hadn't signed up for the card. If you have the $250, you'd be smart to use it to pay down your debt.

Live Within Your Means

To avoid adding to your problem as you pay down your existing debts, ask yourself, "Am I living within my means?" If you aren't able to honestly answer this question, you have a problem with budgeting, denial, or both. If the bills keep coming in and you don't know where you stand, you're not managing your money effectively. You'll likely continue to charge more than you can afford going forward, which will make your existing financial problems even worse.

Certainly, if you have a pile of bills, not only are you paying a lot in interest, but those bills are preventing you from making the most off your money. Moreover, until your lifestyle changes and you no longer pay credit card interest, you won't be able to truly benefit from card perks. Fortunately, it's easy to make some simple changes that will make a big difference.

Find Extra Cash

The more you can pay toward your bills, the faster and cheaper it will be to get rid of your debts. Here are some tips to help you find extra money as you rein in your lifestyle a bit:

- Reduce housing costs. You could move to a smaller house, but remember that moving is not free. What about a roommate? When I was struggling to pay off my debt in Dallas, Texas, my rent payments were pretty steep. I decided to move back home to Arkansas to live rent-free in a small house my parents owned. Think creatively.

- Conserve. Set your thermostat a couple degrees higher in the summer and a couple degrees lower in the winter. Check with your electric, gas, and water companies for conservation tips.

- Distinguish between wants and needs. Do you really need high-speed Internet, satellite or cable television, a cell phone for every family member, a new living room set, high-priced sneakers for the kids, and so on? You get the idea.

- Don't go overboard, but do get the whole family involved in cutting back. A family meeting might be just the thing to help facilitate change. Be realistic, though: Too much deprivation is bound to backfire.

But remember, some belt-tightening changes might need to be only temporary.

- Become a one-car family, especially if your city has good public transportation or well-developed bike routes. Not only will your financial health improve, but your physical health could as well.

- Get a second job. Although it might be humbling, temporarily being willing to work in any type of environment will likely leave you with a feeling of purpose and control over your finances.

- Quit your vice. How much do you spend a month on shoes you don't need? Maybe now is a good time to finally kick the smoking habit. Or did you ever think about how much you spend a month on coffee or soda?

- Lead yourself not into temptation. Buying name brands at a trendy boutique or eating out at fancy restaurants is nice, but if you can't afford it, don't even go there. Rummage through your closets for something that's back in style (after all, what goes around, comes around), and cook a great meal at home.

- Cut entertainment costs. Watch free movies from the library and make your own popcorn instead of going to the theater and buying high-priced treats there. Take a walk at sunset. Play board games. (It's so much easier to recover from a bankruptcy playing Monopoly than from one in real life!)

- Use your savings. The interest rate we earn on savings accounts is typically far lower than what we have to pay on credit card balances. It makes sense to use money earning in the range of 1% to 5% to pay off bills at much higher rates. Then when your debt is paid off, work to replenish your savings. Note, however, that I'm not suggesting that you deplete your entire emergency savings fund.

- Declutter and sell some of that extra "stuff." There's money to be made off whatever is taking up space in your house or apartment. Have a garage sale, go to a flea market, or use an online auction site, such as eBay. How many televisions, sweaters, baseball cards, pieces of Depression glass, and so on do you need? Dust less and put the money toward your debts.

- Throw a party. As Danny Schechter put it in his documentary *In Debt We Trust,*

    In America's earliest days, there were barn-raising parties in which neighbors helped each other build up their farms. Today, in some churches, there are debt liquidation revivals in which parishioners chip in to free each other from growing credit card debts that are driving American families to bankruptcy and desperation.

Don't Fall into the Minimum Payment Trap

Paying only the required minimum amount will often keep you in card debt for decades. These minimums typically range from 2% to 3%, and the lower the percent, the less you're required to send in every month. The less you send in, the more you'll pay over the years. For example, consider a $5,000 credit card debt at 17% with differing minimums (see Table 5.1).

For the total cost, add $5,000 to the interest cost. Paying only the minimum on Card A, for example, would result in a total cost of $30,354 ($5,000 + $25,354).

Look at the numbers in bold. If you send in only the minimum, you could spend anywhere from $25,354 down to $4,296 to pay off the exact same amount, at the same interest rate. Isn't that amazing?

Table 5.1 What a Difference a Fraction of a Percent Makes

Card	Minimum % Payment	First Month's Payment	Interest Cost	Years to Pay Off
A	1.67%	$83.50	$25,354	81
B	2.00%	$100.00	$11,304	40
C	2.50%	$125.00	$6,210	24
D	3.00%	$150.00	$4,296	18

Table 5.1 reprinted with permission from *Slash Your Debt: Save Money and Secure Your Future,* by Gerri Detweiler, Marc Eisenson, and Nancy Castleman (Financial Literacy Center, 1999).

There's just a $50 difference between Card B's and Card D's first month's required payment, but Card B ends up costing an additional $7,000 over the years. Wouldn't you rather have that money than send it to a bank?

Although the 3% minimum would clearly be much better on your wallet, remember that all minimums are set up to make the card issuers money, not you.

Until recently, sometimes companies set the minimums so low that 100% of a cardholder's monthly payment might be applied to interest and fees, with none of it going toward the original card balance. Then in 2005, in response to growing criticism, the Office of the Comptroller of the Currency (OCC), which regulates national banks, issued new guidelines regarding minimum payment policies.

Now the minimum monthly payments must be high enough to cover all fees and interest—and pay down at least a small portion of the debt. Some minimum payments have gone up, but there hasn't been any dramatic change. Most members of the CardRatings.com forum report minimum payments in the range of 2% though minimums do vary. Some issuers, for example, compute minimums as 1% of your balance plus any interest charges and fees.

Even with a higher required minimum payment, you'll save more money by *always* paying more than that amount. Even paying a little more than the minimum can result in significant savings.

Create a Repayment Plan: The Do-It-Yourself Strategy

It's not hard to create a repayment plan that will work for you. Take it one step at a time, and you'll have a strategy in place in no time.

Face Your Debt

If you're like many people in debt, you don't have a clear idea of how much you actually owe. Let's find out—it's not hard.

Gather your most current card statements, and call the toll-free customer service numbers, or go online to find out the most up-to-date balance, interest rate, amount due this month, due date, and minimum percent. Don't forget about your other debts, including student loans, car loans, and mortgage.

You can make a simple spreadsheet on your computer with a program such as Microsoft Excel, but a handwritten chart will certainly work. Your spreadsheet might look something like Table 5.2 (leave room to add two more columns):

Table 5.2   How Much Do I Owe?

Card	Balance	Interest	Minimum	Due		
#1	$ 2,750	14%	3% ($83)	On the 5th		
#2	$ 3,800	12%	2.5% ($95)	On the 15th		
Up-scale store	$ 900	20%	3% ($27)	On the 10th		
#3	$ 4,500	13%	2% ($90)	On the 25th		
Total	**$11,950**		**($295)**			

If these were your debts, you'd owe a total of $11,950, and you'd have to come up with $295 this month just to make the minimum payments. Believe it or not, if you stop charging and can come up with that same amount every month from here on, you can get out of debt in just a few years.

Create a similar chart for *your* debts, and I'll show you how you can achieve incredible savings, just like I did.

Find the True Cost of Your Debt

Unfortunately, because of the interest and fees you'll pay over time, the real cost of your debt is usually much more than the total of what you owe ($11,950, in our example).

To take a look at the impact of interest and fees over time, let's compare how much you'll pay if you send in only the required amounts to how much you'll pay if you keep sending in this month's required payment. We'll get the computer to do the math, so it'll be easy—as well as eye-opening.

Start by adding two additional columns to your spreadsheet. Label them "Cost in Dollars and Years—Minimum" and "Cost in Dollars and Years—Early."

This is when an online calculator comes in especially handy. On CardRatings.com, click on "Credit Calculators" and then choose the calculator called "The Minimum Payment Trap."

Plug in the info from your spreadsheet for the first debt—your balance, interest rate, and minimum percent (where it says "How is your minimum payment calculated?"). After you select the minimum percent, you'll see how much the calculator thinks you should send in this month. Make sure it squares with the number on your spreadsheet.

The last question to answer before you press the Calculate button is "What fixed payment could you make each month?" For now, let's assume that you can send in as much as you sent in this month. Type in that same amount, and then select a payment schedule based on a fixed payment. (Can't afford this amount? There's debt-management advice tailored to you toward the end of this chapter.)

Presto, the calculator shows the difference between paying each month's required minimum and paying the first month's minimum every month. Add the numbers to your spreadsheet.

Go back and run the same calculations for each of your debts. After you do the first one, it'll be a snap. Table 5.3 shows the spreadsheet for our sample bills.

Table 5.3   How Much Will My Debts Cost Me?

Card	Balance	Interest	Minimum	Due	$/Yr— Min	$/Yr— Early
#1	$2,750	14%	3% ($83)	On the 5th	$1,629 13 years	$753 3.6 years
#2	$3,800	12%	2.5% ($95)	On the 15th	$2,380 16.8 years	$1,077 4.3 years
Up-scale store	$900	20%	3% ($27)	On the 10th	$866 10.3 years	$425 4.2 years
Bank #3	$4,500	13%	2% ($90)	On the 25th	$4,951 25.9 years	$2,016 6.1 years
Total	$11,950		($295)		$9,826	$4,271

If these were your debts, paying the minimums would cost you $9,826, plus the $11,950 you owed in the first place (assuming there are no additional charges to the cards). Remember, these are after-tax numbers. Assuming that you pay 28% in taxes, you'd have to earn $13,647 to cover that $9,826 interest tab. Also, you'd be paying on all the bills for more than a decade, when the up-scale store charge would finally be paid off. You'd be paying Bank #3 for almost 26 years.

Now look at what happens if you continue to send in this month's required minimums until the balances are paid off. There's a dramatic difference. Although you'd pay $4,271 in interest, simply by sending in your first month's minimum payment each and every month, there's another $5,555 in interest you would never have to pay ($9,826 – $4,271). It would cost you $7,715 before taxes to come up with that $5,555.

Isn't it amazing? Simply by sending in the same amount you managed to come up with this month (a total of $295, in our example), you'd save 57%, compared to just paying the minimums. All your debts would be retired in around 6 years instead of almost 26 years!

If you're wondering how this could be possible, it's because you'd be *putting the power of compound interest to work for you, not for the bank.* Over time, more and more of each payment would go to paying off what you owe. The less you owe, the less interest you have to pay.

Always pay more than the minimum, preferably a fixed amount every month. I suggest a fixed amount so you can see in advance how much you'll save. You can use that same calculator on CardRatings.com to plug in any steady early payment amount. Play around with the numbers a little, and you'll hopefully get encouraged.

Here are a few examples, and to keep you from glazing over all the numbers, I'll keep it simple. We'll start with the same $11,950 debt, but we'll pretend it's all on one card that charges 14% a year and has a 2.5% minimum.

If you add another $100 to the first month's required amount and send that in

TIP

When you've crunched the numbers for your debts and know how much you'll save, give yourself a little extra motivation. Write that number in big, bold print. Put it someplace where you will see it regularly.

every month until the bill is paid off, your interest bite would be $2,840. Consistently paying $100 above the minimum would save you more than $7,400.

If that's more than you can afford, how about paying another $25 a month? Your interest tab would be $3,771. You'd have over $6,400 more to use however you saw fit, and you'd be completely out of debt in four years.

More Proven Techniques to Pay Down Debt

Here are some other tactics that can help you get out of debt.

Ask Your Credit Card Company to Work with You

Calling your lenders and asking them to work with you is always a good move, especially if your situation is only temporary. Many people assume this is a waste of time, but studies show just the opposite. Also, I know this works from personal experience. I've already explained how to call and negotiate with your card issuer for a lower interest rate (see Chapter 3, "Unlock the Key to Huge Savings: Master Credit Card Rates and Transfer Offers"). You can also ask to be enrolled in a hardship program or ask for a break as you try to pay them back.

Most consumers don't realize that a card issuer has a lot to lose if you end up defaulting and/or declaring bankruptcy. According to John Ventura, Director of the Texas Complaint Center at the University of Houston and author of *Managing Debt for Dummies* (Wiley Publishing, 2007), depending on the type of bankruptcy you file, they might never see another dime from you. It's definitely in their best interest to work with you (more on bankruptcy at the end of this chapter).

These are tough times for creditors as well, who are reporting significant increases in "serious delinquencies"— that is, accounts that are at least 90 days late. They're giving up on an increasing number of these accounts and are planning for continued problems with delinquencies throughout the rest of 2008 and even into 2009.

Before cutting you any breaks, a creditor might require your participation in a debt-management program (DMP) run by a credit counseling agency (more about DMPs soon). Bottom line: Always ask the banks to work with you—the worst they can say is no.

If you're wondering why the banks want people in credit counseling, it's not out of the goodness of their hearts. Gerri Detweiler says lenders do this to get a fair shake. They know all your creditors will generally be asked to participate, and all creditors will be treated fairly. American Express doesn't want to settle for less in interest if you're still paying Chase full price.

Pay the Highest-Rate Card First

To save the most money, first focus on paying off the balance at the highest interest rate. Be sure to pay the minimums on all your other bills, and pay them on time. The last thing you want is to be hit with a more than 30% default rate because of late payments.

Every month, send in as much additional money as you can toward the balance at the highest rate. When I tackled my $45,000 credit card debt, I made lifestyle changes and put all that I could toward my highest-rate card. When that card was paid off, I tackled the one with the next-highest rate, and so on.

If at all possible, be sure to keep sending in at least as much every month, as you go from debt to debt, and you'll be out of debt faster than you ever thought possible.

Pay the Lowest Balance First

This tactic is sometimes more of a mind game than a sound financial strategy because your lowest balance could very well have your lowest interest rate. The idea here is to give yourself a "quick fix" so you can benefit from a dose of immediate gratification. The hope is that if you knock off a card's balance fast, you'll gain confidence and be motivated to move on to the next balance. Please note: I would only recommend this strategy if your lowest balance is very small (under $1,000 or so). Otherwise, you will likely pay much more in finance charges than if you paid off your highest rate card first.

Keep paying the minimum on all your credit cards except the one with the lowest balance. Send in as much as you possibly can above the required amount. When you've paid off the card with the lowest balance, choose the next balance to pay off.

Do you need another quick victory, or do you want to save the most money and pay off the card that charges the highest rate? Or is there another debt you'd rather wipe out? You decide. Keep plowing in at least as much every month, and you'll save big!

Consolidate and/or Get an Unsecured Personal Loan

Debt consolidation is invariably a hot topic. Wherever you look, someone is advertising new ways to consolidate your debt into "one low payment," at rock-bottom rates. As you might expect, there are a few hitches with the hype.

First, if you're not careful, that low payment will cost you more over the long run than if you stick with the payment plan that you have now. To finance that low monthly payment, there's usually a higher interest rate and/or a longer **term** for the new loan. Although all your payments might be lumped together and you pay less a month than you do now, your overall tab will go up, not down.

It pays to consider a debt-consolidation loan only if it offers significant savings and it comes from a reliable source. You can use the calculators on CardRatings.com to compare possible loans to your current card balances.

Another problem with these heavily advertised loan offers is their use of phrases such as "up to" and "as low as." For example, Alecia, an active member of the CardRatings.com forum, got an offer with a 7.99% rate advertised on the front of the solicitation, but when she got to the fine print, the rate was from 7.99% up to 19.99%.

When you get a consolidation loan from a bank, it's normally considered an **unsecured loan,** with only your word for collateral. Therefore, don't expect a very low rate—and bear in mind your credit score will often have a strong bearing on the rate you qualify for. Also, you might get a better deal at a credit union because they often have lower rates.

If the rate and terms are better on an unsecured loan than what you're currently paying on your credit cards, do a "gut check" and decide how much you can realistically afford to pay every month. Can you count on yourself to meet the new monthly payment? Great! As with credit cards, when you can afford to send in more, do it, and you'll save even more.

Friends and Family

Have you considered asking a family member or a well-to-do friend if you can borrow the money you need for debt consolidation? Such a loan might be an excellent financial arrangement for both parties.

But watch out. You might start with the best of intentions—to pay a higher interest rate to your brother than he can get for his savings account—but if you don't follow through, it can tear your family apart.

I recommend getting some tax advice, making a formal agreement about how much you'll pay back every month, and committing to that agreement in writing. The website VirginMoneyUS.com can help you with this.

Don't go for a family loan unless you can really trust yourself to pay it back. But if you can trust yourself, you can save a lot while you bring in some extra income for your loved one. This can be a win-win situation.

On a related note, check out Prosper.com, which offers unsecured loans directly from other people throughout the country (a new type of lending known as "peer-to-peer lending" that is gathering momentum). Because financial institutions aren't part of Prosper, rates tend to be lower than with traditional loans. Prosper is particularly a good alternative if you don't have any family or friends willing to loan you money! ☺

Balance Transfer Offers

I can personally attest to the benefits of using low-introductory-rate balance transfers to get out of debt. They were a tremendous help when I winnowed down my $45,000 credit card burden.

Although these offers can help you dramatically slash your interest charges, unfortunately, some lenders seem to be shortening the length of introductory offers and increasing the rates and fees. No-fee offers are very rare—make sure to carefully check the fine print to understand exactly what fee you will be charged. Also, there aren't as many 0% offers for 12 months as there once were, although they're definitely still out there. Now there are more offers in the 1.9%–4.9% range that last only three to nine months, which means you are more likely to have to resort to multiple balance transfers if you have the sort of debt load that I had and you want the best rates.

If you're carrying a significant amount of debt, consider a balance transfer offer that has a low fixed rate for the life of the balance. The entire balance you transfer will remain at that low rate for as long as it takes you to pay down your entire balance. Rates on these offers are typically around 3.99% to 6.99%. True, the rate won't be as low as cards hawking 0% to 2.9% teaser rates. But the interest savings can still be huge, and you won't have to worry about transferring balances every 6 to 12 months. The other big advantage of locking in at a rate for life is you eliminate the risk of not qualifying for another balance transfer offer when your current teaser rate expires and/or there are simply no other attractive balance transfer offers available.

Home Equity Loan/Line of Credit

Using a home equity loan or home equity line of credit (HELOC) to pay down credit card debt has become very popular with homeowners in the last several years. And, despite the fact that these type of loans are harder to qualify for now thanks to the recent problems in the mortgage industry, utilizing your home equity is still an option worth considering. Home equity loans have two distinct advantages that I was glad to take advantage of when I paid off my debts. First, you will probably be able to get a lower interest rate. Second, you might be able to deduct the interest on your tax return (which you can't do with credit card interest).

Consolidating with home equity does come with downsides, however. You might have to pay closing costs and other fees. Also, some home equity loans come with a large final payment (called a balloon payment) that you need to figure into your repayment plan. Analyze the finer details and remember that lower payments don't always equal lower cost. BankRate.com is a good place to search for the latest rate offers.

Another downside to using your home equity for debt payoff is that you're tying up what is often your most valuable financial resource. According to Jordan Goodman, author of *Everyone's Money Book on Credit* (Kaplan Business, 2002),

> *I hear people say to me all the time that they are now out of debt since they used their home equity loan to pay off their credit cards, when in fact all they have done is shift their debt from one place to another and put their largest asset, their house, on the line at the same time. If you've used the equity in the house to pay off your credit card bills, your remaining home equity won't necessarily be available when you have a real need for a lot of capital, like when the first college tuition bills come rolling in or you have a major medical emergency that is not covered by health insurance.*

The most alarming aspect of using a home equity loan is that you're putting your house in jeopardy. Unlike card debt, which is unsecured, a home equity loan is a **secured debt,** with your house as collateral. Failing to make credit card payments does lead to a lot of negative consequences, but defaulting on your home equity loan puts your home at risk. If you can't completely trust yourself to make every single payment, putting your home on the line simply doesn't make sense.

Is It Time for Professional Help?

Sometimes tackling your debts alone isn't the best option, but you might resist getting help and even wonder whether you need it. Take a look at some of the following statements, and see if they apply to you:

- You haven't been successful in working out a reasonable repayment plan.
- Your repayment plan stretches many, many years into the future. You should typically be able to repay credit card debt within five years or so.
- Your total monthly debt payments, not including your mortgage, equal more than 20% of your take-home pay.
- You can't pay the minimum amounts due on your cards every month.
- You're consistently late paying one or more regular bills (for example, utilities and car loans).
- You're hounded by creditors and collection agencies.

Do any of these statements ring true to you? If so, let's talk about some ways to get help.

Credit Counseling

A certified counselor at a reputable credit counseling agency (ideally, a member of nfcc.org) should offer several helpful services, including these:

- A personalized budget based on your income and expenses
- A repayment plan based on your total debts and how much you can pay each month
- Lower interest charges

- A monthly lump sum that you send to the counseling agency, which then distributes it among your various creditors
- The timely and accurate payment of all creditors
- A lots of free educational material

Look for these characteristics when deciding on a credit counseling agency:

- Accreditation by the National Foundation for Credit Counseling (NFCC) or the Association of Independent Consumer Credit Counseling Agencies.
- A nonprofit agency—but don't be swayed just because a company is nonprofit. According to Jim Young, CEO of Accelerated Debt Management (link at CardRatings.com/Book), many nonprofits don't have your best interest at heart. In fact, the Internal Revenue Service has revoked the licenses of many nonprofits in recent years.
- A clean bill of health. Contact the local Better Business Bureau or your state Attorney General's office to see if any complaints have been filed against the company. If so, find out how the issue was resolved.

> **TIP**
>
> Accelerated Debt Management is the only company I know of that discloses the interest rates you can expect to pay with various card issuers if you enroll in one of its programs. There's a link to this valuable information at CardRatings.com/Book.

- Referrals. If none are volunteered, be sure to ask for some, and make the calls.

Be sure to ask these questions before you sign on with a credit counseling agency:

- What services do you offer?
- What educational materials are available for free?
- How will you help me with my debt problem in the short term?
- Will you help me develop a plan to avoid debt problems in the future?
- What are your fees?
- What if your fees are too high for me to afford?
- Are you licensed to offer services in my state?
- Are your counselors accredited or certified? If so, by whom? If not, what training do they receive?
- Is there a formal agreement or contract to sign?
- From what other sources do you receive funding? Who regulates and audits your operations? Are you certified by the International Standard of Operations (ISO)?
- Will you keep my personal information confidential and secure?
- Are your employees paid a salary or on commission? If they are paid by salary, high-pressure sales tactics should be absent.

Watch out for these red flags:

- Large up-front fees. Most reputable agencies have monthly fees, but they should be reasonable. According to Linda Tucker, Director of Education and Marketing for Consumer Credit Counseling Service in North Little Rock, Arkansas, a basic monthly service fee ranging from $15 to $25 is charged, to everyone who enrolls in its debt-management plan (DMP). This is a reasonable fee. (Bear in mind, though, that fees will vary depending on which part of the country that you live in.)

- Agencies that require detailed information about your situation before sending out free information about the services they supply.

- Agencies that charge for educational materials.

- Agencies that won't help you because you can't afford their fees.

- Agencies that push you to enroll in their paid DMP before they will fully analyze your financial situation.

- Employees paid on commission instead of salary.

- An agency whose counselors are not trained by an outside, unaffiliated source.

- Unrealistic promises, such as erasing your credit history. No one can do that. Under the Fair Credit Reporting Act, accurate information about your accounts stays on your report for up to seven years.

A credit counselor should spend at least an hour analyzing your finances with you (ideally, in person). If you both agree that a DMP is beneficial to your particular situation, you'll want to ask another set of questions:

- Will you continue to provide budget counseling if I choose not to enroll in the DMP? If the answer is no, find another agency.

- How does your DMP work? Look for a program that pays your creditors before the due date and in the current billing cycle. If the agency makes late payments or misses payments, it will only hurt your credit history.

  Cathy, a member of the CardRatings.com forum, had a bad payment experience with a credit counseling company. According to Cathy, "They paid one account late, though I didn't know it." Because of this error, she has had ongoing trouble with a major card issuer. Her advice: "Proceed with caution with any consumer credit counseling agency or debt-management program."

- Will I continue to receive monthly statements from my creditors? If not, what types of reports do you send and how often? *It's your credit history on the line* so make sure the program offers ways to keep track of your interest rate, payments, and balances.

- Will you work to get my creditors to lower or eliminate interest charges and fees? If they say yes, it's a good idea to verify it personally with your creditors.

- What debts are not included in the plan? This is especially important information. You must continue making payments to creditors that are not included in the DMP.

- Do I have to make upfront payments with any creditors before they will accept me? If a counselor tells you yes, call the creditor personally to verify.

- Will my past-due accounts be "re-aged" (meaning brought current)? If so, how long will it take? Note that re-aging accounts does not delete past delinquencies or late payments from your credit report. Also, according to federal law, re-aging can only take place if the account has not been re-aged in the past year and no more than twice in last five years.

As the DMP is being established, it's important to keep paying your creditors so you aren't charged late fees and penalties. This will also keep negative information from appearing on your credit history. After you've enrolled, contact each creditor to confirm that it has accepted the terms of the proposed plan.

Debt Settlement and/or Negotiation

Ads for debt settlement companies are rampant and many claim to be able to settle your debt for a fraction of what you currently owe. While these ads may sound very tempting, don't confuse a DMP with debt settlement or negotiation. Consumer advocates generally don't promote debt settlement or negotiation plans, but these can be a viable alternative for consumers who owe a lot of money and are considering bankruptcy.

As with credit counseling agencies, debt settlement companies normally have you send monthly payments to them instead of your creditors. They promise to hold the funds until all parties have agreed upon a negotiated balance, and they typically claim to have the power to reduce the full amount you owe by 50% or more.

> **BEWARE!**
> Creditors are not required to negotiate with debt settlement companies, so whatever you're told or read, know that there are no guarantees.

To enroll in a debt settlement program, your accounts must normally be in default or past due by 90 days or more. This means that you've stopped paying creditors, who are now charging you interest at a high default or penalty rate. You're racking up late fees as well, and if your credit line is exceeded in the process, even more fees will be added. Your credit score has already likely plummeted or will soon do so, and your debts are typically growing at an astronomical rate.

Debt settlement companies often require you to pay separate fees, such as a setup fee, a monthly service fee, and even a percentage of the amount you save. Finally, the IRS can step in and tax as income any amount of debt that has been forgiven above $600, so it's important to consult a tax advisor before you pursue any type of debt settlement plan.

Although many negative aspects are involved, if you owe a lot of money, are 90 days or more behind on your accounts, and can't afford to pay the minimum requirements of a DMP, you should consider both debt settlement and bankruptcy.

If you decide to try a debt settlement firm, make sure you contact the state Attorney General to see if debt settlement companies are required to be licensed in your state. They can also tell you whether a particular company is licensed. Additionally, it's always a good idea to check with the local Better Business Bureau to see if any complaints have been filed against the company.

One final piece of advice: If you're serious about this option, explore the possibility of taking a do-it-yourself approach to debt settlement first. You can do anything that a debt settlement firm can do and avoid all the steep fees in the process. (Unfortunately, you will still be subject to taxes on any amount settled.)

Several members of the CardRatings.com forum have successfully settled their own debts. Visit our forum for pointers on doing so. If you need some limited guidance, consider the services provided by ZipDebt (follow the link at CardRatings.com/Book), which offers an impressive one-year money-back guarantee on any of its three Do-It-Yourself Debt Negotiation Training & Coaching Programs, which are much less expensive than what a traditional debt settlement firm would charge.

> **TIP**
>
> Go to CardRatings.com/ Book for a list of companies offering these services that I know are reputable.

Bankruptcy

Most of us see bankruptcy as the ultimate sign of failure or chronic overspending, when it's often nothing of the sort.

The overwhelming debts that often drive people into bankruptcy today are more often than not related to illness, job loss, and divorce.

The doctor and hospital bills might be piling up from an accident you had a few years ago. You might have lost your job and health insurance, gone through your emergency fund, and are using credit cards to keep food on the table and fill prescriptions. You might have tried at least some of the ideas I've shared here, and you've spoken to a credit counselor. But the bill collectors keep calling, the stress is unbelievable, and you feel as though you've run out of cash and options.

In a situation like this, depending on the type of debts you have and how long it would take you to pay them off, bankruptcy should be considered. As MSN's Personal Finance Columnist Liz Pulliam Weston puts it,

> *If, despite your best efforts, it would take more than five years to pay off your credit cards and medical bills, or you would need to use assets that would otherwise be protected in bankruptcy—like retirement accounts and home equity—then you should at least consult with a bankruptcy attorney about your options.*

Student loans, child support, and alimony are types of debt that generally cannot be discharged through bankruptcy.

One thing to consider is that you must be willing to withstand a *major* blow to your credit report, the effects of which can last for up to a decade. It will be harder to obtain credit, your credit lines will be limited, and you'll usually have to pay much higher interest rates on the credit you do manage to get, as well as higher premiums on insurance policies. (Visit the CardRatings.com forum for tips on how to rebuild your credit following bankruptcy.)

If you've weighed all the other methods of resolving debt and really see no clear way out, I agree with Weston: The best person to speak with about your options is a bankruptcy attorney. Visit NACBA.org to find one. Probably the most significant sign that it's time to approach a lawyer is if you've tapped out all your resources, and your home or car is on the line. (Bankruptcy laws can generally protect these items.)

The Two Types of Personal Bankruptcy

A **Chapter 7 bankruptcy**, which remains on your credit report for ten years, wipes out your unsecured debts (such as credit card bills). You usually can keep your home and automobile if you keep making payments on them, as well as your retirement accounts, but you must sell other assets to pay down some of what you owe.

A **Chapter 13 bankruptcy**, in which you repay more of your debts, remains on your credit report for "only" seven years, assuming that you successfully complete the requirements. It enables you to keep your property, and you agree to a three- to five-year repayment plan. Successful completion of the plan results in a discharge of your remaining unsecured debt.

You Are Not Alone

If you're contemplating bankruptcy, you're not alone. The number of personal bankruptcies filed throughout the years has seemingly climbed right along with the popularity and increased use of credit cards. The Bankruptcy Abuse Prevention and Consumer Protection Act of 2005 was touted as a solution to the problem.

Many consumer advocates and personal finance experts would argue, though, that this legislation has actually worsened the consumer debt situation because it has become harder and more expensive to file. The same advocates contend that the legislation was enacted only to appease creditors, including those in the card industry.

"Though the law cracked down on debtors, it did nothing to rein in the credit card issuers and other lenders whose practices helped fuel the bankruptcy boom," explains Weston, also the author of *Deal with Your Debt: The Right Way to Manage Your Bills and Pay Off What You Owe* (Prentice Hall, 2005).

Even though it is harder to file now than it was before 2005, the number of U.S. bankruptcies continues to surge. Filings in February 2008, for example, were up 28% over the same period in 2007.

Even if bankruptcy is your only option, and although it might seem impossible at times, I want you to know that you can conquer your debt. There's even life after bankruptcy! With the information and resources I've provided, along with your determination and persistence, you will be able to manage your finances and control your debt instead of allowing your debt to control you. Good luck on becoming debt-free—and please let me know of you progress by dropping me a note or by posting in the CardRatings.com forums.

CHAPTER 6

Watch Out: Traps and Scams
Can Cost You Big Bucks!

The record is clear—when debt booms, fraud booms. Consumers who find themselves in trouble are vulnerable because they are often scared and a little desperate. It's frightening to have debts that are unsustainable and it's very easy in that situation for people to make a quick decision they come to regret.

—Travis Plunkett, Consumer Federation of America[1]

Credit cards come with hidden hazards that can cost you big bucks, to say nothing of a lot of time and aggravation. Card issuers aren't the only ones trying to make money off us. Far too many profiteers are eager to capitalize on your card use to steal your identity and/or rope you into credit repair schemes that profit only them.

Fortunately, forewarned is forearmed! When you know what to watch out for, you won't be an unknowing victim being taken advantage of by card issuers or scammers. What you learn here will save you money and grief, no matter who is trying to profit off you. Let's get going and

---

[1] As quoted in the *Staten Island Advance* February 3, 2008.

make sure all the money to be made from your credit cards goes to *you*, not to some fraudster or greedy lender.

First, I point out some of the traps card issuers set that you might unwittingly fall into when you least expect it. Even when and how you pay your credit card issuer can get dicey.

Grace Periods Are Shrinking

If you pay your balance in full every month, you get to take advantage of an interest-free loan from your lender for between 20 and 25 days. Known as the grace period, as you may remember from Chapter 1, "It's Not Just Plastic— It's Money!" it's generally the amount of time between the date your billing cycle ends and your payment due date. Grace periods, when used wisely, are a significant benefit of using a card as they can help you improve your cash flow.

Unfortunately, grace periods are shrinking. Not too long ago, 30-day grace periods were common. Now many issuers offer only a 20-day period. (Visit CardRatings.com/ Book for a listing of the grace periods of major issuers.)

> **TIP**
>
> Diners Club charge card offers a generous 28-32 day grace period. The card does come with a $95 annual fee, so consider whether you'll get enough in benefits to make paying the fee worthwhile. (This card does offer a lot of benefits.)

Keep your eyes out for fine-print notices from lenders telling you that your grace period has shrunk a little. Make sure you *always* pay by the new date, or your interest savings will go out the window.

I won't be surprised if lenders eventually institute even shorter time frames, meaning less interest-free money for us. Use it wisely while you can, folks! Pay attention and always pay your balance in full by the due date.

Give yourself a grade of A+ in credit card smarts whenever you take advantage of a grace period to *buy things you would have purchased anyway.* Charge these items on a card that also gives you cash or freebies, and you get a gold star. Just don't be lured by the interest-free money to buy things you can't afford.

Please be aware that grace periods usually don't apply to balance transfers, and they very rarely apply to cash advances. To benefit to the max, be sure you know the details about your cards' grace periods.

The Three Grace Periods

1. Typical Grace Period: If you don't carry a balance, you have between 20 and 25 days from the end of your current billing period to pay in full for that month's purchases before you owe any interest. If you pay in full, no interest is charged. When you do carry a balance, you're immediately charged interest on all new purchases.

2. Full Grace Period: Whether or not you carry a balance, new purchases aren't included in the average daily balance interest calculation for the current month's billing cycle. As you might expect, full grace periods are quite rare!

3. No Grace Period: You pay interest immediately on new purchases, regardless of whether you pay your balance in full or not. Though rare, a few subprime cards have been known to not have grace periods. Steer clear of such graceless cards!

A final tip that will help you avoid getting squeezed by a shrinking grace period is to pay your card bills online. If you make your online payments in the morning or early afternoon, most issuers will credit them the same day. And Bank of America and Discover Card's cut-off time for online payments isn't until 5:00 PM ET. Discover even lets you phone in payments until 5:45 PM ET.

Verify the cut-off time with your issuer, and *never* be late. Hang on to any payment confirmation numbers—as we all know, computers aren't perfect all the time.

Confusing Cash Advance Fees

You already know that cash advance fees can be very costly. Most issuers calculate these fees on a percentage basis, which typically is 3%. (I've seen fees as high as 5%, though.) On top of that, most issuers charge a minimum "flat fee," regardless of the amount of the advance.

Although you normally don't get hit with two separate fees, it shouldn't come as a surprise that you'll be charged whichever fee is higher. For example, an issuer might charge 3% on cash advances with a $20 minimum fee—whichever is greater.

Where to Find No or Low Cash Advance Fees

Although card issuers are known for steep advance fees, a few issuers, particularly smaller ones, have more consumer-friendly terms. Pulaski Bank doesn't have a fee at all. And although Simmons First National Bank charges a 3% fee, it caps the fee at $50 (caps on cash advance fees are very rare). I'm proud to say that both banks are located in my home state of Arkansas.

A few issuers have even more complicated computation methods. Amber Ray, vice president of Operations for CardRatings.com, discovered the following interesting clause in the fine print of an HSBC Bank card: "The transaction fee for cash advances is $5 for each cash advance of $100 or less from any ATM or convenience check; for all other cash advance transactions, $15 or 4%, whichever is higher." Fortunately, most fee structures aren't quite this confusing!

> **TIP**
>
> If you must get a cash advance, avoid using ATM machines owned by other financial institutions, which normally charge you an additional fee of $1 to $3.

Small Cash Advances Have Sky-High Interest Rates

Take a look at just how pricey smaller advances can be, and you'll hopefully never consider one. Here we add the cash advance fee to any interest charges and ATM fees to get the total cost for one month. Then we multiply by 12 to get the rate for a year, aka the **annualized finance charge** (AFC), which most experts think is a more accurate way of disclosing the true cost of credit.

Although cash advance APRs are typically more than 20%, very few consumers realize that their annualized finance charge can easily be more than 200%! Let's say you get a $100 advance with a 4% fee, a 24% cash advance APR, and a $15 minimum fee from your own bank's ATM. Your annualized finance charge would be 204% (see Table 6.1).

Table 6.1 How $100 from an ATM Can Cost 204% in Interest

Amount of Finance Advance	Advance Fee	Minimum Fee	ATM Fee	APR	Charge
$100	4%	$15	0	24%	
Costs for One Month	0	$15	0	$2	$17
AFC (17 × 12)				204%	

> **TIP**
>
> Avoid convenience (credit card) checks that are treated as cash advances, too. They normally have high fees and rates, no grace period, and a greater risk of identity theft. They also make it very easy to get in over your head, which can damage your credit score, and you generally can't file a merchant dispute with your card issuer if you use a credit card check.

Consumer Action compares small cash advances to payday loans. Although I agree in principle, a finance charge of more than 200% isn't nearly as bad as the 372% to 869% rate charged by some payday lenders, according to Arkansans Against Abusive Payday Lending. Having said that, it's still pretty darn high!

To avoid getting stung with an APR of more than 200%, read the terms of your card agreement very carefully. Fee calculations can get tricky and quite costly. If you want to profit from your cards, consider an advance only if you're in a *dire* emergency!

Trailing Interest: A Phantom Interest Charge

Another costly finance charge is called **trailing** or **residual interest**. It can rear its ugly head when you pay your bill in full after having carried a balance in the previous month (and, thus, forfeiting your grace period). "If you were carrying a balance for more than two months, residual interest is charged right up until the day your payment is actually received," explains Consumer Action's Linda Sherry.

How a Trailing Interest Charge Works

I've borrowed this real-life example from my friends at Consumer Action. Let's say that you buy a $3,000 big-screen TV using your 17% credit card and decide to pay off the balance in three payments. Let's assume that you're not carrying a balance when you buy the TV, you aren't going to make any new purchases while you pay off the balance, and your payments will always be credited by the due date.

Based on these assumptions, here's how your payment schedule would look:

Month	Payment	Interest Charges	Principal Paid	Current Balance
1				$3,000
2	$1,025.11	$37.50	$ 987.61	$2,012.39
3	$1,025.11	$25.15	$ 999.96	$1,012.43
4	$1,025.09	$12.66	$1,012.43	$ 0.00
5		$ 7.59		$ 7.59

I used one of the user-friendly calculators on CardRatings.com to crunch these numbers.

Notice the $7.59 interest charge in the fifth month? How can that be? The current balance in the previous month was $0.00. This $7.59 is, as you might have guessed, the trailing interest charge. It's based on the balance of $1,012.43 for 20 days, the time between the close of the billing cycle and the due date, which is when the payment of $1,025.09 was credited. In short, interest charges continued to accrue after the statement was printed up until the date the payment was actually posted.

Most cardholders assume that after they pay their balance in full, they don't owe a penny. They don't find out about a trailing interest charge until they get their next bill—and then, only if they look carefully. Linda Sherry points out that if a cardholder checks online, they would likely see a zero balance, with no mention of any additional charge. That's because trailing interest isn't added until the close of the subsequent billing cycle. Clear as mud, huh?

According to Consumer Action, several major card issuers have cards that can charge residual interest. One notable exception is Discover Card. As long as Discover cardholders pay the full balance on their statement each month, they are not charged residual interest.

> **TIP**
>
> To avoid residual interest and minimize its effects, call your issuer when you're getting ready to pay off your balance in full. *Ask for the payoff amount on your account* as of the date when you plan to make your payment. If you're paying by mail, allow at least five days for processing your payment.

Credit Discrimination: Retirees and Race

The history of racial discrimination in this country is centuries old, thus it is not a surprise that people of color often don't get fair treatment from lenders. More recently, seniors have been at risk for credit discrimination, often because of their reduced income and lack of credit history. Fortunately, credit discrimination is against the law, and you can take action if you—or someone you love—experiences this type of treatment.

The Rules

It's perfectly legal for lenders to consider our income, expenses, debts, and credit histories when they are determining our creditworthiness. However:

1. A creditor may not discriminate against you because of your sex, marital status, race, national origin, or because you receive public assistance income.

2. A creditor may not consider your age when deciding to give you credit unless:
   a. You are not old enough to sign contracts (usually under 18).
   b. The creditor will *favor* you if age 62 or older.
   c. It helps the creditor determine other factors of creditworthiness (for example, you might be ready to retire and your income may drop).
   d. Your age is used in a scoring system that benefits consumers age 62 and older.

3. Public assistance, regular alimony, child support, Social Security benefits, pension, annuity, part-time employment and retirement plans cannot be discounted or refused for consideration when a creditor is evaluating your income.

Dealing with Discrimination

If you find that you've been a victim of credit discrimination, it's important to protect your rights and take action immediately. Here are some steps you can take.

> **TIP**
>
> The Federal Trade Commission has a brochure detailing consumer rights according to the Equal Credit Opportunity Act (ECOA), which can be downloaded from ftc.gov or requested by calling toll-free: 877-382-4357).

- Let the creditor know you are aware of your rights under the law. That may be enough to get the lender to do the right thing.

- Contact your state attorney general to find out if the creditor violated any state laws. If so, it's possible the state will prosecute.

- Report the discrimination to one of the government agencies listed below. The creditor must give you the contact information for the appropriate agency if you were denied credit. Although some of the agencies listed below won't help with individual issues, it helps them see patterns to investigate certain creditors.

- Hire a lawyer and take the case to the federal district court. You can recover damages and compensation for attorney's fees and court costs if you win.

- File a class action suit with others who have been discriminated against by the same creditor. As a group you may win the lesser of up to $500,000 or one percent of the creditor's net worth.

Where to Turn for Help

Type of Company	Address
Retail or department store, small loan and finance, mortgage, oil, public utility, state credit union, government lending program, or travel and expense credit card.	Consumer Response Center Federal Trade Commission ftc.gov Washington, DC 20580 877-FTC-HELP 877-382-4357
Nationally-chartered bank (National or N.A. is part of the name)	Comptroller of the Currency occ.treas.gov Customer Assistance Group 1301 McKinney Street, #3450 Houston, TX 77010 800-613-6743
State-chartered bank insured by the Federal Deposit Insurance Corporation but not a member of the Federal Reserve System	Federal Deposit Insurance Corporation fdic.gov Division of Supervision and Consumer Protection 550 17th St NW Washington, DC 20429 877-ASKFDIC 877-275-3342
Federally-chartered or federally-insured savings and loan association. Complaints must be lodged with the appropriate regional office. Visit the Web site or call the toll-free number to find out where to register your complaint.	Department of the Treasury Office of Thrift Supervision ots.treas.gov 800-842-6929
Federally-chartered credit union. This agency also requires complaints be filed at a regional office. Visit the Web site or call the toll-free number to find out where to register your complaint.	National Credit Union Administration Consumer Complaint Center ncua.gov 800-755-1030
Not sure where to turn?	National Consumer League Fraud Center fraud.org 800-876-7060

Credit Card Fraud and Credit-Related Scams

Now that you know what to do to avoid the traps that lenders set, it's time to turn our attention to the crooks who prey on our credit. Do you often feel as though you have to be on the lookout at every turn because some people out there are just waiting to rip you off? I'm sad to say it, but you have every reason to be cautious.

The Federal Trade Commission's 2007 Consumer Fraud Survey showed consumers reporting fraud losses totaling more than $1.1 billion. The median monetary loss was $500. Not surprisingly, the FTC found that individuals with high levels of debt are more likely to be victims of fraud.

Perhaps the most disturbing statistic involves identity theft. For the seventh year in a row, identity theft topped the list of all consumer complaints, accounting for 36% of all complaints received by the FTC.

Although identity theft can occur in other ways, credit card fraud is the most common form and is the culprit in a quarter of all identity theft cases. This stat underscores the strong need to know what to look out for so that we can protect ourselves, our credit, and our money. To that end, let's examine some popular scams.

Pay-First Guarantee Scams

The FTC receives frequent complaints about advance-fee loan scams, in which a consumer pays a fee for a "guaranteed" loan or credit card. The truth is no reputable company will give a 100% guarantee that everyone who applies will be approved for a major credit card.

One example of a "pay-first guarantee" involves what is called a catalog card. Aimed at people with no credit or poor credit, catalog cards are advertised as a sure-fire way to get a credit card that can be used to purchase all types of merchandise.

What's not made clear is that consumers often pay an inflated fee for these cards, which can be used only to buy items in specific catalogs. The cards can't be used in other stores, restaurants, or any other place that accepts plastic. Although the catalogs do have a wide selection of merchandise, the merchandise is usually significantly overpriced. (Significantly is putting it nicely!)

> **TIP**
>
> Some catalog card companies "use a name that sounds like an actual credit card company to lure unsuspecting consumers with bad or little credit history," reports Gee, a member of the CardRatings.com forum. "They offer tempting, high credit limits...and...overpriced products on credit—and often require at least 20% and more as a down payment. 'Buyer beware' applies here." Gee's advice? Simply avoid catalog cards at all costs, which is exactly how I'd put it!

Moreover, catalog cards typically don't report to all three major credit bureaus, and most that I've reviewed report to only one or to no bureau at all. Although they guarantee credit, they generally do little to help their cardholders build credit.

Credit Repair Scams

Credit repair scams vary, but most charge their customers a fee to "erase" bad credit—yet the companies offering such services can't legally do anything of the sort. According to John Ventura, author of *The Credit Repair Handbook* (Kaplan Publishing, 2007), only the credit bureau or the creditor can remove negative entries from a credit report.

Some repair schemes encourage consumers to apply for an IRS Employee Identification Number and then use this

> **TIP**
>
> If you're just too busy or frustrated to repair your own credit, credit expert Mark Enderle offers one of the few paid services that I recommend. Enderle provides a personal credit consultation for a flat fee. For more information about his services, visit this link on my website: CardRatings.com/Book.

number, which has the same number of digits as a Social Security number, to apply for credit and loans. What they don't mention is that it's a federal crime to misrepresent your Social Security number. The companies promising such quick fixes are rip offs, and their actions are illegal.

A few legitimate credit repair companies exist, but most consumer advocates, including me, recommend that cardholders don't pay anyone for credit repair. You can repair your credit for free! Chapter 9, "Your Credit Report and Score: The Better You Look, the More You Profit," provides some guidance, and the CardRatings.com forum is a great place to get the latest in free tips on credit repair.

A do-it-yourself approach to credit repair is a wonderful way to take charge of your financial life—and then to make the most of it. I firmly believe that this is the most effective approach for most consumers, *including you*. After all, it is *your* credit!

Debt and Fraud: Two Peas in a Pod?

Debt and scams go hand in hand, and the folks who can at least afford it are the prime targets of unscrupulous offers. According to credit guru Gerri Detweiler, people with debt problems are often easy prey because they're looking for a quick fix. "People avoid dealing with debt problems because they face unpleasant decisions and they're searching for a perfect solution," she explains. "The problem is, there usually isn't one perfect solution for debt troubles."

By the time some folks get around to dealing with their debts, they are completely overwhelmed by them. At that point, Detweiler says, they're so desperate for a solution that they try things that don't sound or look legit, even to them.

"In order to steer clear of scams, you have to go with your gut," says Detweiler. "There is no quick and easy fix—only time and effort on your part will bring debt under control."

Fraud Protection Scams

In an ironic twist, some fraudsters encourage cardholders to buy protection or insurance in case their cards are stolen and used to run up a big bill. These offers often prey upon the fears of the most unsuspecting among us. Yet, as mentioned in Chapter 1, federal law already protects cardholders from fraud, with consumer liability capped at $50.

What's more, many card issuers offer free "zero liability protection policies," so you don't have to pay a nickel if your card is used fraudulently. Just say "No!" to sales pitches for fraud protection because such pitches are the true fraud.

Elder Fraud

Unfortunately, fraudsters often target seniors with contests, home repair scams, and credit repair offers. Although they're only about 12% of the population, 35% of all victims of fraud are seniors, who are, for example, three times as likely to fall for home equity scams that put their homes at risk of foreclosure.

In fact, about a third of reports to the National Consumer League's Fraud Center (fraud.org) come from the 60 and older crowd, who fall for magazine sales scams, prizes/sweepstake scams, among other common cons. Some estimates show that seniors are scammed out of $40 billion a year in telemarketing fraud alone.

It's not that seniors are less savvy than younger people. They're often simply less accustomed to mistrusting people or doubting the credibility of offers they receive. Scammers exploit seniors' trust, using fast, friendly chatter and slick promises, trying to convince their victims that they just can't pass up "this once in a lifetime offer."

Credit card come-ons with phony promises are often targeted at seniors who have no credit history or a poor one. In one common scenario, the scammer gets the senior to pay an up-front fee before they can receive a "guaranteed" credit line. Unfortunately, in a lot of cases, the so-called issuer doesn't exist, and the victims lose their money. The golden rule to follow when considering any unsolicited offer is that if it sounds too good to be true, then it probably is!

Retirees tend to be the victims of credit fraud, and fraud in general, for other reasons too. First of all, they are the most likely to be home when the scammers call or stop by. Second, they are the least likely to report it. Any number of reasons exist for their reluctance, but include not knowing how to report it or who to report it to, shame that they fell victim to fraud, and not wanting others to think they have lost the ability to manage their own finances. Also, when they do report it, often times memory makes it difficult to answer detailed questions about the crime, especially if several months have already passed.

Have You Been a Victim of Fraud?

- Visit ftc.gov or call the Federal Trade Commission's toll-free hotline to report a scam or get more information about fraud and how to prevent it: 877-987-3728.

- Visit the website of the Office of the Comptroller of the Currency, where you can file complaints against card issuers: occ.treas.gov/customer.htm.

- Visit the National Consumer League's Fraud Center (fraud.org) for reports on unscrupulous companies as well as good advice.

- Contact your local consumer protection agency, state attorney general, and/or local Better Business Bureau (bbb.org).

- Consider sharing your experience on the CardRatings.com forum as well.

Phishing

Phishing typically begins with an email sent to unsuspecting consumers by scammers claiming to be from major credit card companies, banks, retailers, or similar companies. The goal of these scams is to acquire sensitive financial information such as bank account information and credit card details so the thieves can take our money and use our credit.

To trick us, they do everything they can to imitate legitimate firms, for example, copying their logos. Sometimes it's truly difficult to distinguish between what's real and what's a fraud.

The emails seem legitimate enough. Many start by saying "We're updating our computers and need to verify your account number, password, Social Security number, or credit card number. It will just take a moment of your time."

For example, Ira Stoller, a senior member of the CardRatings.com forum, received a fake email that did a pretty good imitation of being an eBay consumer alert. "The message relayed that eBay was updating their database and needed to verify my credit card information," says Stoller.

Although the email looked credible, Stoller knew at the time that eBay didn't house credit card information. Someone was phishing for his credit card information.

The email included a link to a form where Stoller could fill in the requested information. Had he followed instructions, clicked on that link, filled in the form, and sent it off into cyberspace, he would have handed over his credit card number and its expiration date to a scam artist.

Instead, Stoller did something that not enough consumers do: He reported the phish on eBay's consumer complaint page. I encourage you to follow his lead. If someone starts phishing in your email inbox, report it to the company being used as bait.

Here's another phishing example, which was posted on the CardRatings.com forum by Mantras. The email she received said it was a "Security Notice from no-reply@google.com":

We recently have determined that different computers have logged onto your Online Banking account, and multiple password failures were present before the logons.

We now need you to re-confirm your account information to us. If this is not completed by September 22, 2007, we will be forced to suspend your account indefinitely, as it may have been used for fraudulent purposes. We thank you for your cooperation in this manner.

To confirm your Online Banking records click on the following link: www.bankofamerica.com/ OnlineBanking/index.jsp

Thank you for your patience in this matter.

Bank of America Customer Service

Please do not reply to this e-mail as this is only a notification. Mail sent to this address cannot be answered.

© 2007 Bank of America Corporation. All rights reserved.

Look at how legitimate the details look, right down to the copyright! Fortunately, it's easy to protect yourself from phishing. Here are two sure-fire ways:

- Assume that any email or phone call you receive requesting account numbers is a scam. No financial institution will ever ask for your personal or account information that way. Don't provide your credit card numbers, Social Security number, or mother's maiden name to anyone making such a request—even if someone says the call is from the Social Security Administration, Medicare, or another government agency.

- *Never* click on any links contained in questionable emails. No point giving scammers access to your computer or risking the possibility that you might download a computer virus. The only thing you should click on is your Delete key. (It's also a good idea to mark such emails as spam.)

Skimming

Skimming is often an "inside job"—a dishonest employee, for example, may steal your credit card information when you charge something. The thief could photocopy your receipt, swipe your card through a small magnetic reader hidden in his or her pocket, or merely jot down your number and its expiration date. It's easy to imagine how skimming can happen in a crowded restaurant or a bar. You give your card to pay the bill, and the bartender walks off with it. Out of your sight, it's a snap to skim your card.

Another form of skimming occurs at ATM machines. In one typical scenario, a criminal creates a magnetic stripe reader that fits neatly and unobtrusively directly over the magnetic stripe reader on an ATM machine, and the person making a withdrawal is often none the wiser. The thief can also capture the customer's PIN number with a small camera mounted in the skimmer itself or at another location near the ATM.

Although the industry is continually working on ways to protect your card from skimming, you can help by staying alert and closely monitoring your account. As soon as you're aware of a questionable charge, call your card issuer immediately. While you're on hold, think about the various places where you paid for something with your card and it was taken out of your sight.

Popular Ways Thieves Rob Your Identity

- Stealing your mail
- Looking through your trash (often called "dumpster diving")
- Stealing your wallet or purse
- Stealing records from businesses
- Skimming and phishing
- Stealing personal information from your home

Life after ID Theft:
A Step-by-Step Plan of Action

Remember that 1995 Sandra Bullock movie *The Net*, where the self-imposed home-bound computer expert's identity gets stolen? After years of working from home, ordering take-out online, and avoiding her mom, who suffers from Alzheimer's, no one knows what she looks like. The bad guys easily stole her identity, and she had to brave bullets and high-speed car chases to get her lifeback. Back in 1995, we could all breathe a sigh of relief because, after all, it was just a movie, highly unrealistic and no real cause for concern.

It's amazing how quickly technology can change things. Now identity theft is a very real threat to virtually everyone. Back in 1999, when the Federal Trade Commission (FTC) began keeping track of identity theft, it logged a grand total of 1,380 complaints. Fast-forward to 2006: The FTC logged 246,035 complaints of identity theft. According to FTC estimates, more than eight million of us are victims every year, which results in some $50 billion in lost business!

Id Theft: A Living Nightmare

After your identity is stolen, the thief can get credit cards, open lines of credit, drain your bank accounts, open a wireless phone service, get a job, and even file for bankruptcy—all in your name. The imposter can take out a lot of additional credit "on your behalf," use an inordinately large amount of that credit, and then not pay the bills. As a result, your credit reports can take quite a hit. Then your credit score suffers, which has its own long list of serious implications. Top it all off with a warrant for your arrest when the imposter fails to show up for some court date, and you have a real nightmare on your hands.

> **TIP**
>
> As you reclaim your identity, you'll save yourself money, time, and aggravation if you keep detailed records of all telephone conversations. Include the date and time of the call, the number called, the name of person who helped you, and an outline of what you discussed. Also be sure to keep copies of all correspondence.

> **Biggest Security Breach**
>
> According to 2007 court documents, approximately 96 million Visa and MasterCard accounts were compromised at TJX, the parent company of T.J. Maxx, T.K. Maxx, Marshalls, HomeGoods, and other stores. This is the largest computer data breach to date.

If You Think You *Might* Have Been a Victim of Identity Theft...

Quickly take the following steps to reduce the chances of becoming a victim:

- Notify your card issuers. Contact all the card issuers of accounts you think might have been compromised. Some issuers allow you put a temporary hold or freeze on your account without actually closing it out. Change your PIN and ask to add a password, to make it more difficult for someone else to use your card.

  Other lenders will close the account and issue you a new card with a new card number. If you open new accounts, be sure to secure them with a password.

> **TIP**
>
> Choose a nonsense mix of letters and numbers for your PINs and passwords. Don't use something obvious, such as your mother's maiden name, any part of your Social Security number or phone number, your birthday, or even consecutive numbers. Sure, they're easy for you to remember, but that's what also makes it so easy for others to crack your "code."

- Place an initial fraud alert on your credit report. Contact one of the major credit bureaus—Experian, Equifax, or TransUnion (see "Identity Theft Recovery Checklist" for contact information)— which, in turn, will alert the other two agencies. You'll be required to provide proof of your identity, including your full name, date of birth, Social Security number, and address. Don't be surprised if you have to provide other personal information to verify your identity.

This initial alert stays in your file for 90 days. It means that creditors must use "reasonable policies and procedures" to verify your identity before issuing credit in your name. If you're on active duty in the military, ask for an Active Duty Alert, which remains in effect for a year.

You'll also receive a free credit report from each of the three credit bureaus. Double-check every little detail for accuracy—your name, Social Security number, addresses, and employers over the years. Keep your eyes out for accounts you didn't open, debts you didn't incur, and unexplained credit inquiries from companies you did not contact.

You'll need to get fraudulent and inaccurate information corrected. Each credit report should include information on how to dispute the errors you might find in your report, even if you haven't been victimized by identity theft. Studies show that 25% of our credit reports contain errors that are so serious, our applications for credit could be denied. (See Chapter 9 for more on credit reports and scores.)

It's a good idea to get new copies of your reports a few months after you get your initial reports. Verify that any corrections and changes have been made, and make sure no fraudulent activity has occurred since your initial reports.

If You *Know* You're a Victim of Identity Theft...

One day you might find fraudulent activity on your credit report—for example, new bank or credit card accounts you never applied for—or you might get a call from a bill collector about a debt you never incurred. You have my sympathies—and my recommendation is that you take the following steps:

- Immediately place an extended fraud alert on your credit reports.

- Contact one of the major bureaus. Your **extended fraud alert** will remain in effect for seven years (instead of 90 days) at all three bureaus. You'll need to provide the agency with an **identity theft report** that you must file with a federal, state or local law enforcement agency (see my "Identity Theft Recovery Checklist" for more info on this report).

  When the extended fraud alert is on your report, potential creditors must actually contact you or meet with you in person before they issue you credit. And unless you request otherwise, your name will be removed from marketing lists for prescreened credit offers for five years. You'll also be entitled to receive two more free credit reports from each of the three bureaus within the next 12 months.

- Contact creditors and collection agencies. You need to speak with someone in the security and fraud department of every company connected with the identity theft. You want to get the fraudulent accounts closed immediately. Ask for any special forms that you might need to fill out and specific

---

TIP

With both the initial and extended fraud alert, you can request that a victim statement be added to your credit file. Your statement could say something like this: "Victim of Identity Theft. Please verify identity before extending credit. The telephone number where I can be contacted is _____. Many thanks!" Choose a number where you can be contacted easily, such as your cell phone.

TIP

When the dispute is resolved, request a letter from the creditor stating that the fraudulent accounts have been closed and discharged. Finally, keep all the documentation you received in connection with the identity theft.

addresses for correspondence. Don't be surprised if you have to follow up in writing and provide copies of all supporting documents (such as the identity theft police report). Send all correspondence via certified mail, return receipt requested.

Ask for copies of all relevant paperwork from the creditors, including the application submitted by the identity thief and any transactions that occurred on the account. This paperwork will help prove you're a victim. For example, you can show that the signature on the application isn't yours, and you might find valuable clues, including an address, that will help law enforcement find the crook. Companies have 30 days to meet your request for information.

It's a good idea to opt out from receiving offers by phone or mail from these creditors or their affiliates.

- File a police report. Contact the police in the community where the identity theft took place. Ideally, you want to file an identity theft report. These reports have more than the usual amount of detail about the crime—so that the credit bureaus and businesses being scammed can verify that you are a victim and figure out which accounts are under the control of the identity thieves. Normal police reports often don't have these details.

You might need to be persistent if local authorities tell you they cannot take a report. If they won't take the case, go to the county or state police. You can also contact the state attorney general's office for guidance.

When reporting your case to the police, submit copies of all pertinent documents. Also helpful is a list of the creditors you know are affected, showing your account number and the amounts involved.

Make sure you get copies of the police report. Don't worry if you don't have all the information at the time you file the report; you can always make changes later. Just remember to get copies of the updated report.

- Contact the Federal Trade Commission (FTC). Call the FTC at 877-ID-THEFT (877-438-4338; TTY 866-653-4261), or visit its website, ftc.gov/idtheft, to report your fraud case. The "snail mail" address is:

  Identity Theft Clearinghouse
  Federal Trade Commission
  600 Pennsylvania Avenue, NW
  Washington, DC 20580

  While you're at it, request a copy of the FTC's booklet *Take Charge: Fighting Back Against Identity Theft.* (A free PDF version is available online for instant download.) It contains an "Identity Theft Affidavit" that you can use to report the theft to many companies, sample letters, and great advice for guarding against identity theft, including how to protect your home computer.

Identity Theft Recovery Checklist

☐ Contact one credit reporting agency and place an extended fraud alert on your reports.

Experian: 888-397-3742; Experian.com/fraud

Equifax: 888-766-0008; Equifax.com

TransUnion: 800-680-7289; TransUnion.com

☐ Request a credit report from each credit bureau.

Check your Social Security number, addresses, names, and employers for accuracy.

Look for accounts you didn't open, unexplained debts, and credit inquiries from companies you did not contact.

☐ Contact all creditors and collection agencies.

Existing accounts: Request a new account number, change your PIN, and add a password.

Fraudulent accounts: Request copies of fraudulent applications and all transactions.

Request forms needed and the address for sending correspondence.

Opt out from receiving future solicitations.

Request written statements of accounts closed and discharged when the dispute is resolved.

☐ File a police report.

☐ Contact the Federal Trade Commission.

Credit Freezing

Putting alerts on your credit reports is certainly advisable, but some consumer advocates also suggest placing a "credit freeze" on credit reports, which totally prevents all potential creditors and other third parties from accessing your credit reports, unless you lift the freeze. Sandra Block, a personal finance columnist for *USA Today,* equates the extra protection of credit freezing to an "impenetrable deadbolt" on a house or apartment.

As with fraud alerts, credit freezes are mainly effective against new credit accounts being opened in your name— but they're not likely to stop fraudsters from using your existing accounts or opening new accounts in your name when credit isn't checked, such as with some new telephone or wireless accounts. Most states have laws that permit credit freezing. However, some states limit the freeze to consumers who have been victims of identity theft. Residents of most states also must usually pay a nominal fee, typically around $3, each time they freeze their credit file. Indiana, however, doesn't charge for freezes. In addition, several states are considering laws that would make freezing free.

Experian, Equifax, and TransUnion recently started to allow credit freezing as well for a fee of $10 each in most states. You must freeze your accounts with each bureau, so the cost would be $30. To unfreeze (say, because you want to get a mortgage), it's another $10 each. Plus, it can take three to five days before you can count on the bureaus to have "defrosted" your account.

Is ID Theft Insurance the Answer?

Identify theft insurance is being increasingly touted as a way to combat the growing risk associated with identify theft. According to Willard B. Carpenter, who has marketed identity theft products through Pre-Paid Legal Services, Inc. (see the link at CardRatings.com/Book), for the past two years, this niche of the insurance market is really exploding.

Unfortunately, many consumers purchase insurance out of fear and don't fully understand the benefits and coverage. Questions abound. For example, JaneiR36, a senior member of the CardRatings.com forum, posted the following:

> *The latest pitch I got is from the Discover Card customer service department. Can anyone think of a reason why the victim would have to hire a lawyer? Apparently, they offer up to $25,000 for paying for a lawyer's services should you need to hire one after being a victim of identity theft. Thoughts?*

Since you asked so kindly, JaneiR36, in the vast majority of cases, identity theft insurance is usually not worth the price. Federal and state laws protect consumers for free. If you consider this type of insurance, definitely do your homework. More on related credit insurance products in Chapter 10, "Maximize the Benefits of Your Cards by Taking Advantage of Additional Free Perks."

Paying for Free Benefits

Lifelock, a popular identity theft insurance company whose CEO proudly proclaims his Social Security number in every advertisement (as supposed proof of effectiveness of the service), charges customers $10.00 a month for its service. One of the main benefits of the service is the ability for customers to place temporary fraud alerts with each credit bureau every 90 days. While this does help automate the process, you can place your own fraud alerts for free.

Protecting Yourself from Fraud

You can take an active role in preventing ID theft and fraud by following these tips:

- Always take credit card, debit card, and ATM receipts with you when you leave a cash register. Never throw them in a public trash container. Shred them at home when you no longer need them.

- Carefully review your credit card statements for unauthorized use as soon as you receive them. If you suspect unauthorized use, contact the customer fraud departments immediately and follow the other steps I outlined earlier.

- Look at junk mail before you shred it. Make sure it's not a notification of a change in terms or other important communication from a lender. When you know the contents, either act on them or shred them.

- Run everything with personal information on it through a shredder, including unused preapproved credit card solicitations and convenience checks.

- Visit the Federal Trade Commission's site for great information and tips on how to prevent credit and identity theft: ftc.gov/idtheft.

- Encourage simple fraud solutions. Gas stations and retail stores, for example, are increasingly asking for the zip codes of their credit card customers at the point of sale. Obviously, the effectiveness of this deterrent depends on whether a thief can guess or knows where the victim lives. If a wallet is stolen, there's a good chance that the thief already knows the victim's zip code. Even so, I think such measures are definitely a step in the right direction and should be encouraged.

The FBI's Twelve Tips to Avoiding Online Fraud

1. Use your credit card only on secure and reputable websites. Realize, too, that the tiny padlock icon that appears for a secured site is a good sign, but not a 100% guarantee of security.

2. Find out what type of security measures the site is taking.

3. Research the company to confirm its legitimacy.

4. Obtain a physical address and phone number before making a purchase. Call the number to verify that it works.

5. Email the company to verify that the address is active; if they use a free email service, be wary.

6. Call the Better Business Bureau in the company's locality.

7. Check other web sites for references to the company. RipoffReport.com is a site that I like to use.

8. The appearance of a website is not always a good way to judge the company. In other words, a professionally designed website could be designed by a professional scammer.

9. Be wary of special offers and unsolicited email.

10. Use caution when dealing with people outside your country.

11. Because you can dispute charges made with a credit card, using one is the safest way to shop online.

12. Keep a secured list of all your credit cards, account information, and contact information, in case you detect fraud and need to contact the issuers.

Virtual Account Numbers Offer Extra Online Security

If you've ever purchased anything on the Internet, you're probably a big fan of the ease and convenience of making online purchases. As far as I'm concerned, there's something very enticing about shopping in bed! The growth of online shopping has been staggering. Jupiter Research predicted that U.S. consumers would spend more than $39 billion online during the 2007 year-end holiday season alone.

Unfortunately, many folks associate online shopping with an increased risk of identity theft and fraud. Stories of cyber criminals breaking into company databases to steal customer information stop many people from making online purchases. In reality, some studies show that online fraud is no worse than offline fraud. The problem might not be as bad as some people think, but online shoppers should definitely take precautions to protect themselves.

With the boom in e-commerce, card companies have much at stake when it comes to security issues. As you might expect, companies are continually working to calm their customers' fears. One solution that I'm a proponent of involves "virtual" or temporary credit cards.

Each virtual card is a unique random number that is typically issued for a one-time use with a particular online merchant. Virtual numbers are linked to your card account, but your actual credit card number is never revealed. Although these numbers are normally associated only with individual transactions, some cardholders use the same virtual number for multiple purchases from the same merchant.

American Express, a pioneer is this area, introduced its Private Payments service in 2000. Cardholders could shop online using a temporary number instead of transmitting their actual American Express number over the Internet. Since then, many other companies, including Discover, Citibank, Bank of America, and PayPal, have begun to offer virtual numbers. Unfortunately, American Express pulled its program in 2004, reportedly due to lack of cardholder interest. Although I'm a satisfied AmEx cardholder, I sure wish that a lot of cardholders had signed up for the program while it was still being offered—myself included.

Visa offers a similar free service called Verified by Visa; cardholders get password protection for purchases made at participating online merchants. For more information, visit usa.visa.com/personal/security.

Virtual Numbers: What's the Point?

Although virtual numbers are generally free, they haven't caught on with consumers, for several reasons, including a lack of awareness and the perception that the service is too much of a hassle. That's a false perception, so do call your card issuers or go online and find out what's involved.

Despite the lack of consumer interest, virtual numbers can be quite beneficial. If nothing else, they can give you peace of mind by making your online shopping experience as secure as possible. And who wants to be exposed to the inconvenience of fraud, even if you ultimately don't have to pay a dime? Virtual numbers help alleviate that hassle and add an extra layer of security.

Online merchants also benefit. Merchants' security concerns might not be a big concern for you, but charge-backs from fraudulent purchases associated with online identity theft cost merchants billions of dollars. Those costs, of course, are passed on to you and me.

One final note regarding virtual numbers: If you have to present your actual credit card to complete or confirm the purchase, use your real number online. Examples include airline and movie tickets. When in doubt, simply double-check with the merchant.

Some Final Tips

Here are some final tips to keep you and your credit safe:

- Never tell. Don't give out your card account number, bank account info, Social Security number, date of birth, and so on, unless you're familiar with the company and know why the information is necessary and how it will be used.

- When in doubt, go with your gut. It works! Also remember the old rule of thumb: Any offer that sounds too good to be true probably is.

- Be in the know. You don't have to be an expert on credit, but it'll serve you well to keep up with the latest developments from card issuers. Also keep an eye out for new scams or identity theft schemes. As new technology emerges, so will new schemes and scams. CardRating.com's forum is a great place to keep up-to-date.

- Monitor your credit regularly. Consumer advocates recommend checking your credit reports at least once a year. Personally, I'm in favor of checking your reports more frequently. Taking a proactive approach can only help minimize your exposure to fraud and identity theft. More on credit reports and scores in Chapter 9.

Paying Monthly Credit Monitoring

Some consumers go so far as to subscribe to an automated daily credit monitoring service. These services send email alerts of key changes to any of your three credit reports. Credit bureaus, banks, and other organizations offer them, usually at about $10 to $30 a month, but I generally don't think they are worth the cost in most cases. You can find out more info about such services by going to CardRatings.com and clicking on "Credit Information."

- Pay attention to details. For example, look at every credit card statement and guard your cards. I can't stress enough how important it is to manage your credit carefully and to vigorously protect your identity. Your financial health and, ultimately, your whole identity (no pun intended) depend on it.

Avoiding traps and scams doesn't require a lot of work, but it does require you to be ever-vigilant. Having an ever-vigilant mindset can go a long way in helping you avoid the latest scam or credit card pitfall. Ultimately, being vigilant means that you will be able to keep more money in your pocket, which I think is definitely worth the effort. Good luck!

CHAPTER 7

Start Out on the Right Foot: Credit Cards for Students and Saving for College

College campuses have become a key stomping ground for credit card issuers. Through the Internet, mail, and on-campus promotions, they offer freebies, food, low introductory rates, preapproved credit card applications, bonus airline miles, and all sorts of other incentives to entice students to sign up for their cards. Unfortunately, far too many students carry a lot more plastic in their wallets than they can handle. In the process, they rack up thousands of dollars in debt.

Sure, cards offer many benefits to students, but young people who don't understand credit basics are in no position to make the most of their cards. Instead, lenders are making the most money from them. Here I show you not only how to avoid becoming another sad statistic, but also how to use a credit card to your financial advantage.

Whether you're a college student, a parent, or simply someone who cares about the next generation, understanding the relationship between card issuers and college kids will save you grief and hopefully motivate you to help today's young adults avoid ending up as far too many do—overwhelmed by debt.

The time spent in college can be costly primarily due to rising tuition costs, but it doesn't have to be the beginning of an adult life strapped with card debt. Read on to learn what college students—and even high school students—should know to get started on the right foot with credit and to avoid card debt.

Why Do Credit Card Companies Court College Students?

Dr. Robert Manning, author of *Credit Card Nation* (Basic Books, 2001), explains:

> *Credit card companies encourage fantasies of easy money because students are so profitable. Teens have financial naiveté, high material expectations and responsiveness to relatively low-cost marketing campaigns, high potential earnings, and future demand for financial services.*

The current generation of teenagers also has more purchasing power than ever, and companies are spending millions each year just to get the attention of teens.

Another reason card issuers tap into the student population is brand loyalty. When students get a card in their wallets, they're likely to keep that card and its upgrades for years to come. Over time, issuers hope to develop other financial relationships with these young people, ranging from bank accounts and car loans to mortgages and retirement funds.

Although this might seem ironic, considering that most students won't have a sizable, steady source of income for years to come, Dr. Manning says this is one example of how the card industry has changed radically in the past decade or so. "Previously, conservative rules deemed a good customer as one who paid their bills on time," he says. "Now, a good customer is one who can't repay his or her debt."

"Credit is no longer an earned privilege," continues Dr. Manning. "It's now considered a social entitlement, and the screening criterion [for card applicants] is weak."

Banks make money off cardholders by charging interest on unpaid credit card balances as well as fees. Cardholders who don't pay their balances in full each month are now the most desirable type of customer. Say you're a student who graduates with a balance of $7,000 at a 17% interest rate. If you faithfully make the minimum monthly payments (2% of your balance) and don't charge anything else to the account, you'll pay $16,162.92 in interest, and it will take you almost 45 years to repay the bill. (You'd pay more than twice as much in interest than you owed in the first place!)

The banking industry has learned that college students will draw upon various sources of income to pay their debts—such as student loans, money from part-time jobs, and their families. Still, the picture on student cards is not all rosy from the lenders' point of view. According to Arkadi Kuhlmann, CEO of the online bank ING Direct USA, a record number of 18- to 25-year-olds are filing for personal bankruptcy—200,000 did so in 2006.[1]

Mixed Marketing Messages

If you want to see how pervasive the marketing efforts of card issuers are, visit a college campus during the first few days of class. You'll probably spot tables stockpiled with T-shirts, iTunes cards, and credit card applications. Buy a few books in the college bookstore, and in your bag you'll find marketing pieces promoting a carefree college life "when you have the right credit card." And don't be surprised if a student asks you to sign up for a card. Some

[1] Arkadi Kuhlmann, "Don't Leave Financial Instruction Behind," *Fort Worth Star-Telegram*, 13 December 2007.

lenders pay them bonuses for bringing in more business. Through various media, students are often solicited several times a week.

You can't place all of the blame for such marketing efforts on card issuers, though. Ironically, universities play a key role as well. Many universities have lucrative marketing deals with card companies—a fact few people realize. These cards, which often display the school's name and logo, are marketed to students, faculty, and alumni. By contracting with a credit card company, a university can see multimillion-dollar profits—some up to $20 million over the course of several years. In exchange, the card issuers might get exclusive marketing rights at school events (for example, football games), as well as the students' contact information for direct marketing purposes.

The schools might receive money for signing the contract, a fee for everyone who signs up for the card, and a percentage of charges made to it. Although additional money for education seems like a worthy cause, some consumer advocates view this type of arrangement as a conflict of interest.

New State Laws Restrict Student Card Marketing

Several states have passed laws restricting the marketing efforts of card issuers on college campuses. Texas, for example, limits campus marketing to certain locations on certain days of the year. California doesn't allow the use of free gifts on campus to entice students. Hopefully, other states will follow suit.

The New College Order

So what's the effect of this inundation of card offers on the college campus? The vast majority of college students have at least one credit card. According to ING's Kuhlmann, by their senior year, they typically have $3,000 in credit card debt with 10% owing more than $7,000. Some have even heavier burdens, and most will be in debt for a long time. A 2004 study by NellieMae.org, the largest nonprofit provider of education loan funds, found that two-thirds of college students make only the minimum payment on their card debt, and 11% cannot even pay that much.

High card debt has many implications for students. A few end up dropping out of college so they can work full-time just to pay their card bills. In fact, financial debt is a leading factor affecting the college drop-out rate.

If students stay in school but ruin their credit in the process, it can affect their ability to rent an apartment, afford insurance, and even get a job to help pay off their debts. Financial stress can cause relationships to suffer and lead students into depression. In a few cases, it has been a contributing factor to suicide.

I certainly had a very hard time coping with the anxiety and stress caused by the $45,000 I owed on my credit cards by the time I finished graduate school. It's one of the primary reasons why I established CardRatings.com.

Whenever I recall that time, I think about Sean Moyer, who attended my alma mater. He committed suicide in 1998, overwhelmed by his card debts. I feel a special bond with Sean not just because we both attended the University of Texas in Dallas. The harsh reality is that what happened to him could easily have happened to me.

Remembering Sean Moyer

Sean worked hard to get himself out of debt. But even after credit counseling, a move home to save money, and two jobs, he couldn't make ends meet. Sean had a dozen cards at the time of his death, according to his mother, Janne M. O'Donnell, who is outraged by the aggressive marketing tactics lenders use on college campuses.

"I believe something must be done to stop card companies from preying on 18, 19, and 20 year olds," Janne said when she joined forces in 1999 with the Consumer Federation of America to expose the huge costs credit card debts impose on many college students. "How those companies can justify giving a credit card to a person making minimum wage is beyond me."[2] (It is worth noting that most issuers don't require any source of income in order to qualify for a student card.)

I discuss what happened to Sean whenever I speak to college or high school classes about card debt. His story moves me to this day, and I really admire Janne's attempts to reach out to others, as well as the legacy she has created in her son's honor.

How Students, Their Families, and the Industry Can All Win

Fortunately, more people are now recognizing the need for a better balance between marketing credit cards on campus and educating students about how those cards can affect their future. To ensure that the universities make deals that are mutually beneficial to their bottom line and to their alumni, faculty, and, most important, their students, people are requesting a more public and transparent view of the contracts that schools have with the credit issuers.

[2] Consumer Federation of America, consumerfed.org/pdfs/ccstudent.pdf, 8 June 1999.

It's definitely doable. For example, one of the most interesting win-win situations that I've heard about was a study conducted by Wells Fargo. The company sent a mailing to almost 78,000 randomly selected new college cardholders, offering a 60-minute phone card in exchange for completing an online credit education program.

The good news is that the students who completed the program had much better payment records than a control group—despite using their credit cards more. Moreover, they were less likely to carry a balance. Those who did carry a balance had lower balances and paid off more of them. They used their cards more responsibly than the control group. The results show that teaching people about credit early on seems to benefit both the students and the bank.

Even though the sample was very small, Wells Fargo sees the possibilities in this situation and has offered online education to all new student accounts for a few years now. I think that's great! These days, the incentive is a free matinee movie ticket from Fandango, which probably appeals more to college students than a phone card. ☺

Chase's +1 card, which was released in 2006, takes it one step further. The +1 card revolves around a group page on Facebook, a popular social networking website heavily populated by college students.

Cardholders earn reward points by signing up for the card, joining the Facebook group, referring friends, and more. What I like most about this card is that cardholders also earn points for completing credit education modules. I commend Chase for using reward points in such a creative and meaningful manner, and I hope other issuers are paying attention. After only one year, the Chase +1 Facebook group had close to 34,000 members.

Chase is smart to team up with Facebook, and we'll no doubt be seeing a growing online marketing effort as issuers continue to compete for college kids' business. Wherever college students go, lenders will continue to find ways to entice them there, on and off campus, and increasingly online.

Citibank has the only card I know of with a similar incentive program. The Citi MTVu card, which is associated with MTV, gives cardholders reward points for making on-time payments—and even for good grades!

You Have to Start Somewhere: Money Management 101

The sooner teens learn about the reality of finances and credit cards, the better. As very young children, they learn that plastic is often the preferred way to pay for things. (Monopoly's latest version uses debit cards instead of cash.) As kids mature, parents should explain more about credit—and how those flashy plastic cards aren't real money. They need to know that we have to pay interest when we can't pay the bill, and how that interest can quickly double or even triple the original price of an item.

The more money-management skills you share with your teens—*before* they go off to college—the easier a transition they'll make into the world of credit. When teens leave home for college or work, they'll be bombarded with credit card offers. Incoming college freshmen amass an average of $1,500 in credit card debt, according to NellieMae.org. That's the average—many soon max out their cards.

A sound understanding of credit will educate teens about the potential pitfalls of "the too good to resist" offers they'll soon encounter. By investing some time before they go off to school or a job, you'll help them establish good credit, which will give them countless advantages when they're on their own, looking to purchase a car or a house, trying to get insurance or a job, and so on.

Teaching teenagers about credit involves more than mere calculations of fees, interest rates, and balances. Teens also need to understand the advertising messages, the difference between wants and needs, and the lure of money. Although talking about these things with your teen can be difficult, the payoff is tremendous. Show me a teenager with a healthy, realistic perspective on money and material possessions, and I'll show you someone who will probably make wise financial decisions in the future.

Sam X. Renick, a financial educator who created the engaging cartoon character "Sammy the Rabbit" to teach kids about money issues, sums up the need for financial education:

> *With easy access to credit, hyperaggressive advertising campaigns targeting youth, and a global drive to cashless societies, it should be evident to everyone, regardless of their social, economic, or ethnic strata, that credit card education is of paramount importance to anyone wishing to avoid a life filled with stress, misery, disappointments of dreams, and relationships devastated by debt.[3]*

So how do you teach the basics of personal finance? One of the best ways to get started is by helping your children establish a budget and a sense of financial responsibility instead of giving them free rein to purchase anything they want.

A good resource for this task is Dr. Manning's website, CreditCardNation.com. Along with a financial literacy assessment quiz, the site includes easy-to-read, entertaining mini lessons for students about credit, including "The Discussion That Mom and Dad Never Had with You OR

---

[3] Sam X. Renick, itsahabit.com, private communication to Curtis E. Arnold, 2007.

What Should Have Followed the 'Birds and the Bees' Talk" and "What the Credit Card Companies Don't Want You to Know."

Another excellent resource for teen financial education is the Jump$tart Coalition for Personal Financial Literacy, which is based on the premise that average high school graduates lack basic money-management skills. Jump$tart develops and distributes educational resources and encourages curriculum enrichment to ensure that K–12 and college students learn basic personal finance skills. (I believe so strongly in this organization that I'm the co-chair of the Arkansas chapter of Jump$tart, and CardRatings.com is a national partner.)

JumpStart.org has a searchable clearinghouse of materials, including an online database of national training programs to assist educators, parents, and students in obtaining personal finance knowledge and skills. Major topics in the Jump$tart program include income, money management, ways to save and invest, and tips on spending, including consumer credit.

Should My Teenager Get a Credit Card?

This is a tough one. Both sides of this issue have valid arguments. If you decide it's time to teach your child the golden rules about credit with hands-on training, the first thing you'll want to investigate is the types of cards available. This will help you match your teen with a card that meets your needs as well as your teen's. Responsible teaching on your part can make your teen's entrance into the world of plastic smooth, fun, and successful, and it might just make you feel a little more secure, too. ☺

I can hear you saying, "I'm supposed to feel secure about giving my teenager a credit card?!?" Although I'd never advocate a card for every teen, you might feel more secure knowing that your teen has a backup in emergency situations. Using plastic is also safer than using cash, and if your teen's card is lost or stolen, you'll generally pay nothing for unauthorized purchases. But most important, you'll find comfort in knowing that your teenager has experience with credit cards and all their entrapments before being deluged by the offers.

Numerous cards geared to precollege teens are now available. For example, Visa's Buxx card is promoted as a parent-controlled reloadable payment card and a great way for parents to teach budgeting and money management to teens. The Buxx card sparked a great deal of discussion when it came on the market in 2001. Several versions of this type of card exist today, with a variety of enrollment and reloading fees. The fees can add up quickly, so read the fine print carefully and shop around if you decide to pursue this option.

An option for parents with a higher risk tolerance is to co-sign for a low-limit, unsecured credit card (that is, a *real* credit card). If you're brave enough to choose this option, make sure you limit your risk by asking for a very low limit on the card, such as $200 or $300. Bear in mind that your credit rating is the one that will be on the line because you'll be the primary account holder. (See Chapter 9, "Your Credit Report and Score: The Better You Look, the More You Profit," for more information about credit reports and credit scoring.)

Here are my tips for making sure your teen's first credit card experience is a good one:

- Get a card with a low limit and no annual fees.
- Discuss the details of the card with your teen, including the interest rate on purchases and cash advances, fees, due dates, and grace periods.
- Review all transactions every month and discuss them with your teen.

- Show your teen what finance charges will apply if the balance is not paid in full and on time. This includes any interest and fees.

- Realize that when teens reach a college campus, they'll be inundated with card offers and will be able to get one, even if you are their sole financial support or are unaware of it.

- Be a good role model for your children. Show your teens your credit report and a credit card bill. If you have high credit card debt, explain how it happened and what you're doing to get out of it. You don't have to be perfect to set a good example!

- Discuss how everyone needs to limit card use. Explain that you'll be setting limits before your teens head off for school, and explain what will happen if they run up bills they can't pay. Will you be able—or willing—to bail them out, or will they be on their own? Lay out the consequences. It's much better that they know in advance.

Foundations for Good Credit: Tips for College Students

If you're a college student, you probably have a credit card already—if not, you might plan to get one or more soon. If the card issuers have anything to say on the subject, you'll have a lot more cards in your pocket by the time you graduate.

> **TIP**
>
> While the following section is geared toward college students, it never hurts any of us to do a little review!

Even though you might feel in limbo, some place between your teen years and adulthood, if you have a credit card, it's time to take charge of your finances and manage them as an adult. The sooner you do, the sooner you'll feel the satisfaction of controlling, saving, and spending your own money, and being sure decisions you make now won't haunt you for the next seven to ten years of your life—*and beyond.*

Three Times Three: The Good, the Bad, and the Ugly

The Good

1. College students can easily get credit cards.
2. Credit cards can help young people establish a good credit history.
3. Credit cards are helpful and/or necessary when buying items such as airline tickets and when shopping online.

The Bad

1. College students can easily get multiple credit cards.
2. Having multiple lines of credit can mislead students into thinking they have a lot of money to spend.
3. Managed incorrectly, credit cards can lead to large debts and ruin a credit report.

The Ugly

1. Credit card debt doesn't magically go away, and bankruptcy has serious financial consequences for many years.
2. Too many students underestimate interest payments. Minimum payments mean the things you buy might cost you two or three times what you paid for them. You'll be in debt for years, paying for today's tacos long after *your* children graduate college.
3. The average total debt of a college senior is almost $30,000 (which includes student loans and credit card debt).

Keeping It Good

According to a national survey conducted between October 2007 and February 2008 by the U.S. Public Interest Research Group (PIRG), 66% of college students reported that they had at least one credit card. That number swells to 91% of seniors according to NellieMae. org—and for good reason. Credit cards are so convenient, making it easy to shop online for everything from textbooks to concert tickets, to music downloads. They're also a big help when you're in a jam, whether it's a medical emergency or vehicle breakdown. Used wisely, cards can be an advantage throughout college, and they can help young people develop crucial financial-management skills.

As soon as you get your first card or loan, you enter the world of credit reports and scores. Credit reports contain information such as your identity, debts, and credit cards.

Lenders develop credit-scoring systems to help them determine your "creditworthiness." They include information from your credit report, such as your bill payment history, the number and type of accounts you have, any late payments and collection actions, and your outstanding debts.

How you manage credit has a profound effect on your ability to get car loans, home mortgages, and other types of credit. It can also impact future jobs and insurance premiums. If you pay your bills on time, your first credit card will help you establish a solid credit history. But making late payments or no payments now will negatively impact your financial future.

Developing a New View about Credit

Dr. Mary Ann Campbell, CFP, founder of MoneyMagic. com and a money educator, cites unrealistic expectations as a major reason for student debt. "Many students' expectations of their earning potential after college far exceed what their actual income will be," she explains. Some students use their cards with reckless abandon during college, planning to pay off their debt when they land that great job after graduation. They forget that they usually need to climb a few rungs starting with a low-paying entry-level job before they get to the top of the career ladder.

Dr. Manning's website, CreditCardNation.com, contains a great resource if you're looking for a realistic view of life after college. Using his Budget Estimator, which he designed for students at the Rochester Institute of Technology, where he is a professor, you can see how your money is best distributed. Begin with the average starting salary for jobs in your major—or you can choose a different amount. The program then automatically pops in cost estimates for taxes and Social Security.

Then it's your turn. Plug in your likely expenses: housing, car payments, utilities, food, insurance, telephone, Internet, clothing, credit card bills, student loan payments, entertainment, and so on. Then presto, the Budget Estimator tells you whether your budget is balanced. If not, you can adjust the numbers to see how you can make ends meet.

Advice to Grow On

When it comes to credit cards, some of the best advice for students comes from other students.

- Heather, a college junior from Arkansas, recommends getting one card with a low credit line. "This limits the amount of credit you have access to and, therefore, removes the temptation to spend more than you have or more than you can pay off immediately," she says.

- Dwayne Blew, a member of CreditBoards, a forum dedicated to credit issues, was careful about what he charged and paid his card balance in full each month during college. Now he is reaping the benefits of a good credit score. As he puts it,

  One of the reasons you're going to college is to improve your lifestyle once you graduate. After putting so much effort into school, why let something small like a credit card end up ruining it all?

Good point!

- Another student recommends selectivity. "Don't sign up for a card that charges an annual fee to use it, and read the terms of the card before applying. You wouldn't believe how many students don't know what an APR is." I would add only that I'm constantly amazed by how many adults don't know their APRs, either.

Consider these other important recommendations for making the most of credit in college:

- Enroll in a personal finance course as soon as your schedule allows, recommends Dr. Campbell.

  If it's not required coursework, take it as an elective. You'll learn a set of life skills that will help you not only right now, but also after college and for the rest of your life.

- Open a line of communication. Find a trusted source, someone you can talk openly with about money issues. Not understanding financial problems or hiding them won't make them go away.

- Find gratification and rewards in activities that don't require you to spend, spend, spend, like shopping does. Instead, participate in intramurals or campus organizations, volunteer for local non-profits, take a hike…or you can always get a job.

- Appreciate the true magic of compound interest when it's working for you—earning you money at the bank or in the stock market. But recognize that compound interest can lead to true devastation when it's working against you—racking up your interest tab with a card issuer. Even when you buy something on sale, accumulated interest alone can double or triple the price.

- On a related note, my advice is that the first month you don't pay your entire balance in full, you should ditch your card as soon as possible and start using cash or a debit card. I feel very strongly about this as I personally know how card debt can start very small, but can quickly snowball.

- Avoid the lure of reward cards, particularly if you are a freshman or sophomore, until you have proven to yourself that you can use a plain-Jane card (that is, a nonreward card) responsibly. Studies show we all spend more on reward cards, and I don't think using a reward card is a good way to get started on the right foot.

- Account for everything. Keep records of your interest rate, fees, balance, due date, and purchases. You can easily set up a spreadsheet in Excel that will keep you organized and on time with your payments. (See Chapter 5, "How to Slash Your Debt and Keep Your Hard-Earned Money for Yourself," for instructions.)

- If you're already in debt, stop charging and always pay more than the minimum. If you're carrying a balance on more than one card, you'll save the most if you focus on paying off the one with the highest interest rate first, then go to the card with the next-highest interest card, and so on. (For more information about paying down debt, see Chapter 5.)

- Credit scores can make all the difference in your world—for good or for bad. Because it can take many years to recover from a bad credit score, it pays to keep yours in good shape. (Learn how in Chapter 9.)

- Use your cards responsibly—it's vital for your future. Credit is a privilege, and it's your personal responsibility to make sure it doesn't become a peril. "The magic comes from you," as Dr. Campbell often says.

- If you're not sure you can trust yourself to use a card responsibly, use it only for emergencies. "And if you can eat it, drink it, or wear it, it's not an emergency!" That's what David Hunt, the former president of AT&T Universal Card, said when he gave his daughter a credit card when she started college.

Saving for College Tuition

Let's shift gears and discuss college tuition. Parents are often most impacted by the high cost of college—even with scholarships, the costs can be staggering. Unless students pay their own way by working or securing student loans, the parents usually foot a good portion, if not all, of the bill.

If you've thought about or have even started a savings mechanism specifically for your children's college education, you're ahead of the curve. If you haven't, start now.

One of the best methods of saving for education is a 529 college savings plan. Named after Section 529 of the Internal Revenue Code, 529 college savings plans were created to encourage families to save money for college. Typically operated by a state or educational institution, participants invest after-tax money into their 529 accounts, where their earnings grow tax-deferred. Qualified distributions from the account that are used to pay for college costs are tax free as well.

Interestingly enough, these 529 savings plans are so popular, card issuers have created incentive programs around them. Although credit cards don't typically come to mind when you think about saving money, 529 rebate credit cards (aka college savings cards) can indeed help you put aside money for college. Let's review the 529 basics before we look at how the cards fit in.

The ABC's of 529's

There are two types of 529 plans: savings and prepaid plans. Both are managed—that is, a fund manager chooses how to invest the money for the plan. 529 savings plans are operated by a state with the purpose of saving money for any accredited college. Prepaid plans, which are run by states or educational institutions, allow investors to lock in future tuition costs at participating schools.

The advantages of opening a 529 plan should be obvious: It's a tax-exempt fund that helps you save money tax-free for future educational goals. As with any investment fund, the sooner you start, the more compound interest you'll potentially earn. Research plans nationwide and invest in the one that meets your criteria, has the lowest fees, most flexibility, and so on. Savingforcollege.com is an excellent resource to help you comparison shop.

Spending to Invest

Growing healthy investment accounts requires making an initial investment. Start small, if you have to, because even investing a small amount each month can build a good foundation. If your investments could use a little boost, or if you're the type who loves a good incentive program, take a look at the 529 rebate cards that can add a little more to your fund.

Three such programs are frequently in the news: BabyMint, Upromise, and FutureTrust (go to CardRatings. com/Book for the links). Each program partners with vendors that have agreed to rebate a percentage (which typically ranges from 1% to 10%) of the purchase cost. The rebates are credited to a member's account, and can then be invested into a 529 savings plan. As an added bonus, each program offers a credit card that will provide members with additional rebates on all purchases made, not just on qualified products.

When these programs were first introduced, a limited number of partnering 529 plans were available. As of this printing, Upromise administers the 529 plans of several states, including Arkansas, Colorado, Iowa, Missouri, New York, North Carolina, North Dakota, and Pennsylvania. Investors can direct BabyMint savings into almost any state 529 Plan. Through BabyMint, you can also choose to have your rebates sent to you via check, have them deposited directly into your college savings account, or make payments toward your student loans.

If you already contribute to a 529 Plan, check to see if your plan is affiliated with a card. If you haven't started a fund, when you research the plans, find out about the programs they have with card issuers.

TIP

To get your savings to accumulate quickly, ask grandparents, other family members, and even friends to join and have their rebates directed to your child's savings account. Each of these programs offers this option.

Fidelity Investments offers a similar educational savings credit card, the Fidelity 529 College Rewards American Express card, which automatically deposits a flat rebate of 1.5% on retail purchases directly into a 529 savings plan. Friends and family can also carry this card and direct their rebates to your child's account. The only catch is that Fidelity must manage your 529 account. So if you already contribute to a Fidelity-managed 529 or you are ready to start one, this could be a good option for you.

Overall, these are great programs to assist you in your quest to save for education. Partner first with a 529 plan that has no or very low maintenance fees and shows a good return. For reward cards, be sure to compare all of the benefits and restrictions. However, when you think of saving and credit cards in the same breath, extra care is in order. Keep these tips in mind when using cards to save for college:

- Take a thorough look at each of the incentive plans, including restrictions. Spending an hour or two researching will likely be a good investment of your time.

- As with any rewards card, be sure you pay off your balance each month. If you don't, the amount you'll pay in interest will probably cost you a lot more than your savings rebate.

- Purchase judiciously. Instead of saying to yourself, "Oh, if I buy that, I'll get a rebate toward our education account," think about the money you'd save if you didn't make the purchase in the first place. To keep your spending down, choose the card that's affiliated with vendors you already use, and don't let yourself go overboard with new products.

- Remember, card rebates alone can't finance a college education. Even if you make every effort to max out the amount of rebates every year for 18 years, at the very most, you'd probably earn enough to cover part of your expenses for only a semester or two (and that's being quite optimistic). Also remember that to achieve rebates, you have to spend money in the first place.

- Before signing on, commit to making your own direct contributions to the 529 account, to see maximum growth. This will help you to spend and save wisely.

- Start early—say, when your child is starting to master crawling. That way, you have the advantage of time to help your savings grow. If your child is starting to master calculus and plans to enter college in a year or two, 529 plans might not be your best option. Investigate other saving and financing programs at finaid.org.

- Don't hesitate to enlist other family members and get them to sign up for the cause. Used judiciously, these programs can help turn your family's spending into a small but significant contribution to you and your child's future.

Tax Savings and Card Rebates: A Win-Win for Cardholders

I love the thought of allowing credit card rebates to grow tax deferred in an investment account and then not paying any taxes on qualified redemptions that are used to defray college costs. This is a savvy way to get the most bang for your buck and is exactly what college savings cards offer. Keep more money in your pocket and give less to Uncle Sam. What a concept!

You Are in the Driver's Seat

In closing out this chapter, let's shift our focus back to student cards. I am very passionate about student credit issues and speak regularly on college campuses. My message to every incoming freshman is this: Card issuers are extremely eager to get your business—so eager, they spend millions and millions of dollars each year aggressively marketing their cards on campuses across the country. It's part of their long-term plan—to develop long-term financial relationships with you and everyone else in college today. According to critics, they're willing to do almost anything to accomplish this goal.

Use the keen competition among card issuers to your advantage. Given how much they want you, there's no benefit in settling for the first offer that comes your way. Be proactive and compare offers by reading the terms and conditions carefully and then choosing the one that's best for you.

Keep in mind that college cards often come with high interest rates (usually in the mid to upper teens). This is how lenders make money and protect themselves against the risks students pose…. Students generally have limited incomes, brief credit histories, lower credit scores, and higher default rates than other age groups. (Don't take it personally!)

You can find some great credit information online, so it pays to surf around. Try to educate yourself about credit cards and credit in general. I've already mentioned most of my favorite sites for students interested in learning more about credit. Last, but not least, is my own site, CardRatings.com, the best place to comparison shop for a student card.

Finally, don't use your credit card as a source of spending money. Although many college students have every intention of promptly paying off their cards when they get a real job, such good intentions are often never realized. Credit reports and scores are ruined in the process.

I know firsthand the potentially devastating effect of relying on credit cards as a source of income during school. If you do find yourself buried in card debt, get help. You're not alone, and it's probably not entirely your fault. Talk to your family. Reach out to a member of the clergy. Consider using a nonprofit debt counseling service. Find someone on campus you trust who can help you figure things out.

Having said all that, I also want you to remember that credit cards are not evil. In fact, cards can be great financial tools. When you're in college, the best way to use one is to help you establish a positive credit history. Think of establishing credit as a sign of true independence. Isn't that what all college students crave?

Just remember that cards require financial discipline and a good measure of prudence. Happy charging!

CHAPTER 8

Use Targeted Cards to Your Financial Advantage

Lenders know that targeting credit cards to certain specific groups is an effective way to grow their businesses. Student cards are a good example, but several cards are marketed to people with particular needs, such as folks who have never had credit, who need to rebuild credit, or who want business credit. Some cards are marketed to people with particular habits, ranging from shopping at certain stores, to supporting certain causes, to living the life of the rich and famous.

You'll be fascinated by what the very wealthy can get for free from their cards, including free companion airline tickets and personal shoppers (an actual person who does your shopping for you) at stores such as Saks and Gucci! No matter what your income, there's a card for everyone these days as issuers "slice and dice" us into fairly specific demographics and then try to create cards that will appeal to us.

After you've read this chapter on targeted cards, you'll have a unique advantage: You'll be able to find the cards that will benefit you the most, regardless of how they're marketed.

Need to Rebuild or Build Credit? Get a Secured Card

Tom, a member of a forum called CreditBoards, filed for Chapter 7 bankruptcy protection and now is in the process of rebuilding his credit. Although this isn't an easy task, Tom's patient persistence is rewarding him with steady improvements. He checks his credit reports regularly and takes the time to get every mistake corrected, even the smallest ones (more on this in the next chapter). But the most important thing he's doing to improve his credit score is using the right **secured credit card**—in the right way.

A secured card can be a very useful tool if you're rebuilding or building credit. I'm a big fan of them and applaud Tom's efforts.

What Is a Secured Credit Card?

Most credit cards are *un*secured—that is, you don't have to put up any collateral to get them. But you do with a secured card: Your deposit into a savings account serves as the collateral. The amount of the required security deposit varies from card to card, but the minimum amounts generally range from around $200 to $300. You might even earn interest off your funds, just as you would in a normal savings account.

Your credit limit is usually the same as the amount you deposit into the savings account (matched dollar-for-dollar). With a few cards I've seen over the years, the limit has even been higher than the required deposit. For example, a secured card might advertise an initial credit line of 130%, so your deposit of $300 would get you $390 in available credit.

A secured card is often the best answer if you can't get a traditional card. Secured cards are accepted wherever credit cards can be used, and certainly come in handy for emergencies and for transactions when having a card is advantageous, such as when you're renting a car.

Secured cards function just like other cards. If payments aren't made in full each month, you're charged interest. The lender will *not* tap into your savings account for the interest—or the payments. If you're late with a payment, the rate goes sky-high, just as high as it would with an unsecured card. And if you use the card irresponsibly, you'll damage your credit. The security deposit won't help.

What Are the Benefits of a Secured Credit Card?

If you can squirrel away the $200 or $300 needed for a security deposit, it's likely that you can get a secured card, which will help you:

- Establish credit. If you've never had a credit card, secured cards are a good first step in building credit. "A secured card is most useful for the person starting out on their credit history," explains Dr. Jerry Plummer, an economics professor at Austin Peay State University, "since it says that the person is willing to take the extra step to establish credit."

- Reestablish credit. If your credit history is damaged (Dr. Manning estimates that 40 million U.S. consumers have bad credit), you might not be able to qualify for a traditional card. But you'll probably be able to qualify for a secured card, unless you've had to file for bankruptcy. Generally, you won't be able to get a secured card until the bankruptcy has been discharged.

- Gain built-in debt protection. Was excessive spending partly to blame for your bad credit? A secured card can act as a safeguard, making it harder for you to get in over your head again. You'll know that your credit is secured with *your* own money. If your account becomes delinquent, it will likely be closed and your security deposit will be seized. Knowing this will help safeguard you from racking up more card debt.

- Avoid *subprime or fee-harvesting credit cards*. These cards are known for gouging and preying on people with bad or no credit. The fees on subprime cards can easily total $200 to $300 in just the first year, which is about the size of the credit lines they offer. Don't fall for a subprime card and have almost all of your credit line eaten up by fees. The issuer is the only one who benefits from these cards!

Tips for Finding Your Best Secured Card

Important! Not all secured cards report to the three major credit reporting companies (Experian, Equifax, and TransUnion). To build or rebuild credit, it's smart to get a card that does report to all three. Fortunately, many secured cards report to them all, but make sure before you apply.

Where to Look

Most companies don't actively advertise secured cards. But CardRatings.com lets you compare offers and even apply online. Just click on "Poor/No Credit" from our home page. It's also a good idea to check with your local bank or credit union.

Fees

It pays to find a low-fee secured card. You could spend more than $100 a year on a few cards, with their annual fees and hidden processing charges (for "registration" and "setup," for example). Many alternatives exist, so there's no point in paying fees like that. Fortunately, the total yearly fees on many secured cards are less than $50. In fact, several have annual fees in the range of $25 to $40, with no processing or up-front fees.

Interest Rates

Just because you have no credit or poor credit doesn't mean you have to settle for the highest rates known to mankind! You should be able to find an ongoing purchase APR in the midteens, although rarely I have even seen rates around 10%. Definitely avoid any rates in the upper teens or above 20%. Shop around, and visit CardRatings.com to see what issuers *and* cardholders are saying about the newest offerings.

Unfortunately, secured cards normally don't have introductory rates. One notable exception is being offered as of this writing by Wells Fargo, just to its banking customers: a secured card with a teaser rate of 5.9% for six months. Maybe your bank will be running a special promotion for depositors. Ask!

Fine Print

I can't stress enough the importance of always reading the fine print. It's the only way to find out key facts: For example, what happens if you're late with a payment? And what's the length of the grace period? Making sure you're clear on the details will help you get on the right path and build a solid credit history.

> **TIP**
>
> Be ever vigilant folks! I recently took a careful look at a secured card offer we were reviewing on CardRatings.com and realized this particular card didn't have a grace period at all! This was a shock as I haven't encountered a card that did not have a grace period in many years. Fortunately, we do a lot of the leg work for you on our website. ☺

Earned Interest

It's a good idea to choose a secured card that helps you make money on your deposit. The good news is that many do, but you should verify this before you make your final choice. You might earn only 1% to 2% in interest, but that's definitely better than getting 0% on your hard-earned money. Also, if you have to carry a balance on your card, you can effectively offset your finance charges by 1% to 2%.

Best Kept Secret!

Citibank offers a unique secured card that pays a rate of return comparable to what you'd normally get with a CD (certificate of deposit). The rate of return is 4% (as of the printing of this book). The downside is that you must commit to keeping the account for at least 18 months. However, most secured cards require that keep you account open for at least 12-18 months before you are able to qualify for an unsecured card. In other words, I really don't think this requirement is a big deal.

If You're Denied a Secured Card

Hopefully, it's just a mistake, so first check out the advice I give about fixing errors on credit reports in Chapter 9, "Your Credit Report and Score: The Better You Look, the More You Profit." Bear in mind that not everyone can get approved for a secured card, though. If you still can't qualify for a secured card, consider applying for a prepaid card—everyone can be approved for one. The fees can be steep, but for some people, prepaid cards are the only option. Although prepaid cards generally don't help you establish or build credit, they can come in handy when you have no alternatives. (Go to CardRatings.com/Book for the only prepaid card that I know of that allows you to build credit.)

How to Use a Secured Card to Help You Build or Rebuild Credit

Here are my top tips for using a secured card to build or rebuild credit:

- Stick with only one card and keep spending to a minimum. The goal is to pay off the card each month so your credit score will improve as quickly as possible.
- If you can't pay your full balance in a given month, be sure to promptly pay at least the required minimum amount by the due date. It's a good idea to get into the habit of always sending in more than the required minimum.
- Never be late. Otherwise, you could become a victim of a domino effect. Before you know it, you're charged late fees, and then your interest rates are raised, privileges are lost, and your credit history takes a beating.

When Will I Qualify for an Unsecured Credit Card?

Although there's no hard and fast rule, using a secured card responsibly can help you rebuild or establish credit much quicker than you might anticipate. I've heard from many cardholders over the years who have qualified for a regular card with decent rates in as little as 12 to 24 months. A good indicator that you're on the right track is an increase in solicitations by mail for cards with rates around or a little above the national average. (Visit CardRatings.com/Book for the current average rates.)

> **TIP**
>
> It's wise to check your credit score before you even apply for a secured card and then check again after you've used the card for a year or so. You can usually qualify for an unsecured card with a decent rate when your **FICO score** is in the 670 range. (See Chapter 9 for more on credit scores.)

It's a good idea, though, not to be in too much of a hurry and instead to focus on developing a good credit record. Using a secured card responsibly should help you learn healthy habits. Then when you do get an unsecured card, you'll remain in control of your spending and credit.

How Your Business Can Profit from Cards

Many owners of small businesses use their personal credit cards to get their businesses off the ground. Although this is sometimes the only alternative during the start-up phase, continuing to use a personal card isn't the wisest choice when a business is established.

Benefits of Business Cards

Like many, Gina Baker used her personal cards in the early days of her business, which she has been running for more than five years. As her business grew, and continues to grow, she finds her needs changing.

"It was becoming hard to gauge how much money I was making while using my own credit cards and cash," Baker explains on the CreditBoards forum. "I needed to separate my business and personal cash flow."

Having a card in your business's name offers many distinct advantages, including the following:

- The ability to build a credit history in the business's name
- The capacity to account for expenditures accurately
- Easy itemization for tax purposes
- Vendor discounts

"The perks are great," Baker says. "With a business card, you get discounts on business purchases from wholesalers and retailers who wouldn't give a second glance to a personal card."

Business cards offer many other benefits as well: travel accident insurance, collision coverage on rental cars, free or inexpensive additional cards for employees, the ability to set individual credit lines for each employee who has a card, detailed financial transaction reports, and so on.

American Express, which markets its cards under the name "OPEN for Business—Small Business," offers many business cards designed to appeal to small business owners. For example, all OPEN cards come with automatic discounts at FedEx, Delta, Courtyard by Marriott, Hertz, Yahoo! Search Marketing and Small Business, Logoworks, 1-800-Flowers.com, and more. All OPEN cards allow you to customize online expense reporting, create account alerts, add employee cards, and download data to your in-house accounting system.

Advanta Bank Corp., another popular business card issuer, mainly focuses on the small business market and often has great deals. For example, as of the printing of this book, its no-fee Platinum Business Card with Rewards offers a 0% rate on balance transfers for 15 months (transfer fee applies), followed by a 7.99% fixed rate. In addition, this card offers up to 5% cash back or travel rewards with no limit on your total rewards. Advanta also enables business owners to truly personalize their cards by putting their company name and logo on the card. I really like this feature—suddenly your card can become a unique marketing tool!

This is just a sampling of the cards available to you and your business. Given how keen the competition is among lenders, I expect to see many more small business cards in the next few years. For the latest deals that might appeal to you, visit the Business section of CardRatings.com.

Credit Criteria for Business Cards

Getting a business card based purely on the credit of your business is very difficult. According to Gerri Detweiler, co-founder of Business Credit Success and president of Ultimate Credit Solutions Inc., unless the business has been incorporated for at least two years, has about 25 employees, and brings in around $2 million a year, a business credit card usually has to be personally guaranteed. In other words, the issuer bases its credit decision largely on your personal credit history...as it takes time to build a credit history for your business.

> **TIP**
>
> If your personal credit picture isn't rosy and you're trying to establish or rebuild credit at the same time you're applying for business credit, you might need a secured card. As of now, Wells Fargo is the only issuer I know that offers a secured business card to its bank customers. The card boasts up to a $50,000 credit limit, which is secured by, and equal to, your collateral deposit (works basically the same as a personal secured card). Another added benefit is that this card reports your payment history to Dun and Bradstreet (D&B), a company that compiles business credit information and is the world's leading source of commercial information and insight on business.

Gina Baker built her business credit from the ground up. She started small by applying for a card from Office Max with a $250 limit. She also obtained lines of credit from Federal Express and Staples. Although some of these cards required a personal guarantee to prove her credit-worthiness, Baker established credit for her business fairly quickly. With good credit management, she noticed offers coming in from larger lenders within six months, with some offering credit limits of $10,000.

A Little Known Way to Quickly Build Business Credit!

It is important to check if any potential creditors you are considering will report your payment history to D&B. Reporting to D&B will help you build credit in the name of your business. Experian and Equifax are two other large companies that compile business credit info. Ideally, you want to choose a creditor that reports to as many business credit reporting companies as possible. Visit CardRatings.com/Book for more information on which cards report to which bureaus.

How to Play Your (Rebate) Cards Right

The small business card market has really exploded in the last few years. In fact, as Sastry Rachakonda, director of Discover's Business Card division, recently wrote to me, "Lenders have good reason to be interested in this market, as small business owners make an estimated $250 billion in purchases on business cards on an annual basis."

Small business spending has been growing at a very healthy clip. Even better from a lender's point of view is this consideration: "The charge volume associated with a typical business card account is generally three to four times higher than that of a consumer card account," Sastry explains.

Discover is a fairly new entrant into the business card market. Its Discover Business Card and Discover Business Miles Card both offer fee-free PurchaseChecks, a very unique offering that allows cardholders to pay merchants or suppliers who don't take credit cards. Cardholders also earn rewards with PurchaseChecks and get the same standard APR and payment grace period as they would with regular card purchases.

One outgrowth of the strong interest in this market is increasingly aggressive business rebate offers. Although rebates on business cards often parallel rebates on consumer cards, business rebates tend to be a little more generous when it comes to cash-back rewards, travel rewards, and so on. For example, the business card of choice in my wallet is a cash-back card from American Express that gives me 2% on all purchases above $10,000 annually with no earnings cap. I don't know of any consumer cards that offer this level of rebate on all purchases.

To put things in perspective, if your business charges $100,000 a year, a 2% rebate would represent a year-end cash-back bonus of around $2,000. Not a bad deal just for using a particular card!

Although most small-to-medium businesses have traditionally used airline reward cards, I personally prefer cash-back cards, for basically the same reasons I prefer consumer cash-back cards over consumer airline reward cards. Granted, a business airline reward card makes sense in a few instances, but I encourage you to carefully compare rewards, as we did in Chapter 2, "Show Me the Money! Credit Card Rebates."

Also, it's worth noting that some business reward cards offer greater rebates in certain expense categories. To maximize your profits, find the business card that most caters to your spending habits.

Other Items to Consider

Choose your business card based on these criteria:

- Rate—Make sure you're getting the best interest rate you can. As of this writing, the average business card rate is 12.04 %.[1] Several cards feature introductory rates as low as 0%. (Watch for balance transfer fees!)

- Fees—Are there annual fees or other types of fees? If so, will you get enough from the rebates to justify the fees?

- Perks—What kind of perks will benefit your company the most? If you travel a lot, look for cards that earn miles with no blackout dates. If you make a lot of business purchases, look for the cards that offer cash back or vendor discounts at the places where you're most likely to shop. This could easily add up to hundreds of dollars in savings fairly quickly. I love that our AmEx business card offers a 5% rebate with certain online retailers.

- Ability to monitor spending—How often does the issuer send reports on spending and how detailed are the reports? Can you monitor individual employee expenditures? Can you view spending online or be notified by email or a text message when you reach preset spending limits? Can you download the reports into your accounting system (Quicken, Money, and so on)?

---

[1] Based on card data published by CardRatings.com as of March 1, 2008.

- Flexibility—Can you set different credit limits for different employees and adjust them whenever you want? Can you grant some employees access to cash and restrict others?

- Card acceptance—If you travel a lot, particularly abroad, be sure to get a card that's widely accepted. I always carry a backup MasterCard in my wallet, in case a particular merchant doesn't honor my American Express card. (Visa and MasterCard are the more widely accepted.)

- ATM—If you or your employees travel frequently, choose a card with a national ATM network that you can use if you're faced with emergency cash needs. Watch for fees.

- Grace period—Think of the grace period as an interest-free loan and a great cash-flow management tool. The grace periods of business cards are comparable to those for consumer cards, so look for one with a 25-day grace period.

Plum Sweet!

American Express introduced the Plum Card in 2007, which allows you to pay as little as 10% of your balance, and you can then defer payment on the remaining balance for up to 2 months, interest-free. If you are having cash flow problems, this card could be very helpful! Visit CardRatings. com/Book for more info.

As always, comparison shopping is a good idea. Perusing the ratings, reviews, and applications for business credit cards on CardRatings.com will help simplify this process.

Retail and Department Store Cards: Worth a Look?

Many retail and department stores are very aggressive in marketing cards branded with their own logo (aka charge cards). Lately, it seems that every consumer purchase is prefaced with an offer to apply for a card and get instant savings: "If you apply for a {fill in the name of the store here} credit card today, you will receive a 15% discount on your purchase."

Oooh! What diehard shopper wouldn't be tempted?

Sometimes these cards have a Visa or MasterCard logo, but traditional store cards aren't affiliated with any larger payment network (such as Visa or MasterCard) and can be used only at the store that issues the card. JCPenney was one of the first retailers to issue such cards back in 1958. Since then, a lot of stores have recognized the profit to be made by operating their own credit cards.

You've probably heard the spiel from The Gap, Macy's, Kohl's, Dillard's, Target, Best Buy, Wal-Mart, Banana Republic, Saks, Nordstrom, and more. Before you jump to get 15% off your next purchase, though, let me fill you in on the full implications of succumbing to this form of instant gratification.

These are the pros:

- Store cards can be a good way to establish credit because the approval requirements are often less stringent than for major credit cards. Credit expert Gerri Detweiler points out, "A selective consumer can establish a positive credit history with retail store credit cards, which usually have lower credit limits and are easier to obtain."

- You may also receive special financing offers for larger purchases, such as computers, appliances, or furniture. These **same-as-cash deals** allow you to pay smaller monthly installments with no interest for a specified period of time, usually ranging from 6 to 36 months. A few offers don't even require any monthly payments for a certain period of time.

- Beyond introductory discounts, you might also get to take part in exclusive savings events or shopping promotions. The store might open early just for cardholders on certain days, for example.

- Reward programs are often available. As with credit card reward programs, you can typically earn one point for every dollar you spend at the store. The points are normally redeemed for store gift cards or store credit. Some store cards offer more

Star Light, Star Bright

Macy's offers four different levels of card membership based on how much you spend on your card. You earn Gold Star Rewards when you spend at least $500 annually on your Macy's Card, and among other things, you're entitled to exclusive offers four times a year. If you spend $2,500 or more, you can qualify for the Elite Star Rewards Visa Card, where you'll earn a 3% rebate on Macy's purchases. Earned rebates can be redeemed toward $25 Macy's gift cards.

aggressive rebate percentages, which are often based on the amount of your annual spending level.

- Some store cards offer other benefits that aren't based on your spending level. Examples include free gift wrapping, free alterations, and free shipping. These perks are definitely worth looking into at your favorite stores.

Now consider the cons...

One of the biggest problems with store cards is their high-flying interest rate, often above 20%. The perks rarely outweigh the finance charges, so if you won't be paying off your balance in full every month, I advise just saying "No!" to store cards.

To get a great rate, you might have to fulfill a minimum purchase requirement. For example, you might be required to spend $1,000 or more to qualify for a 0% rate. Although this shouldn't pose a problem—if you have budgeted $1,000 for the purchase—don't be tempted to spend more than your budget allows!

Watch Out for "Buy Now, Pay Later, No Interest" Offers

If you go for one of these special financing deals, be sure to pay off the *full* balance before the interest-free period comes to an end. If your balance isn't paid off to the penny, **retroactive interest** often is applied from the date of purchase, even if you've faithfully paid on your bill every month and have a balance of only $1 or $2 at the end of the promotional period!

For example, say you buy $2,000 worth of furniture on January 1 and take advantage of a 0% for a year offer. You pay $150 every month, and when you realize there's still a balance of $200 in late December, you send it in right away. Unfortunately, it doesn't get posted until January 2, so you're hit with a 25% retroactive interest rate and have to pay more than $350 extra—or even more, if you don't quickly pay off the new balance.

The moral of the story, according to Marc Eisenson, author of *Invest in Yourself: Six Secrets to a Rich Life* (Wiley, 2001), is that you shouldn't get involved with a "pay no interest until..." deal unless you're absolutely certain that you'll make the full payment by the due date. Unfortunately, good intentions often aren't enough. Make sure you can trust yourself!

Applying for Multiple Accounts Can Cost You in More Ways Than One

The store clerk says that if you open a line of credit today, you can get one year of free financing on the new appliances you just purchased. "Well then, sign me up!" you exclaim.

You know to make sure you pay off the "buy now, pay later" deal before "later" comes around. But what you might not know is that opening multiple credit accounts will negatively affect your credit rating. And if you're not careful, you might find yourself opening several lines of credit within a relatively short time frame.

Aside from all the appealing sales pitches, applying for multiple accounts can be particularly problematic if you use store cards only once or twice just to take advantage of the instant rebates. You can soon forget that you ever had them in the first place, but your credit report won't forget. (More on this in the next chapter.)

"Limit yourself to applying for only one or two cards during any 12-month period," Gerri Detweiler recommends. "Any more is typically considered a risk factor on your credit report." On top of that, having several open accounts can be a source of temptation and can result in too many overindulgent shopping sprees! ☺

It's a Balancing Act

Now that you know the pros and cons of store cards, how do you figure out if one is worth its weight in gold—or in store credits, in this case? As you might expect, you need to do a little math.

Let's say you come across an offer at the mall for a card with no annual fee that has a six-month promotional APR of 0% on purchases of more than $500 and an ongoing purchase APR of 22%. The perks include 10% off your first in-store purchase, as well as 10% off your first online purchase. You also get free shipping on all online purchases of more than $100. On top of that, for every dollar you spend in the store, you earn one point. When you earn 1,000 points, you automatically receive a $10 gift certificate in the mail.

> **TIP**
> If you're likely to carry a balance, don't even bother to crunch the numbers. An APR of more than 20% on a $1,000 store card bill trumps any rewards you might get just about every time.

Although that's a very nice set of incentives, ask yourself this question: Will you have to spend more than you normally would to earn the perks or take advantage of the promotional pricing? If so, that's extra spending you're putting on a card just to get some discounted merchandise, which won't be discounted for long. When that teaser rate is over, the interest rate will balloon to 22% and your debt could mushroom quickly if you're not careful.

But if you...

- Frequently shop at the store...
- Pay off the balance in full every month...
- Don't exceed your monthly budget in the process...
- Don't apply for too many other cards...

...then you can fully enjoy the perks, knowing that you earned them "free and clear."

With so many great offers out there, it really pays to take the time to think through the benefits of a particular store card before you sign up for it. I know performing math is a lot to ask when you're at the checkout counter with an armload of new purchases. But never sign on for a card without reviewing the fine print and finding out exactly what you'll get. It might take away some of the fun of a shopping splurge, but in the long run, you'll be happier if you slow down a bit and safeguard your credit.

Ask the clerk to hold your items, take the application, and find a place where you can sit down and read it. You should find the Schumer Box and the other terms and conditions right there. While you're at it, take a minute to think about what you were going to buy. Then consider this money-saving thought: That hip outfit from The Gap won't likely be so hip in a few months anyway!

For current store card offers, visit the "Card Reports" section of CardRatings.com. See what cardholders are saying about their store cards in the "Consumer Reviews" section, and feel free to post your review there as well.

Maximize Your Cash Flow with a Generous Grace Period

Kohl's offers a unique "Interest Free" (no finance charge) option to some of its cardholders. If you reside in AR, CO, CT, DC, DE, MD, NJ, NY, PA, TN, VA, or WI, you have the option of avoiding a finance charge in any billing period as long as you pay one-third of your new balance—but not less than $50. If your new balance is $50 or less, you must pay the entire new balance to avoid finance charges in the following month. Kohl's also offers a generous grace period to all cardholders (regardless of where you reside) of between 28 and 31 days. Just make sure you stay within the grace period, otherwise you'll be hit with a 21.9% APR on your balance! Ouch. ☺

Affinity Cards: Using a Card to Help Others

Chances are, a few nonprofits tug at your heart strings. It's great to be a part of something larger than yourself, but who has enough time and money for all the do-gooders we'd like to support? At times, it can be difficult to find extra money in your budget to contribute to even your favorite cause. When your budget stretches you to the limit and your charity or nonprofit beckons, an affinity card might be the perfect solution.

What Is an Affinity Credit Card?

Remember the airline reward cards we discussed earlier? They're a perfect example of an **affinity** (aka cobranded) **card**, which brings together two organizations for their mutual benefit. One is the card issuer, and the other is usually a nonfinancial group, such as an airline.

Sometimes the nonfinancial group is a nonprofit. I want to focus on this segment of the affinity cards market because I think it deserves your special consideration.

Affinity cards offer you the possibility of an expanded relationship with your favorite charity. All you have to do is use the card to make everyday purchases, and the nonprofit receives small donations from the card issuer. That's right, you can support the cause with no out-of-pocket cost, just by using its affinity card on your weekly run to the grocery store. What used to be a chore is now a charitable donation benefiting your favorite nonprofit!

For example, the Humane Society of the United States (HSUS), which started its affinity card program through Bank of America more than 12 years ago, has 60,000 open accounts and consistently receives "well into six figures each year," according to Steve Putnam, HSUS vice president of Business Development and Corporate Relations.

How It Works

Bank of America gives HSUS $.25 for every $100 in purchases. During the writing of this book, Bank of America was also providing an additional $50 for every new HSUS account it got through an email promotion. (Cardholders also can earn reward points that can be redeemed for cash rebates, gift cards, or free airline tickets.)

HSUS depends on the affinity card to support many programs, he says, including efforts to strengthen animal cruelty laws, resolve conflict with wildlife, protect wildlife habitat, offer humane education programs in schools, spay and neuter dogs and cats, promote shelter adoptions, and provide disaster relief for animals.

The variety of affinity cards is incredible. Whatever your interests, chances are there's a card for you. Would you like to support your child's education? Check out the Target affinity card, which donates to a local school of your choice.

Want to help less fortunate and homeless people? Love Elvis? With the Elvis Presley Visa Card, offered through Bank of America, a portion of every purchase is donated to the Elvis Presley Charitable Foundation, which provides homeless families up to one year of rent-free housing.

> **TIP**
>
> Another benefit of using an affinity card is that it provides the nonprofit group with free advertising. Swiping your card at your local grocery store could lead to a conversation with the cashier about your cause!

Alumni organizations, professional associations, and children's causes, such as the St. Jude Children's Research Hospital, are just a few more of the many nonprofits you can help. To compare affinity card offers, visit the "Rewards Card" section of CardRatings.com.

An Objective Approach to Affinity Cards

Although your interest in supporting a nonprofit organization should determine whether you use a particular affinity card, it pays to understand a few possible catches:

- Some affinity cards come with high APRs. If you won't be paying off the card in full each month, you are likely to end up paying more in interest than the organization receives through the affinity program. As Chris, a member of the CreditBoards forum, puts it:

> *Since you identify yourself with the card, it tends to be the primary card in one's wallet, unless you are a person who watches spending carefully, it's real easy to charge high amounts on the card and get trapped in a financial quicksand.*

If you'd end up carrying a balance, it'd probably cost you less if you gave a small donation directly to the organization (and avoided the card altogether).

- The amount the nonprofit receives could be very small—as low as 25¢ for every $100 you spend. For example, Dan, another member of CreditBoards, used a card that benefited his alumni association, but the percentage was only 1/2%. By switching to a card that offered a 1% cash rebate, he was actually able to double his support. Find out exactly how much will actually go to supporting your nonprofit before you sign up for a card.

- Understand what it takes to make a donation. In general, organizations receive donations only on actual purchases, not on cash advances or balance transfers.

- Personal perks are often limited with affinity cards. Airline miles and cash rewards for your own benefit are usually scaled back. Moreover, many of these cards offer no personal rebates.

- You normally can't deduct contributions made through your affinity card on your tax return. Of course, if you choose to use a standard cash-back card instead and write a check to your nonprofit, like Dan did, you should be able to claim a tax deduction. Consult your tax advisor for more information.

I really like tax deductions, so I personally favor standard cash-back cards over affinity cards. But affinity cards offer definite benefits, not the least of which is the convenience factor: The whole donation process is on autopilot. Thus, these cards have a "forced savings" component.

Be as objective as possible when you consider affinity cards. The bottom line is that you should make sure it's a good deal, both for your favorite deserving cause...and for you.

> **Big Bucks for Ducks**
>
> Ducks Unlimited, a Memphis-based organization devoted to wildlife conservation efforts, has raised nearly $70 million from its affinity card program since it launched in 1986!

Credit Cards for the Rich and Famous

So you've worked to improve your credit record and, color by color, metal after metal, you've climbed the credit card ladder. Blue, silver, gold, platinum, titanium. Very impressive. Think you've reached the top? Maybe not!

Not long ago, having a platinum card in your pocket meant that you were at the top of the card game. However, the reality today is that possessing a platinum card is the rule, not the exception. The credit industry has succumbed to the "keeping up with the Joneses" syndrome, and card companies are beginning to aggressively market cards with "elite benefits."

Do free companion airline tickets, free upgrades to first class, special deals with hotels, personal shoppers at stores such as Saks and Gucci, travel planning and concierge services, and bonuses and rewards galore tickle your fancy? If you're in a position to take advantage of perks such as these, a "prestige credit card" could be your best option.

Even if you don't think you're in that league, read on. You might be surprised to know that you already qualify for an elite card, and you just might find reason to apply for one.

American Express Centurion

By reputation, the most well-known prestige card has been the American Express Centurion, popularly known as the Black Card. Introduced in 1999 and available by invitation only, Black is reportedly only for people who charge at least $250,000 a year.

Other undisclosed eligibility requirements exist as well, but the card is so exclusive that it's hard to get reliable information about it! Here's what is clear: Centurion has a $5,000 initiation fee...plus an annual fee of $2,500! Stories about the rich and famous who use Centurion abound.

"The Centurion Card is built for a very discerning, high-wealth individual who enjoys travel and the best life has to offer," explains Desiree Fish, vice president of Public Affairs for American Express. "The perks of the Card cater to their needs and lifestyle."

Although the price tag is very steep, the perks could well be worth the fee—if you live a certain lifestyle. According to various blogs, Centurion card members seem to be frequent travelers, and the card caters to their needs, offering bigger and better frequent flyer rewards, perks, and upgrades at hotels. Often discussed are complimentary companion airline tickets on certain international flights with the purchase of a full-fare ticket.

Carte Blanche

If the price tag and eligibility requirements of Black seem out of reach to you, don't despair. (You're not alone, trust me!) Several other elite-type offerings have more palatable fees and requirements. The Diners Club Carte Blanche Card, for example, has an annual fee of "only" $300 and offers many high-end benefits:

- Unlimited international companion tickets on British Airways. Cardholders receive a companion ticket each time they purchase a round-trip, full-fare, nonrestricted ticket from the United States or Canada to London or beyond (certain restrictions apply).
- Complimentary concierge service and full-service travel planning.
- Private jet access. "This exclusive service is an ideal alternative to charter flights or commercial air travel," explains the Carte Blanche website, "offering a variety of jets and hourly flight plans to choose from, thousands of worldwide destinations, and no hidden fees or charges—plus, no large up-front commitments."

Visa Signature/World MasterCard: Elite Benefits for the Rest of Us

If $300 is still out of your price range, consider Visa Signature Cards and World MasterCards. They have a lot of enhanced benefits, many at no additional cost, and are targeted to middle-income Americans (usually, but not exclusively, upper-middle-income). Surprised? Don't be. Remember, card issuers are in fierce competition, and they want business so badly they are willing to dangle bigger and better carrots in front of us.

Some of the perks these cards come with include hotel discounts and upgrades, no preset spending limits, rebates on travel, extra travel insurance, 24/7 concierge service, VIP reservations at expensive restaurants, special discounts at stores and spas, early ticket purchasing for concerts and sporting events, flexible, generous rewards, and more.

Sound enticing? The good news is that you might already have a card issued by a bank that would happily give you Visa Signature or World MasterCard privileges— assuming your credit is good to excellent. The offers change frequently, but it's quite likely that you can find a card with no annual fee or a low one (up to around $85), and as reasonable an interest rate as you'd get on any other reward card. I personally got an offer from Citibank recently to upgrade my platinum account to a World MasterCard that included many enhanced benefits. The offer was free, so I gladly accepted!

Go to CardRatings.com/Book to take a gander at the current crop of freebies that these elite cards offer.

Keep Your Spending in Check

Although these cards have a lot of attractive features, these same features can do more harm than good. If you decide to pursue an elite card, be sure to not let the lure of the extra benefits tempt you into charging more than you can afford.

Also be sure that any extra fees are a good investment of your hard-earned money. If you pay $300 a year for the coolest perk on the planet but never actually take advantage of that perk, you're just wasting money.

For the opinions of actual cardholders, check out the "Consumer Reviews" section of CardRatings.com. You'll find several reviews on elite cards, which can help you choose the one you'd like to have in your wallet. Even if you don't qualify, it certainly doesn't hurt to dream!

Final Thoughts

We've gone through quite an assortment of specialty cards in this chapter, haven't we? Each type of card has its own unique characteristics, benefits, and marketing ploys. Put yourself first, and choose cards that will maximize your returns at the least cost. Good luck on making these unique cards work for you!

CHAPTER 9

Your Credit Report and Score: The Better You Look, the More You Profit

You need to stay on top of your credit because it really does affect your whole financial life!

—Liz Weston, *MSN Money* Personal Finance Columnist and Author of *Your Credit Score* (FT Press, 2007)

Your credit report and credit score are two of your most powerful financial tools. The better you look on paper, the less cards are going to cost you, and the more money you can make off them. Your rates on other loans and your premiums on insurance policies will likely be lower as well. And the next time your credit is checked when you apply for a job or an apartment, you'll likely pass with flying colors.

If you have a lousy credit picture, you'll pay more for everything—not just this year, but for the next seven years and maybe longer. You won't be offered great deals on cards, and, what's worse, you might be putting your family finances at great risk.

If the slightest thing happens to make you look worse on paper, you might go from just squeaking by to facing financial devastation. The rates on all your cards might quickly jump to as high as 30%. Then, if you lose your job, it could be harder to find a new one. Soon you might be facing bankruptcy. But it doesn't have to be that way.

If you keep your credit report in good shape and as error-free as possible, your credit score—that three-digit number lenders use to decide how much of a risk you are—will be as high as possible. With a high credit score, you'll have a powerful foot in the door for negotiating low-rate loans. A credit report in tip-top shape will also mean lower insurance premiums and better job opportunities.

With so much at stake, it seems only natural that everyone would want to accurately maintain their credit profiles. But until the Fair and Accurate Credit Transactions Act (FACTA)passed in 2003, that wasn't an easy thing to do.

FACTA has helped consumers gain better access to their credit reports and, fortunately, it's a lot easier now for you and I to manage our credit. In this chapter, I tell you what you need to know about credit reports. I explain how to get any errors on yours corrected and tell you how to keep your credit report in tip-top shape. Then I show you how to improve your credit score—which might be easier than you think, even if your credit is currently in bad shape.

Improve Your Credit Report

To improve your credit report, you first have to get a copy of it and then scour your report, looking for mistakes. Here's how to go about it:

Get Your Free Annual Credit Report

Experts have recommended for years that consumers check their credit report annually for errors and signs of misuse. It's good advice because you'll likely find errors, and, in many cases, your credit report provides the first sign of identity theft.

The three largest credit reporting agencies previously charged fees if you wanted copies of your credit reports which, by the way, were also very hard to understand. Since FACTA, you're entitled to a yearly free credit report from each of the three major credit bureaus. Not only are the reports now free, but they're also more comprehensible. So set a yearly date—perhaps tax day, the first day of winter, or even your birthday—and order a free copy of your credit report from each bureau. You need to get reports from each bureau because your credit history as reported by each will likely vary. This will result in three unique credit reports—three unique opportunities for error.

Better yet, stagger the reports by ordering one every four months from a different bureau. That way, you'll be able to keep closer tabs on your credit record throughout the year—and make sure your identity hasn't been stolen. Please note that your credit history as reported by each bureau will likely vary. This will result in three unique credit reports.

The best way to obtain your free credit reports is to visit annualcreditreport.com, which is the official site set up by the federal government and sponsored by the three main reporting agencies—Equifax, Experian, and TransUnion. You can request a report online, download the request form and mail it in, or simply make a toll-free call to 877-322-8228.

As part of the verification process, both online and over the phone, expect to answer some questions that only you should be able to answer. If you make your request online, you'll be able to see your report as soon as your identity has been verified. Phone and mail requests take up to 15 days to process.

Remember these two important tips when requesting your credit report:

1. Watch out for spam. Annualcreditreport.com will not request personal information through emails, phone calls, or pop-up ads. If you receive any of

these, assume it's spam or a scammer. Do not click on any links, respond to any emails, or provide information over the phone.

2. Don't go to the individual credit bureaus' sites to request your reports. If you do, you might have to sign up for a free 7-day or 30-day trial to get it. If you don't opt out of the service before the trial period expires, you'll be charged a monthly fee. There's nothing free about that!

Other Free Reports It Pays to Get

You're also entitled to copies of reports that other companies develop about you. For example, if you've ever applied for an individual life, health, disability, or long-term care insurance policy, your medical information might be on file at the Medical Information Bureau (mib.com). You're entitled to a free report of this information; simply call 866-692-6901 to obtain it.

Other companies compile information about your employment, tenant, and insurance claims history. One of the largest database companies is ChoiceTrust (choicetrust.com).

ChoiceTrust's Comprehensive Loss Underwriting Exchange (CLUE) shows any claims that have been paid on auto and homeowner's insurance. Insurers check the CLUE report before deciding whether to insure your home and, if so, at what rate. It's smart to get a CLUE report before you put your house on the market. When you're thinking of buying a house, get the CLUE report before you make an offer. You can get it through the web site or by calling toll-free 866-312-8076.

What's on Your Credit Report?

Your credit report includes assorted personal details, such as your name, where you live now as well as past addresses, your Social Security number, your date of birth, and your spouse's name (if you have one). Sometimes information regarding your employment history also appears.

Most, if not all, of your credit card accounts and other loans should appear on your report, and for each one, you should be able to see when you opened the account, your highest balance, your current balance, and your payment history.

Your credit report also shows information that's available from public records, including criminal convictions, bankruptcy, tax liens, court judgments, and overdue child support. Negative information such as this can stay on your credit report for seven to ten years, and there's no time limit on convictions.

TIP
The fastest way to build your credit is to ensure that each of your creditors report your payment history to all three bureaus. The good news is most reputable credit card companies report to all three bureaus, but not all do. Some creditors, particularly smaller companies, only report to one or two bureaus—which is a good example of why it's important to get all three reports. And, some creditors don't even report to any credit bureaus.

Finally, your credit report lists **inquiries**—the names of lenders, landlords, insurers, or employers who have viewed your credit report. Some might be from your current lenders, and others might be from banks considering whether to send you a preapproved credit card offer in the mail.

Your Credit Report Rights

You have the right to:

- Be told if information in your file is used against you.

- Know the contents of your file.

- Dispute incomplete or inaccurate information.

- Have credit reporting agencies correct or delete inaccurate, incomplete, or unverifiable information.

- Prevent outdated negative information from being reported.

- Limit file access to those with a valid need.

- Decide if your report is to be shared with employers.

- Limit prescreened credit and insurance offers you receive.

- Seek damages from violators.

- Request a credit score (more on this later in the chapter).

Members of the Armed Forces Have an Additional Right

When you're deployed away from your usual duty station, you can have an "active-duty alert" placed on your credit report, as a safeguard against identity theft. When this alert is in place, creditors can't issue any new credit in your name without first contacting you or your personal representative.

To request an active-duty alert, simply call the toll-free number for one of the major credit reporting agencies, and ask that an alert be placed on your file. It doesn't matter which company you call because the law requires them to notify each other of these alerts. Here are their numbers:

- Equifax   800-525-6285
- Experian   888-EXPERIAN (397-3742)
- TransUnion   800-680-7289

Correcting Credit Reports

Errors on credit reports are common. Twenty-five percent of them contain errors so serious that they could result in the denial of credit, according to a survey by the U.S. Public Interest Research Group. Having a major error on a credit report is a pretty serious problem, but such errors can usually be corrected fairly easily—although it generally does take time.

First, you have to find the mistakes. Make sure:

- Your name, address, Social Security number, and date of birth are correct.

- All the accounts are yours. If you see any accounts that you don't remember opening, you might be a victim of identity theft. (See Chapter 6, "Watch Out: Traps and Scams Can Cost You Big Bucks," for advice.) Someone else's account also could have been "given" to you by mistake.

- No late payments are showing for accounts you know you paid by the due date.

- Outdated information doesn't appear, such as a tax lien that you straightened out a decade ago.

- Each account shows only once. You don't want the same exact account showing twice on your report.

- No accounts are missing.

- Nothing else is incorrect, outdated, or incomplete.

Typical Credit Report Errors

Here are five frequent problems with credit reports:

1. Confusion between your report and the report for someone who has the same name—It might be as simple as the difference between "Sr." and "Jr." or John L. Smith and John M. Smith. Maybe you use your middle initial for some accounts and don't use it for others—or maybe someone in the bureau keyed your name incorrectly. This is a good example of what's called a "split file" in industry lingo—which "can be a problem, since all the 'good' credit accounts may be split between two files," explains Mark Enderle of Preferred Credit Solutions. (Visit CardRatings.com/Book for a link to Preferred Credit Solutions.)

2. Clerical errors—For example, someone could have spelled your name incorrectly, transposed your Social Security number, or entered an incorrect address—any of these could pose a problem.

3. Inaccurate information from creditors—This might happen if, for example, a lender incorrectly reports an address where you never lived.

4. Incorrect Social Security number—Often, it's simply a typo, but if you're married, your spouse's number might have been entered instead of yours. Or maybe you have other **authorized users** on an account, such as your teens who you let use your card.

5. Merged file—This is where data from one person is combined with the data of another person. "This happens quite often and can be very deleterious to one's score," reports Enderle. One reason why this happens has to do with the way the credit bureaus compare Social Security numbers. "Only seven of the nine digits need to match," Ederle explains, "because they wanted to limit the 'kick outs' on clerical errors." The result is that people with the same or very similar names or similar Social Security numbers are merged together.

> **TIP**
>
> It's not always easy to find these mistakes, but if you see information that doesn't belong to you—or might not belong to you— your identity could have been stolen, and you should investigate. But don't panic—it's quite easy for creditors to mess up our files. Contact the credit reporting agency to inquire. (If an identity thief seems to be at work, see Chapter 6 for advice.)

When You Find Errors on Your Report

If you find errors on your credit report, follow these simple steps:

1. The fastest way to start your "dispute," as they call it, is to go online for detailed and up-to-date instructions (see the following for credit bureau websites). Make sure you follow the directions given by the credit bureau in question.

Dispute Addresses for the Credit Reporting Agencies

Experian
experian.com
P.O. Box 2002
Allen, TX 75013

Equifax
equifax.com
P.O. Box 740256
Atlanta, GA 30374

TransUnion
transunion.com
P.O. Box 2000
Chester, PA, 19022–2000

---

2. Copy and send along these key items with your dispute letter to the credit bureau:
   - Your credit report—Highlight all errors on the copy you'll be sending, numbering each problematic item—1, 2, 3, and so on.

- Any documents that help make your case—*Never* send an original, but always include documentation. If a store card account shows an unpaid balance, send along a copy of your cancelled check. Number these documents to match the ones you attach to your credit report.

- Your driver's license—Including a copy of your driver's license may prevent delays in disputing errors. Always provide as clear of a picture as possible. Make sure your driver's license (or state ID card) is current, showing your correct name and address. The bureaus don't need your driver's license number, so if it makes you feel better, just mark it out.

3. Send disputes in writing.
   - Documented proof—This provides proof that you have disputed an error on your credit report. Make sure you keep a copy for your records.

   - Send your letter via certified mail, return receipt requested. Hang on to the return receipt to prove when the credit reporting agency receives your dispute.

   - Remember the 30-day window. The credit bureaus have 30 days after receiving your letter to let you know the results of their investigation into your complaint. If the information that you are disputing cannot be verified, they *must* delete it.

4. Be sure to include the following in your complaint:
   - Your name—Always give your full name when filing a dispute. Other people might have the same or a similar name, which is often why files become mixed. Follow this format: first, middle, last, Senior, Junior, I, II, III.

- Your Social Security number—Always include your Social Security number, which helps ensure that the credit bureau pulls the right report. In some cases, such as when a father and son live at the same address, the name and address might be identical, but the Social Security number should always be unique.

- Your address—When you initiate disputes, the credit bureaus look at your address, but do not weigh it as heavily as your name and Social Security number in verifying that you are who you say you are. Still, it pays to make sure that you give your current address correctly, and if you've been living there for less than two years, give your previous address as well.

- Your date of birth—Including your date of birth is another way to make sure the bureau pulls the correct credit report.

- The name of the creditor or collection agency—If you don't know the name, just use the spelling as you see it listed on your credit report. If you're listing the name of the collection agency, also list the name of the original creditor below it.

- The account number—Use the number you find on the credit report so they can still follow your complaint even if they have the incorrect account number.

- The reason for your dispute and what you want changed—Calmly, clearly, and politely explain your concerns and your proposed remedy.

- The results of the research you conducted—You want your dispute understood and the next step to be obvious. So it pays to nose around a little to see if you can figure out what happened.

> *I have never had an account with the Yuma Department store. I live in upstate New York and have never been to Yuma. I checked online and see that someone with my name happens to live in Yuma. My hunch is that our reports got mixed up. Could you please remove this account from my credit report? Many thanks.*

- Type your dispute letters. You want to avoid having your dispute delayed just because someone cannot read your handwriting. *Be sure to sign your letter.*

TIP

If your dispute occurs when you're trying to get a major loan, let the credit bureau know that you'd like it to rush the process and that you want the lender to receive an updated copy of your credit report. You can also request that all creditors within the last 6 months be notified of any corrections made to your report and that any employers who have gotten a copy of your report within the last 24 months receive a corrected copy.

Success or Failure

What if...

- You get the bureau to delete an item that was on your report incorrectly. Be sure you keep the notification from the credit bureau. If the creditor later reinserts the same item, the credit reporting agency has to notify you within five business days, and you'll have your proof ready.

- A disputed item is verified as correct and remains unchanged on your credit report. Make direct contact with the creditors or collection agencies that are reporting inaccurate information about you. Explain the errors and request that they make the corrections from their end.

If this doesn't work, you can contact the Federal Trade Commission (ftc.gov) and file a complaint. You can also call 877-382-4357 and request help from the FTC's dispute referral system, which was set up to help solve problem disputes.

Also, you have the right to initiate another dispute. However, it's a good idea to wait 60 days between follow-up disputes. Otherwise, a credit reporting agency might take advantage of its right to deem a dispute as "frivolous," which might happen if you dispute the same item within a short period of time.

- A credit bureau decides your dispute is frivolous. Uh oh. It can terminate the investigation and put the onus on you. You might have to provide documented proof showing cause for the change to be made before a new investigation will begin.

Writing a Statement: A Big Waste of Time?

When you can't get a creditor or merchant to resolve a dispute, you have the right to add a 100-word statement to your credit report that tells your side of things. While this sounds like a good idea, as credit expert Gerri Detweiler reports, "It's a waste of time and doesn't do much, if any good. Sometimes, in fact, the statements remain after the disputed item has been removed!"

You might have more luck simply giving the heads-up to the lender, insurer, or potential boss who will be looking at your credit report, suggests Nancy Castleman, Detweiler's coauthor on a couple of books, including *Slash Your Debt* (Financial Literacy Center, 2001).

I'd say something like this to a loan officer if there was a knotty problem on my credit report: 'I've been trying to straighten out a computer glitch at the XYZ hospital ever since I had my appendix out three years ago. You'll see that it's the only questionable item in my credit file, and if you know someone at XYZ, I'd sure appreciate the referral.

Protecting Your Credit Reports during Bankruptcy

Bankruptcy should always be a last resort. (See Chapter 5, "How to Slash Your Debt and Keep Your Hard-Earned Money for Yourself," for bankruptcy alternatives.) If you haven't filed yet, take your time and don't rush the process. It's more important to cover all your bases and avoid making a mistake that could cost you later.

It's imperative that you obtain the most current payment information if you will be filing for bankruptcy. You need to know how much is owed and where you can send payment. Call each creditor for the information. If the creditor has turned over your account to a collection agency, get that agency's contact information and then call there for the information.

It's important to identify *all* your accounts. Your bankruptcy attorney will need this information to complete the process. If you owe money to creditors or collection agencies that don't show on your credit report, find the most recent billing statements or collection letters that you've received.

The Don'ts of Working with Collection Agencies and Creditors

It's not easy to deal with collection agencies and impatient creditors. They're the pros, and by the time you have to turn to them, you may be feeling pretty low. Here are my tips for getting through the encounter:

- Don't let them bully or upset you about outstanding balances. Just get the information you need. All you have to say is, "Thanks. I'll call back soon."

- Don't give them time for a rebuttal. Just hang up. If they push the matter, then only as a last resort, tell them you will be filing bankruptcy. Give them the name and number of your attorney and end the call.

- Don't play games. Sometimes people call creditors and suggest that they might declare bankruptcy, just for an edge in negotiating a settlement. You absolutely do not want to use this tactic if you plan to follow through with the bankruptcy, as it will likely backfire on you. As noted by bankruptcy expert John Ventura,

  If you are going to file bankruptcy, you should not waste your time talking to creditors at all because your creditors are going to be notified by the court to stop contacting you about the debt as soon as you file.

All Other Creditors

After your bankruptcy has been discharged, your accounts from all other creditors not included in the settlement will appear differently on your credit report, depending on the type of bankruptcy:

- Chapter 13—The accounts included in a Chapter 13 bankruptcy remain on your credit report for seven years. (A Chapter 13 bankruptcy enables you to keep your property, and you agree to a three- to five-year repayment plan. Successful completion of the plan will result in a discharge of your remaining unsecured debt.)
- Chapter 7—The accounts included in a Chapter 7 bankruptcy remain on your credit report for ten years. (A Chapter 7 bankruptcy reduces unsecured debt by discharging or wiping it out. You're usually able to keep your home and automobile if you keep making payments on them.)

The bankruptcy laws were rewritten in 2005 to make it more difficult to file under Chapter 7. If your income is higher than the median income for a family of your size in your state, you must pass a "means test" before you can file under Chapter 7. (For more information on means testing, including median income tables by state and family size, visit usdoj.gov/ust.)

Watch Out for Accounts Handed Over to Bill Collectors

Before you file for bankruptcy, defaulted accounts usually go to collections or charge-off status. When a creditor turns over a defaulted account to a collection agency, it normally stops reporting account information to the credit bureaus. The bill collector then tries to get you to pay and reports account information. The creditor is out of the loop.

By the time your attorney sends your creditors notice of the account being included in bankruptcy, it may no longer be in their computer system. Therefore, they might fail to notify credit reporting agencies to update the account to a zero balance and include it in bankruptcy status. Bottom line: Be very careful during this process so that this doesn't happen to you.

Complaints

If you have a complaint with how a creditor is reporting your account information, you can file a complaint with the FTC and with your state's attorney general. Your bankruptcy attorney can also file complaints against creditors who do not report your information accurately.

When a creditor fails to update account information, an account could be listed in collections or charge-off status when it's not. This could be a serious problem when you apply for new credit. A potential lender might assume that you still owe on the debt and decline your credit application.

The most efficient way to fix this problem is to do the following:

- Obtain a copy of your bankruptcy and discharge papers from your attorney or the courthouse. (You might incur a copy fee.)
- Make three copies of the section that lists all the creditors and collection agencies that were included in the bankruptcy—usually this is called Schedule F.
- Forward all these documents to all the credit reporting agencies (listed earlier in the chapter), requesting that they update each creditor included in the bankruptcy to properly reflect a zero balance.
- Finally, if a creditor or collection agency isn't honoring your bankruptcy and is continuing collection efforts, contact your bankruptcy lawyer. Give your lawyer the name and address of the company bothering you so that he or she can send an official notice. Follow up with your lawyer if the creditor persists in harassing you. Creditors can be held

accountable if they do not cease after bankruptcy notification.

As with all consumer issues, knowing your consumer rights throughout the bankruptcy process is essential. Taking a proactive approach at the onset of the process will help you on your road to credit recovery.

Rebuilding Your Credit

I hope you never have to follow my bankruptcy-related tips for improving your credit report, but if some of the details help motivate you to avoid a bankruptcy, that'd be great.

Do everything you can to limit your spending and to take good care of your credit report following bankruptcy. In sum, if you want to build and keep a great credit report, follow this advice from Gerri Detweiler, Marc Eisenson, and Nancy Castleman, the coauthors of *Slash Your Debt* (Financial Literacy Center, 2001):

> *...avoid late payments, and to have at least one major credit card [a secured card is a good option] that you pay on time, and over time. Some would argue that it's the single strongest reference on a credit report. The reason? Because statistics have shown that people who have paid major credit cards on time in the past are likely to pay new ones on time, too.*

Improve Your Credit Score

Have you ever wondered whether you have "good" or "bad" credit, and how lenders determine whether you're creditworthy? If so, you're not alone. Consumer advocates have wanted this information for decades, but the way creditors determine creditworthiness was shrouded in secrecy for many years. Thanks to FACTA, the legislation that also brought us free credit reports, the magic formula creditors use has been revealed—at least, to some extent.

Now you can request not only your credit score, but also an explanation of the factors used to compute the score. Unfortunately, credit scores generally aren't free, but as I explain, it's money well spent in the cause of improving your all-important credit score.

Fair Isaac and Co. (FICO) develops the credit scores used by the major credit card issuers and in 75% of the nation's mortgage decisions. According to the Fair Isaac website, myfico.com, 90% of the nation's largest banks use FICO scores when evaluating loans.

Free Credit Scores from Washington Mutual

Got a Washington Mutual credit card? If so, you might be eligible to get your FICO score for free. What's the catch? None. Really! You just need to register your Washington Mutual credit card account online for your free score.

As of this writing, a FICO score in the 700+ range is considered attractive, and the average score is 690. However, that might soon change because FICO is refining its credit scores so they're more accurate. The new system, known as FICO 08, will look more closely at delinquent payments and credit histories. If you were more than 90 days late on one credit card bill a few years ago, but you've been promptly paying all your other card bills as well as your mortgage, you'll fare better under the new FICO system. If you tend to be late on lots of bills, your score will be even lower than it is now.

How Do Scoring Systems Work?

Before they give you a credit card or loan, lenders want to be able to predict with some level of certainty that you'll actually pay them back. The riskier you appear when compared to other people, the more you will have to pay, if you can get a loan at all.

Scoring systems compare details on the credit reports of people who pay their bills on time, looking for what they have in common—and, similarly, what people who *don't* pay their bills have in common. The formulas weigh various factors, trying to predict whether a new customer is likely to always pay on time.

As you might expect, credit scoring can get pretty complicated. Nearly every branch of the financial industry has customized scoring systems that serve as a basis to compare the scores of potential borrowers—homeowners, cardholders, and so on.

The higher your score, the better you appear. The more risky you appear...you know the drill. But what you might not know is just how much a low score could cost you. Look at these numbers from myfico.com, which show how your credit score will likely impact the amount you'd pay on a 30-year, $300,000 mortgage (consult the website for the latest numbers):

FICO® Score	APR	Monthly Payment
760–850	5.498%	$1,703
700–759	5.720%	$1,745
660–699	6.004%	$1,799
620–659	6.814%	$1,959
580–619	9.247%	$2,467
500–579	10.253%	$2,689

With a low credit score, you would have to pay $986 more every month than someone with a high score. Isn't that amazing? Similarly, a credit score of around 720 can potentially save you thousands of dollars in credit card finance charges when compared to a credit score in the mid-600s.

What Goes into a FICO Score, and How Can You Increase Yours?

Let's look at a breakdown of the criteria on credit reports that FICO uses to create credit scores.

35% of Your Score Is Affected by Your Payment History

If you fail to pay your bills on time, your score will suffer. The longer you go without paying, the worse the damage can be. The good news is that the damage isn't permanent—the effect of late payments, charge-offs, collections, and judgments normally starts to gradually fade after a few months when you pay your bills on time. Also, late payments on credit cards aren't normally reported to the credit bureaus unless they are 30 days or more late.

30% of Your Score Is Affected by Utilization

> **TIP**
>
> One of the fastest ways to increase your credit score is to pay down debt and increase your credit limits. Some card issuers give instant credit line increases just for the asking, and you can get a credit line increase online in seconds!

Utilization is the difference between the combined credit limits on all your accounts and the total amount you owe. If you have lots of cards and are very close to your limits on them, your utilization will be high and your credit score low. The more of your available credit that you're using, the lower your score. The way the math works, it's much better to have several accounts with low balances than it is to have fewer accounts at or near the credit limit. The basic equation to determine utilization is this:

Current balance ÷ Credit limit = Utilization

Lower utilization is better. Ideally, you should keep your changes limited to 10% or less of your individual credit limits. The lower your utilization, the higher your score is likely to be.

Watch Your Utilization

According to Craig Watts, Public Affairs Manager for Fair Isaac, if your credit utilization is 50 percent or more of your credit line, then you are doing some serious damage to your credit score. When the new FICO 08 scoring model is adapted, if you have a utilization of over 50 percent, you'll be penalized even more than you are under the current credit scoring model.

15% of Your Score Is Affected by Your Established Credit History

The longer you have credit card and other accounts with lenders, the better. When you're first starting out, establishing credit isn't always easy. So apply for one or two credit cards, get a store card, and make consistent, on-time payments. Over time, you'll establish a good payment history, and before you know it, you'll probably be flooded with applications for low-rate credit.

In the past, you could give your credit score a big boost by simply becoming an authorized user on another person's

> **TIP**
>
> When applying for credit, get your own credit report first from each bureau. I recommend all three bureaus because you won't know which report the bankers will want to see. When you get your own credit report, it's called a **soft inquiry** and will not hurt your score. Make sure it's in tip-top shape before you apply for new credit, as I explained earlier in this chapter.

established credit accounts. A common example is a parent adding their son or daughter to one of their credit card accounts. But in 2007, Fair Isaac announced that authorized user accounts will no longer factor into their credit scoring formula. The rollout for this change began in September 2007. Your best bet in light of this announcement? Build up a good, solid payment history in your own name!

10% of Your Score Is Affected by Credit Inquires and New Credit

Unnecessary credit inquiries hurt your score—especially if your overall credit file is small to begin with (which the industry calls a "thin file") or if you have a bad credit history.

Shopping for a mortgage or a new auto? Fortunately, all home loan applications made within a certain period of time count as only one inquiry—it used to be 14 days, but newer versions of the FICO formula make it 45 days. Similarly, all auto-related credit inquiries made within a certain time span are counted as one.

10% of Your Score Is Affected by Your Mix of Credit

Having different types of credit can help your scores. People with the best credit scores tend to have both **revolving credit** (credit cards or lines of credit) and **installment loans** (mortgages or car loans) on their credit reports.

TIP

Keep in mind how much each of these different factors affects your scores. Periodically, you might want to "violate" one of the least consequential factors. For example, to take full advantage of various low-introductory rate card offers, you might want to "let yourself" have more than two or three credit cards because the mix of credit accounts for only 10% of your score. Especially if you have good utilization on your existing accounts, it won't likely be a big problem because utilization accounts for 30% of your score. (Utilization is a much bigger factor than your mix of credit.)

Does Everyone Use FICO Scores?

Of course not, that would be too easy! Although Fair Isaac does provide the dominant scoring models, and lenders use multiple scoring systems and models, often adding additional criteria of their own. Unfortunately, we get access to only a few of these other scores, which generally don't even match the scores creditors see.

Consumers can also obtain other credit scores, which are commonly known as FAKO scores, because they often mimic FICO scores. FAKO scores tend to be less expensive.

An Alternative to FICO

InCharge Institute, a nonprofit organization specializing in personal finance education and credit counseling, offers a proprietary scoring model called BrightScore. You receive an analysis of your

BrightScore, a copy of your credit report in an easy-to-read format, and a customized action plan for better managing your credit. For details, visit CardRatings.com/Book.

Another scoring system worth noting is the VantageScore, which was launched in March 2006 by Experian, Equifax, and TransUnion. This score applies one formula to data from all three bureaus and uses a different scoring range than the 300-850 range associated with FICO. Your VantageScore will fall within a range of 501 to 990, with higher scores representing a lower likelihood of risk. Another unique aspect is that you are given a letter grade on a scale ranging from A to F.

Where Should I Get My Credit Score?

You have a lot of alternatives. As of this writing, you can find a couple of free credit score trial offers on CardRatings.com that include free credit monitoring—click on "Credit Information" from our home page for your current options. If you would prefer not to sign up for a trial offer, you will have to pay for your score(s). The fee is usually around $15 per score.

I recommend picking one system or product and sticking with it. Don't bother looking at multiple scoring systems because doing so can get confusing. Stick with the FICO scores from the three biggest credit bureaus, which you can order through a link at CardRatings.com/Book.

Final Tips

Each time you view your credit scores, you will normally see negative items listed that are hurting your scores. Focus on improving those particular areas, and check your scores regularly to monitor your progress. Persistence will pay off.

Finally, when monitoring your score, it's a good idea to give yourself a cushion, to be on the safe side. One reason for this is that sometimes, lenders will see a different score than you do. As MSNBC Personal Finance Columnist Liz Weston succinctly states, "get your scores as high as possible to give yourself a cushion, since credit scores change constantly and lenders may use different versions of the FICO formula that produce somewhat different results."

TIP

Speaking of lenders, their advice can be useful for getting a loan, but it's not always good for your credit scores. If you're told to consolidate and close accounts, be careful how you go about this. Compliance with this lenders' advice often results in lower credit scores. My advice is to pay down your debts and not close your accounts unless the lender says that you must do so to qualify for the loan, and you have no other options.

There you have it, all the information on credit reports and scores that you need to make yourself look as appetizing as possible to those sharks...whoops, I mean lenders! Remember, the better you make yourself look, the more they'll want you and the better terms you'll enjoy. And the better terms you can qualify for, the more money you'll keep in your bank account. Bon appétit.

Insider Credit Score Secrets

The CardRatings.com forum is a great place to learn free self-help techniques that will improve your credit score. It's not uncommon for members of our forum who are rebuilding their credit to see a 50 to 100 point increase in their credit score within a 12 to 18 month period.

CHAPTER 10

Maximize the Benefits of Your Cards by Taking Advantage of Additional Free Perks

Many other little-known but important card perks are rarely discussed or advertised. As J. D. Power and Associates puts it, most cardholders "are not fully aware of the benefits their card offers."[1]

In fact, chances are very good that you already have these benefits, because some of them are very basic and the law requires others. But you can't capitalize on them if you don't know they exist. After reading this chapter, you'll be able to take advantage of them, and most people still won't have a clue.

Some of the following ten credit card perks are completely free and can save you money, but others come with a price tag and might not be worth a dime...to you. I give you the pros and cons, and then you can decide how each benefit might enhance your bottom line:

- Purchase protection
- Extended warranties
- Special merchandise discounts
- Travel insurance
- Rental car insurance
- Price protection
- Lost luggage help

[1] jdpower.com/corporate/news/releases/pressrelease.aspx?ID=2007232

- International travel discounts
- Card registration services
- Credit card protection insurance

Purchase Protection

We've already discussed the fraud protection cardholders get: If you notify the issuer, you're legally liable for only a maximum of $50 if someone uses your card in a fraudulent manner. And with the zero-liability policies most issuers offer, you probably won't even be out the $50.

But what if the issue isn't the fraudulent use of your card? What if something you bought with a credit card gets stolen or a merchant won't replace a defective product that you bought? You might have protection for those circumstances, too.

Although the details vary by issuer and even by card, you'll typically have some degree of free coverage in case something you bought with a credit card in the last 90 days is stolen, breaks, or gets lost.

I can personally attest to the value of this benefit. My wife and I bought a new lawnmower and some lawn equipment a few years ago and were very distraught when the shed containing our lawn equipment was broken into a few months later. The crooks took everything, and we were so upset.

> **TIP**
>
> Before you count on a card's protection program for pricey purchases, verify what items qualify, what the dollar limits are, what kind of damage is covered, whether eligibility requirements apply, and so on.

When I finally came to my senses after the initial shock, I remembered that our card offered purchase protection. I filed a claim with our card company (a simple one-page form) and received a check in the mail within about 30 days that refunded the full purchase price of the mower and equipment. Although this didn't take away our feelings of being violated, I did feel a great sense of relief when I received the check in the mail. Heck, I almost kissed my credit card!

Purchase Protection for All

We all get basic purchase protection, thanks to the Fair Credit Billing Act (FCBA), which established a process for requesting the credit card issuer's help in billing disputes with merchants.

If you send in a written complaint about a merchant (assuming, of course, that you made the initial purchase on your credit card), the card issuer must investigate your claim. The dispute must be resolved, or you must be told why the lender is maintaining the charge—usually, it's because the merchant disagrees with you. In the meantime, you can withhold payment and you can't be denied credit just because you are disputing a bill. This is a great benefit!

The FCBA also applies when you order something with a credit card and don't receive it, or when you receive shoddy or damaged goods. Technically, this applies only if the merchandise in question costs more than $50, if you purchased it in your home state (or within 100 miles of your billing address), and if you made a "good faith effort" to work out your differences with the merchant.

However, I've found that when cardholders write to issuers for help with merchant-related complaints, lenders often follow through—even if the purchase isn't made in a particular state or within a specific number of miles. They want to keep us as customers, so by all means, promptly and politely complain if you ever have these types of problems. It might take some time to get things resolved, but it's worthwhile to request that the issuer intercede on your behalf to get what you deserve. Let your card issuer do the legwork for you!

For example, when Dustin from New York City tried to return defective merchandise, his request was refused, so he disputed the charge on his Citibank Diamond Preferred Rewards card. "They made it very easy. The first time I called, it was two days after the purchase...they told me to wait three days for the charge to post," Dustin explains on the Cardratings.com forum.

When he called back three days later, Citibank marked the amount as being in dispute and conditionally credited Dustin's account with that amount. "They sent me a letter asking for information. I filled out the form and sent them everything (receipt copy, return policy of the store, explanation of what happened, etc.)," reports Dustin.

It took 90 days for the issuer to reach a final decision because the merchant didn't respond to the form Citibank sent to investigate Dustin's claim. "But I got my money back after making two phone calls and sending in a letter," he concludes.

Extended Warranties

Many card issuers extend the length of a manufacturer's warranty without any cost to you if you use their card to make the purchase. Adding a year to the warranty on a product that already comes with a one-year guarantee is typical. But more is possible, too.

In fact, because the free extended warranties on cards normally provide more than enough coverage, in many cases, you have my permission to spare yourself from even listening to the salespeople's pitches for them—unless you are buying a rear-projection microdisplay television or an Apple computer. *Consumer Reports* recommends extended warranties for only these two items.[2] In virtually every other case, the cost of an extended warranty is too high and the likelihood of needing the coverage is too low.

Warranty Week, an industry newsletter covering the warranty business, has a somewhat different point of view: "We believe there is a price ratio between a product and its extended warranty that even the *Consumer Reports* editors would concede is a good value, if only they took the time to examine the differences in prices and coverages."

On Cyber Monday 2007 (the Monday after Thanksgiving), *Warranty Week* priced a medium-sized Samsung LCD television and a large Philips plasma screen on the websites of 45 different electronic retailers. The results showed great disparities in the price of the televisions and the price of the warranties. *Warranty Week* reports:

> *If the TV is $683 and the extended warranty is $349, it's probably not a good value. But if the TV is $5 more and the warranty is $290 less, it might be worth considering (unless the policy is loaded with exclusions and disqualifications).*[3]

Although that might sound reasonable, if you play your cards right (yes, a pun was intended), you can take advantage of a free built-in extended warranty, courtesy of MasterCard, Visa, Discover, or American Express. So before you buy something for which an extended warranty might be useful, call your card issuers to decide which card to use.

Find out the following information:

- Covered products
- Length of the extended warranty

---

[2] "Why You Don't Need an Extended Warranty," *Consumer Reports,* November 2006.

[3] warrantyweek.com/archive/ww20071128.html

- Any other exclusions, such as store exclusions
- Other terms that might help you decide which card to use

When you know which card will serve you best, you can shop by price alone and save more of your hard-earned cash in the process. I hope you score quite a deal!

Special Merchandise Discounts

Some card issuers offer free merchandise from their catalogs as a reward. Historically, these reward programs have often been a raw deal for cardholders. The goods you get are typically overvalued.

However, some cards offer you discounts at select merchants without requiring you to use any of your reward points, which might be a much better value for you. Using such a card can be a great way to pay less for things you would buy anyway and to try new things for less. The secret is to make sure you don't buy so much at a discount that you bust your budget. More "stuff" won't pay the rent or buy groceries, no matter how great the value. ☺

Keep Your Eyes Out

Merchant discount programs are often time-limited, are offered just to cardholders, aren't heavily advertised, and require you to register. For example, from April through June 2008, Discover Card is offering a special discount 5% rebate program for cardholders who make home- and fashion-related purchases. Specifically,

> **TIP**
>
> Find out if any of your cards have special merchant discount programs or seasonal promotions. If you need to register to benefit, do it. Earning extra cash back when you buy things you need is terrific, especially if it doesn't cost you anything but a few minutes of your time. ☺

cardholders will earn a 5% bonus rebate on purchases at department stores, clothing stores, home improvement centers, and lawn and garden centers.

Getting 5% back by shopping strategically is indeed a good thing. But you might be wondering, what's the catch? The only catch (and it's not really a catch) is that you must sign up for the bonus program. It just takes a two-minute phone call, but if you don't "opt in" to the program, you won't get any of the additional rebates. So, if you have a Discover Card, call now!

Another attractive feature of the program is that Discover changes the businesses where you can get the extra 5% discounts four times a year, depending on the season. For example, in the fall, Discover typically targets back-to-school items, including clothes, shoes, and things you might need in a dorm room. In the spring, home improvement might be highlighted.

Travel Insurance

Technically known as accidental death and dismemberment insurance, this form of life insurance your card offers can be very valuable coverage. And the price is sure right: free. Unfortunately, it's something we never want to need, so this perk doesn't get the attention it deserves.

Although the details vary, chances are, you already have a credit card that provides between $100,000 and $1 million in accidental death and dismemberment insurance. All

> **TIP**
> If you'll be traveling with family, find out if each person will get the same amount of travel insurance, assuming that you charge the tickets at the same time to the same card. If not, you might be better off booking each ticket separately or using more than one card.

244 How You Can Profit from Credit Cards

you have to do is make sure you use that card when you charge airplane flights, cruises, train rides, and bus trips.

So the next time you're about to book a trip, choose your card carefully. Before you make your reservations, have a conversation with the customer service representatives at your card issuers. Find out how much coverage your heirs would receive with each card.

Rental Car Insurance

Every time you rent a car, the sales agent is instructed to ask you if you want to buy collision and liability insurance. If you whip out the right piece of plastic, you can say "no" to that extra cost with confidence.

Collision damage waiver (CDW), sometimes called loss damage waiver (LDW), reduces your responsibility if damage occurs to the car or if it's stolen. Liability insurance covers damage that you do to someone else while driving the rental car.

You definitely want protection, but your personal auto insurance might also cover rental cars. Most policies do provide some coverage, although it might be limited. Look through your policy or check with your agent to find out what you've got. If your insurance covers only a limited amount, you probably need more. But the good news is that you might not have to buy it from the car rental company.

Collision Coverage

Many platinum and gold credit cards offer CDW/LDW coverage for free, so it's smart to use a card with this built-in perk to pay for car rentals. You'll avoid paying extra for something you already get for free. Insurance from the rental car company typically costs an extra $9 to $19 *per day*. That's an extra $126 to $266 for a two-week vacation!

If you're not certain that you have a card that comes with CDW/LDW protection, call the issuer. Give your account number to make sure you hear about the benefits associated with your particular card. (I recommend a bunch of questions you should ask when you call a little later in this chapter.)

TIP

More is not necessarily better. When you buy CDW/LDW coverage from the rental car company, it might invalidate the CDW/LDW perk of your card. If you already have adequate coverage from your credit card, why buy additional insurance from the rental car company?

The CDW/LDW coverage from card issuers is typically secondary coverage, meaning your personal auto insurance policy is tapped first in the event of an accident. However, the Diners Club card provides primary coverage. For a flat fee of $24.95 or less, you may be able to get primary coverage for up 42 days on your American Express card. The American Express coverage is up to $100,000 for theft of or damage to the rental car.

Liability Coverage

Most credit cards don't provide liability coverage, but rental car companies normally give it at no additional charge, so ask. According to the Insurance Information Institute, the law requires these companies to provide the minimum level of liability insurance that your state requires. Additional coverage costs from about $9 to $14 a day.

If you have adequate liability coverage on your own car or you have an umbrella policy on your home or auto insurance, you might want to pass on the extra liability coverage the car rental company is selling. Be sure to verify your coverage before you rent a car.

Find Out What Rental Car Coverage Comes with Your Cards

It's very important to ensure that you have good coverage. There's no point in saving $9 to $19 a day on collision insurance, for example, if you might end up having to pay thousands. Take the time to ask your card issuers these questions:

- How much collision and liability coverage do you offer on rental cars?
- Do you exclude coverage from any types of cars?
- If an accident occurs, what circumstances would cause you to refuse payment? Will you pay if I'm at fault?
- Will the coverage be in effect for the full length of my trip? (Ask if the coverage is active for the amount of time you'll be away, such as two weeks.)
- Will I be covered in another country? How long will it be effective?
- If I buy insurance from the rental car company, does that invalidate your coverage?
- Do you provide any medical insurance? If so, what's covered?
- Do you cover additional drivers?
- Do you provide any roadside assistance coverage?
- What should I do if an accident occurs?

If your credit card coverage is satisfactory, make sure your account is current. Then rent that car and enjoy your savings. Do drive safely and have a great trip!

Free Insurance Comes in Handy on My Nightmare Honeymoon

My wife and I can personally attest to the value of free rental car insurance coverage courtesy of our credit card. We were rear-ended on the first night of our honeymoon in Portland, Oregon. Our rental car, a stylish Mustang convertible, was totaled. Needless to say, we were very lucky we survived and only suffered whiplash. The good news is our credit card company made good on their insurance claims and helped pay for the totaled Mustang. In the end, we managed to have a great honeymoon despite the initial setback!

Price Protection

You might already have this very valuable card perk without even realizing it. Some cards will give you a refund if you buy something and then later see the exact item advertised for less. Each card has its own restrictions on this freebie benefit, commonly known as "price or retail protection," although all seem to limit the time frame to somewhere between 30 and 90 days after the initial purchase date.

Items that you buy online are often excluded, and usually, a print advertisement must show the lower price. For example, if you use a Citi Diamond Preferred MasterCard to buy something and then you see it advertised (in print and within 60 days) for less, you can get a refund of up to

$250 to make up the difference. "Certain conditions, restrictions, and exclusions apply. Details of coverage will be provided upon card membership."

A savvy member of CardRatings.com's forum, spjoink, took advantage of the 90-day price protection on his American Express Platinum card to get $2,400 back on the 12 iPhones he bought for his employees. When Apple dropped the price on these phones not too long after they went on sale for the first time to the public, spjoink called Amex. "After putting me on hold for less than 5 minutes, they refunded me $200 for each phone...they told me they didn't have to do this, but since I am a valuable customer, they chose to do so!"

What a savvy consumer spjoink is! Unfortunately, spjoink's friend wasn't so lucky. He used a MasterCard to buy his iPhone, and it had only a 60-day price protection policy. Apple hadn't dropped the price by the end of those two months, so he couldn't get a penny back from his card issuer.

To take advantage of a card's price protection, you first need to know it exists. I recommend that you do the following:

- Find out which of your cards has this valuable benefit before you charge your next major purchase.
- Watch out for the pesky details such as where you can make your purchase and what you need to show as proof of a lower price.
- Be careful about the deadline. If a 60-day guarantee applies, get to your card issuer before that time frame expires.
- Remember that you have to take the initiative. No card issuer will call and offer to send you a refund. You have to make the call!

Lost Luggage Help

It has probably happened to every traveler. You make it to your destination, but your luggage doesn't. Next time that happens to you, the credit card you used to book your airline ticket might be able to help.

At the very least, many cards offer a toll-free number to call to enlist representatives who can keep you posted on the airline's progress in tracking down your bag. And with some gold and platinum cards, you get even more help when your luggage goes missing. For example, the Chase Freedom card offers lost luggage coverage of up to $3,000 for checked baggage, and it reimburses you for up to $300 in immediate needs if your bags are delayed.

So before you make reservations for your next journey, call your card issuers to see which one has the best lost-luggage benefit. Use that card to charge your tickets if all other things are equal (such as the same number of frequent flyer miles, the same amount of cash back, and the same travel insurance coverage).

Then if your luggage is delayed or lost, you'll be able to whip out your credit card, and call the 800-number with confidence, knowing that you'll get help.

International Travel Discounts

Heading off on an international travel adventure or for an extended stay overseas? Be sure to pack your favorite card.

Credit cards typically offer a much better exchange rate than you or I can get. The reason? Visa and MasterCard usually get the same wholesale rate on international transactions that large banks and corporations get—not the retail rates offered to you and me. Although getting a break on the exchange rate is a definite financial advantage, it's *not* free. Visa and MasterCard levy a 1% fee on all trans-actions made abroad. Not surprisingly, many card issuers pass on this fee to cardholders and even tack on additional fees of their own, often as much as 2%.

This could make your transaction fee as high as 3% of the U.S. dollar amount of every transaction. At $3 for every $100 you spend, those fees can really add up over the course of a two-week vacation, and they can make a huge dent in your wallet if you're traveling or living abroad for an extended period of time.

Choose the Right Cards to Take on Your Journey

A 2008 survey of credit card issuers conducted by Heshan Demel, one of my CardRatings.com colleagues, found the following foreign transaction fees:

TIP

If possible, give yourself some lead time before traveling abroad. That way, if you find out that all your cards charge a 3% fee, you can apply for one of the no-fee cards I mentioned. A smaller bank or credit union might be worth a try as well.

- American Express: 2%
- Bank of America: 3%
- Chase: 3%
- Citibank: 3%
- Washington Mutual: 1%
- Wells Fargo: 3%
- Capital One: No foreign transaction fees
- Discover: No foreign trans-action fees (Note that Discover is accepted only in China, the Caribbean, Central America, and Mexico.)

As this survey indicates, most large issuers do charge a 3% transaction fee. Capital One and Discover are the two notable exceptions. Capital One even absorbs the 1% fee

Visa and MasterCard charge! So you can really save big if you use a Capital One card or Discover Card while on your trip. It's always a good idea to call your card issuers for their current fees on international transactions prior to traveling.

Important Advice for International Travelers

Right before you leave the country, it's a good idea to call your card issuers and give them the dates of your trip. This is a good security precaution. The card company will know that it's you charging up a storm in Paris or Hong Kong, not a thief.

Also watch for special credit card promotional offers for foreign travel, especially if you're among the well-heeled set. For example, the Citi Chairman American Express Card, launched in 2007, is targeted to Smith Barney and Citi Private Bank clients and boasts no foreign currency transaction fees until January 2009.

Card Registration Services

What would you do if your wallet was ever misplaced or stolen, or if you found fraudulent charges on one of your cards? Most of us would probably struggle to remember which cards were in the wallet, and then we'd scramble to call all our card issuers to report the loss.

Credit card registration services (aka card protection services) are a paid option that you might want to consider. For a monthly or yearly fee, card registration services come in handy if your credit and debit cards are ever lost or stolen. Although the fee is usually small, it's up to you to figure out whether the services offered are worth it.

What Does a Registration Program Do?

When you sign up for a card registration service, you arrange for certain benefits that can help you out in a crunch, including these:

- Cancellation of your credit, debit, and/or sometimes calling cards if they are lost or stolen
- Protection from unauthorized purchases made with stolen cards or by fraudulent means

For instance, if your card is lost or stolen and you have a registration service, the company will notify the issuers of all your accounts—that's right, all accounts. You make one call, and the service takes care of the rest. Most services will also request replacement cards for you.

For protection benefits, many registration services tout reimbursement and safeguards from fraudulent activities on your cards. Remember that the FCBA protects consumers from fraudulent charges, regardless of whether you're enrolled with a registration service.

Moreover, as has been mentioned previously, many credit card payment networks, including Visa, MasterCard, and American Express, have also introduced liability policies that provide 100% reimbursement for unauthorized charges, so cardholders don't have to pay a dime for unauthorized charges.

What Are the Advantages of Registration Services?

If your cards are stolen, there's a pretty straightforward procedure: Call each card company, cancel the cards, and get new ones issued.

However, say you're traveling when your cards are stolen. You probably won't have the phone numbers of each credit card company with you, and it might not be easy to find them. Wouldn't it be nice to make one phone call and have that all taken care of, relieving you of the hassle of placing all those calls?

In addition to card cancellation, many registration services offer additional benefits, such as these:

- Change-of-address service
- Easy and secure access to all your credit card information
- Emergency cash advances when credit cards are lost or stolen while traveling
- Credit monitoring after a loss
- Emergency airline tickets
- Three-bureau credit report

Other Options

It's easy to sign up for a registration or protection service. You simply place a call or click on a link and give detailed information about each of the cards you want to register. Many credit card companies, including Discover, offer this service. Registration service fees from most card companies typically range from $20 to $35 a year.

Do your research and shop around to see if any registration services fit your needs. Find out exactly what services you'd receive and what your liabilities are. Let's hope that whether you buy such services or not, your wallet is never lost or stolen.

Credit Card Protection Insurance (aka Credit Insurance)

Credit insurance, which pays off the minimum monthly payment when cardholders cannot make their payments, is sold not only by card companies, but also by stores, car dealers, and more.

Yearly sales of credit insurance totaled $5.6 billion in 2006, according to Insure.com, with the average premium charge being about 50¢ for each $100 of loan coverage per month. For example, if you carry a monthly balance of $3,000, you'd pay about $15 a month for credit insurance. That might not seem like a lot, but small sums add up: $15 a month would cost you $180 a year. If your monthly balance is $6,000, you'd pay $30 a month, or $360 a year, for credit insurance. Ouch.

Several types of credit insurance are available, and many policies cover all the following:

- Credit disability insurance—Pays on your credit card bills if you become disabled
- Credit involuntary unemployment insurance—Pays on your credit card bills if you're fired
- Credit property insurance—Pays to fix or replace items bought on credit or used as collateral
- Credit life insurance—Pays off a debt if the borrower dies

A typical credit insurance policy offers the following:

- Voluntary enrollment
- Cancellation at any time
- Rates regulated by the state insurance commissioner, regardless of age, sex, or health
- Premium fee calculated on current monthly balance

- Benefit equal to the minimum monthly required payment if you are disabled or unemployed
- Full payment benefit in the event of death or dismemberment, with a cap set normally at $10,000
- Personal credit rating maintained in good order, even in the event of disability or unemployment

The key point to remember is what most credit insurance offers don't eagerly highlight: Coverage typically pays only the required monthly minimum each month, except with credit life insurance.

Is Credit Insurance Worth the Fee?

Supporters of credit insurance (usually those who sell it) say it offers great protection for some credit users. For instance, people who carry a large debt or who are in poor health might benefit if they become too ill to work.

Critics argue that it's a grand money-maker for the insurers but a raw deal for cardholders and that consumers' money can be better spent on other insurance coverage. They say a term life insurance policy, for example, would cost less and pay out more in benefits. Seeking better insurance is especially important to people who earn a lower income and don't have several types of insurance—the ones who tend to use credit insurance the most, according to the Consumer Credit Industry Association.

For almost all situations, the expense of credit insurance outweighs the potential benefits. Instead of a policy that makes only minimum monthly payments when a claim is made, a better alternative is usually to set aside funds for life's emergencies, pay down your debts, and carry term life insurance.

If you're unsure of whether your credit card account includes credit insurance, call your issuer and ask.

Although you won't usually be enrolled in a credit insurance program without your approval, it doesn't hurt to double-check. Cancellation is available at any time.

A similar product to credit insurance is debt-cancellation and debt-suspension contracts. Many lenders are offering new card customers these products instead of credit insurance. These products offer to cancel or suspend payments and charges if certain events occur, including death, disability, and involuntary unemployment.

Unfortunately, because federal banking regulators have determined debt-cancellation and debt-suspension services to be "banking products," they are not subject to state insurance regulation. No minimum benefit levels exist, and these products can be crummy deals for consumers.

According to the Center for Economic Justice, the ratio of benefits to fees for a credit card debt-suspension agreement is typically 3% or less. This means for every dollar paid for this product, consumers receive only 3¢ or less in benefits. Ouch!

That's a pretty lousy deal. The credit protector or card protection product your card company offers might fall into this category. The bottom line is that you should proceed with extreme caution when considering any type of credit insurance.

Final Thoughts

There you have it—ten more credit card benefits for you to weigh and use as you see fit. Although you might not have heard of them before, I hope you already have some thoughts on how you can take advantage of one or more of them in the near future.

Just remember to call your card issuer to verify the details instead of relying on some hype you think you saw someplace. While you're on the phone, ask for the other benefits that your card offers. As consumer advocate Marc Eisenson puts it, "Not asking is an automatic 'No.'" And who knows? A terrific unpublicized freebie might be yours for the asking.

CHAPTER 11

Master Advanced Card Techniques to Save and Make Money

Now that I've shared the basics on how to get the most bang for your credit card bucks, let's delve into these advanced topics that can help you maximize the value of your credit card:

- Reallocating credit lines to save money, get extra freebies, and build up an investment fund
- Making biweekly credit card payments to save money and get out of debt faster
- Using cards to make money
- Paying your taxes with a credit card
- Steering clear of universal default

As a disclaimer, some of the card usage techniques presented in this chapter may not appeal to you, and some of these techniques are very controversial. My main intent in this chapter is to expose you to some advanced techniques and let you decide if you'd like to utilize them or not.

Reallocating Credit Lines

Many issuers allow you to reallocate credit card lines—that is, to move the credit limit from one card to another, assuming that the cards are issued by the same lender. You might want to do this to save money, to get extra rewards or other freebies, and to build up an investment fund.

For example, let's say you just got a 0% balance-transfer card with a $10,000 credit limit. It's from a bank where you already have a card with a 13% APR that has a $5,000 credit limit. You might be able to get the bank to move almost all of that $5,000 line on your existing card to the new 0% balance-transfer card, without even pulling your credit report (which can ding your credit score).

If you try this technique, it's usually best to leave a small limit ($500 or so) on the original card. Unless you have a really good reason, there's no benefit to closing an account because it might lower your credit score. Still, that extra $4,500 at 0% will make getting out of debt cheaper and faster for you—unless, of course, you see it as an affordable way to get into debt even deeper. Watch out: That can be a real downside of having access to more and cheaper money.

I've reallocated a credit line myself, with an offer of a 0% rate that's good for the life of the balance transfer (yes, you read it correctly- a 0% forever rate!). A few issuers have periodically offered 0% for life and other enticing low-rate offers, but strings are often attached. The card in my pocket requires that I make two new purchases of any size in each billing period if I want to maintain my 0% rate every month.

I transferred a large balance from another card at a much higher rate and also did a credit reallocation from my existing credit card with the same company, increasing my 0% line by several thousand dollars. The end result was that I was able to transfer even more of my card debt and slash my interest charges more.

I came close to maxing out the combined credit limit on the 0% offer. I could do that because I wasn't concerned about the hit my credit score would take due to high utilization; I didn't plan to apply for any loans within the next 12 months. Moreover, I could trust myself to take advantage of the 0% rate to significantly reduce what I owed in that time frame, so this was worth it.

I make two nominal purchases every month to meet the issuer's purchase requirement, knowing that my monthly payments are being applied to the 0% balance. While my purchases accrue interest at the normal purchase rate, I have paid only around $10 in interest all year on a balance of around $20,000.

Getting the 0% rate and then reallocating my existing credit line has led to incredible savings. Where else can you get a deal like this?!? Even if you are offered a card with a 3.99% introductory rate instead of one at 0%, it's likely a lot better than what you're paying now. If you then reallocate lines on top of that, you'll be amazed by how quickly your savings can add up.

You might be skeptical about such offers, but I'm living proof that if you read the terms carefully and play by the rules (such as always paying the bill on time), you can save thousands in interest as you get yourself out of debt sooner than you ever thought possible.

Going forward, some banks might be cutting down on approving reallocations (you can't blame them for not being thrilled about turning 13% APR credit lines into ones on which they can't earn a dime...unless we mess up). On the other hand, lenders know that keeping existing customers is a lot easier and cheaper than finding new ones, so many will continue to be accommodating.

Cardholders even report different experiences with the same banks. It sometimes seems to depend on the customer service rep you happen to get on the phone. Some cardholders have had no problem getting the reallocations they wanted, and the reps didn't even mention their credit reports. Others were transferred from person to person within the bank. Many report the best success by asking for someone in the credit or balance transfer department. Others had success following this advice from Polonius, a veteran member of CardRatings.com's forum: "If you ask for a *reallocation,* the [customer service rep] may tell you it can't be done. Call it a *consolidation,* and your chances may improve."

Be advised, though, that a few cardholders have had unfortunate experiences when they've requested a credit line reallocation, even losing access to their credit cards: Their credit reports were pulled and the reps didn't like what they saw. For example, if you're behind on payments or if you've recently been granted a lot of new credit, you might be better off not asking. It's also a good idea to ask if the rep will need to look at your credit report (a **hard inquiry**) before you ask for a reallocation.

Making Biweekly Credit Card Payments

One of my favorite advanced card techniques involves sending in biweekly payments on your card bills. This technique can save you thousands of dollars. You'll also cut the length of time it takes to pay off the debt by up to 75%. I know it sounds unbelievable, but it's true—even if you're paying a high rate.

Say you owe $5,000 on a credit card at 17% with a 3% required minimum payment. If you send in only the required amounts, by the time you've paid off that $5,000 (some 14 years from now), your interest bite alone would be $4,119.

Instead, if you make biweekly payments—that is, payments every two weeks—you will save over $2,500 and be debt free in less than 3.5 years! Assuming that this $5,000 debt was yours, this month, you'd be required to send in

$150. Pay the $150 before the due date and send in $75 (half of that $150) every 14 days *without fail* from then on. Believe it or not, that's all you have to do to achieve amazing savings.

Sound too good to be true? Many consumer advocates have recommended this, starting with Marc Eisenson, coauthor of *Invest in Yourself: Six Secrets to a Rich Life* (Wiley, 2001), who came up with the idea.

Here's how it works: A year has 52 weeks. A payment every two weeks results in 26 payments a year, *which is the equivalent of 13 monthly payments,* not 12. The entire extra month's worth of payments goes toward paying off your outstanding balance.

In case you're wondering whether the bank that issues your card will actually credit the payments every two weeks, the short answer is yes. Card issuers are required by law to credit payments when they're received.

Here's How to Use the Biweekly System to Your Advantage

To save the most, pick the bill that carries the highest interest rate, and be sure not to charge anything else to that card. Make certain you get this month's minimum in by the due date. I recommend that you mail it at least ten business days before that date, to avoid any mail-related snafus and make sure you start off on the right foot. Better yet, pay your bill online—your payment typically is posted by the next business day (and often is posted on the same day).

From then on, send in half of that amount every 14 days. As for those statements you get from the card issuer, don't let the due date and minimum payments on them sidetrack you. (But do verify that your payments are getting credited properly.) Just be sure to make your payments like clockwork so they arrive at the lender every two weeks.

It's a good idea to ask your card's customer service rep if there's anything you should know about making your biweekly payments before you start, but don't be surprised if the rep has never heard of this idea. If that's the case, you might want to simply ask for tips to speed up the crediting of your payments.

For example, some card issuers advise that you put your account number on the checks. (I'd rather not have this information floating around as the checks are processed, but many companies say it's helpful if you want your payment credited ASAP.)

WARNING

Although this system can save you a lot of money, you *must* follow these instructions exactly. Otherwise, you might end up with late fees, exorbitant interest rates, and a blemish on your credit report for up to seven years. So unless you can trust yourself to keep up with those payments, you're better off just sending in as much over the required minimum payments as you can, any month you can afford it.

Afraid You'll Forget?

Ask the customer service rep if you can authorize electronic transfers every 14 days. Some companies provide this service for free, while others charge a fee (in that case, skip it!), and others won't help at all.

Also consider the electronic bill-paying service where you bank. If the bank doesn't charge for the privilege and will automatically transfer the funds every 14 days, it's a perfectly reasonable way to go.

Using Credit Cards to Make Money

Warning: Before you read this section, understand that the following strategies are worth considering only if you...

- Are good with details.
- Always meet deadlines.
- Don't have any existing card debt.
- Have good to excellent credit.
- Have a steady cash flow, with money to invest every month.
- Will not need to borrow money or do anything else that will get your credit report pulled. These techniques could significantly lower your score.

I recommend that you not even consider these practices if you are just making ends meet or if you are concerned about the implications of your credit score being lowered. Steer clear at least until you're on more solid ground—ideally, with an emergency fund socked away in the bank. You're better off focusing on the tips I offered in previous chapters.

Also, as a disclaimer, I'm not advocating that you engage in any of the following practices. (Some are quite questionable.) My desire is to simply expose you to these practices and present a balanced viewpoint, with both pros and cons.

Credit Card Arbitrage

In case you're not familiar with the term, *arbitrage* is a fancy way to say "buy low/sell high." Wall Street "arbitrageurs" buy stocks, commodities, or currency at low prices in one market and then immediately sell them at higher prices in another market. These days, a small but growing number of enterprising cardholders practice what is sometimes referred to as credit card arbitrage.

They use cards that offer 0% or very low introductory rates on balance transfers as a source of investment capital. The proceeds from such card offers is invested right away in various types of investments, depending on their risk tolerance and smarts. Regardless of the investment vehicle, I should point out that this practice is definitely not for everybody—MSN Personal Finance Columnist Liz Weston aptly labels practitioners as "0% card daredevils."

Some folks choose to invest quite safely (and intelligently, if you ask me)—say, in liquid investments such as CDs or high-yield savings accounts. Others choose more risky investments, even stocks. Although Wall Street returns might be tempting, the potential losses are equally as large—or larger.

Virtually all personal finance advisors agree that the stock market makes sense only when you can invest funds for at least five years, which is generally long enough to make up for any economic downturns that might occur. Given the current economic climate, I seriously doubt that we'll see a card offering five years of 0% money, but who knows? Who'd have thought we'd ever have seen 0% balance transfer offers for the life of the transfer?

These are the only cards to consider for arbitrage:

- Cards that allow you to write a check to yourself or that will direct-deposit the money automatically into your checking account so you can invest it right away.

- Cards that don't charge balance transfer fees (these are hard to find) or "cap" the fee at a low amount. If you have to pay a 3% fee with no cap on the money you use, for example, the card probably won't be worth it because these days, you'll likely earn only in the range of 3% to 4% with a high-yield savings account, if that much. If you're lucky enough to earn 4%, that would leave you with a 1% return before taxes. Assuming that about one-third of your income goes to taxes of some sort, you'd clear a fraction of 1% after taxes. That's not exactly a great rate of return!

- Cards that will not treat your transaction as a cash advance. Instead of the 0% introductory rate, a cash advance could easily cost you 20%+ in interest.

- Cards that have a relatively long introductory term—ideally, a year or more. Otherwise, your capital won't have much time to grow, and you won't earn enough to make filling out the application worthwhile.

> **TIP**
>
> Most lenders are tightening up their transfer offers, but you can usually find cards that meet most of these criteria, often in your mailbox. To check out the current crop of 0% and low introductory rate card offerings, go to CardRatings.com, and click on "Low Introductory Rate" under "Card Reports".

For Arbitrage to Work

Before you even apply for a card with a transfer offer, call the toll-free number to make sure you can write yourself a check or get a direct deposit, that there's no or a low balance transfer fee, and that your check will not be treated as a cash advance.

Be sure to send in the required monthly payments *on time.* If you're late with just one payment, your 0% rate could quickly vanish, to be replaced by a much higher one—sometimes more than 30%. Also be sure to pay back the total of what you've borrowed before the introductory rate expires. Otherwise, the new—and, no doubt, higher— rate will quickly eat up the interest you've earned.

Don't use your arbitrage card for new purchases because the interest rate on your purchases will be much higher than the balance transfer rate. Even if you immediately send in enough to cover your purchases, your payment will be credited against what you owe at 0%, while the debt at the higher rate will get larger. (As I've already indicated, exceptions to this rule make sense if 0% offers come with strings requiring monthly purchases, just as long as you can keep those purchase amounts really small.)

Pay off what you owe on other cards before you try out arbitrage. It doesn't make sense to use 0% money to earn 3.5% before taxes when you're being charged, say, 13% on another card that has a balance, which you have to pay with after tax dollars. When you factor in taxes, you'll pay around 19.40% on that 13% debt. So use 0% and low-rate cards to pay off your pricier pieces of plastic. When you've lightened your debt load, you can revisit the arbitrage question.

How Much Can You Really Earn with Arbitrage?

Let's say you're approved for a 0% offer for 12 months with a $10,000 credit limit that meets all the criteria I just laid out. Not wanting to take too bad of a hit to your credit score, you write a check to yourself for half of your new credit line, confident that you have enough cash on hand to send in the first month's minimum payment of $100—and enough of a cash flow to meet future required payments.

You immediately deposit that $5,000 in a one-year CD earning 5%. (The best one-year CD rates as of the printing of this book are in the 4% range—go to BankRate.com for a listing of the highest CD rates currently being offered). Assuming daily compounding of the interest, your APR will actually be 5.127%, and at the end of the year, you'll earn $256 in interest...before taxes. Then, assuming that about a third of what you earn goes to taxes, you'll get to keep $171.

The more you can invest, the more you'll make off the card issuer's money. For example, if you invest $10,000, you'll earn $513 before taxes and $341 after taxes. If you invest $75,000, you'll have $3,845 before taxes and $2,576 after taxes. Make sure you can come up with the first minimum payment of $1,500 before you plan to spend that $2,576 a year from now! Also, good luck on getting approved for a card with a $75,000 limit. Although you won't likely end up with a $75,000 credit line, it's not uncommon to have a credit line of $20,000 to $30,000.

Given the amount of money you can make, as well as all the details you'd have to handle, is arbitrage worth it for you? If so, keep reading for the ways arbitrageurs amass credit card funds.

> **TIP**
>
> One simple way to access to more capital is to visit your cards' websites and apply for automatic increases in your credit limits. Over time, they can really add up. Some arbitrageurs even volunteer to send in financial reports to get higher limits. On top of that, many get their lenders to reallocate their credit lines, not to get out of debt, as we discussed earlier, but to be able to get more "free" or low cost money for arbitrage.

App-O-Rama

Many arbitrageurs use a strategy known as "App-O-Rama" to increase their pot of 0% money or attractive rebate offers. They submit a lot of card applications at the same time—sometimes ten or more! Another motivation is that their applications will be approved with nice, high credit limits before all the "hard" inquiries are reflected in their credit scores.

Although the idea of having plenty of "free" money may seem enticing, it's important to know that, sooner or later, getting a bunch of new credit *will* lower your scores. That makes App-O-Rama a very bad move for anyone who might need to apply for a mortgage or any other type of loan within the next 12 months or so.

Another potential problem is that if too much of the new credit is used for arbitrage, App-O-Rama will lead to yet lower credit scores due to high utilization. How much is too much? Experts disagree on this one, but most say anything below 10% utilization is best.

Multiple cards with high credit limits can be a real benefit to people who enjoy arbitrage. If they maintain perfect payment histories on all their cards and keep their utilization relatively low on each card, their credit scores might actually go up. As the combined limits on their collection of cards go up, they use a lower percent of their overall credit limits. As strange as it might sound, that actually can earn them some extra points for low utilization.

One related motivation for arbitrageurs is that the better they make themselves look on paper, the easier it is for them to get more cards with greater credit limits (at least in theory). Stories abound on the Internet of people who have amassed large amounts of credit playing one round of App-O-Rama. I've seen one person brag about getting up to $300,000 (but I haven't personally verified this)! Then, being careful about utilization, a few months later, they might put in a pile of applications in their spouse's name. That can lead to even more available credit.

Playing with the Numbers

Just for fun, let's say someone was able to theoretically amass $500,000 in available credit. Having a $500,000 pot makes the arbitrage numbers far more entertaining. Assuming 50% utilization, that's $250,000 to invest. If the money is put in 5% savings accounts, it would earn $12,817 before taxes and $8,587 after taxes! Tempting, isn't it?

Remember, though, that there's always a chance issuers will reject an application, refuse to renew a card, or deny a request for a credit line increase. In addition, even with perfect payment histories, some lenders have been known to reduce credit limits for various reasons. (There were numerous reports of credit line decreases on the CardRatings.com forum during the first few months of 2008.) In the worst-case scenario, they can reduce your line so that it's just a little more than your current balance, which immediately changes the utilization from wherever it was to around 99%. Ouch! This can and does happen.

Your multitude of new cards also could get an issuer thinking that some "unusual" activity is going on, which could trigger an investigation. A few people interested in keeping their App-O-Rama accounts have had to submit to a fairly detailed financial review, including sending in their income tax returns; others have watched their credit disappear because they were uncomfortable sharing their financial info with their card companies.

Above all, the important point to remember about an App-O-Rama is that if you blow it one time on one card, your investments will likely go from arbitrage to plain old garbage. So this is *definitely* not for anyone who might forget a payment or confuse a couple of bills. It'd be a shame to pay a lot in fees and a higher rate on multiple cards because you were late with one card payment—due to universal default (more on this shortly), one late payment can result in a detrimental domino rate effect.

Finally, watch out for the geometric progression—or, in layman's terms, getting too much going at one time. All the provisos I laid out for arbitrage apply to App-O-Rama. Arbitrage is dicey enough with one card. The more cards you have, the more likely you'll have a problem. Make sure each of these is true for you:

- Each card is appropriate. (Check this before you apply.)

- You can afford to make the required minimum payments and are never late with any of them. (As a reminder, minimum payments vary among issuers.)
- You carefully consider credit scoring implications.

Paying Your Taxes with a Credit Card

The IRS now allows you to charge your entire tax bill, extension or partial payments, and estimated taxes. Although this might sound appealing, especially if you can't afford to pay your taxes or are looking to rack up some serious reward points, you'll want to consider some issues before you decide to pay with plastic.

How It Works

Instead of directly accepting card payments from taxpayers, the IRS has worked out deals with "service providers"—that is, intermediaries who handle the credit card transactions for a "convenience" fee. (Visit IRS.gov for a current list of providers.)

The IRS receives the amount you owe, and your credit card account is billed. In fact, it's billed twice: One charge is listed as United States Treasury Tax Payment, and a separate charge appears for the convenience fee.

Hefty Convenience Fees

Whether you pay online, over the phone, or through tax-preparation software or tax professionals, and whether you e-file or submit a paper return, you have to pay a fee of 2.49% to 3.93% for the privilege of paying by credit card. For example, a 3.0% fee on a $2,000 tax bill translates into an additional $60 payment, which the IRS calls "a nondeductible personal expense."

If you use a typical card to pay what you owe and don't pay off your balance in full when you get your bill, you could be in real trouble. You're up to 3.93% in the hole just because you charged your taxes, and if you aren't using a card with a 0% promotional APR, the interest bite could really hurt. If you're already carrying a balance from the previous billing cycle, you'll be charged interest from the day your tax bill is posted (that is, you won't enjoy a grace period).

Paying Taxes with a Reward Card: Is It Worth It?

Although it might be very tempting to try to earn miles and cash rebates by charging your taxes, the cost of doing so almost always outweighs any rewards. Carefully compare the reward you'd earn to the convenience fee that will be levied.

Some cards offer rebates as high as 5% on certain purchases or at certain retailers, but no standard cards offer a rebate as high as 2.49% on tax payments. Even if you could a 2.49% rebate, you'd only be breaking even, which might be a plus just for the convenience of it, but you wouldn't end up ahead.

One possible exception exists: a rebate card with a generous teaser offer. For example, during the first few months of 2008, the Citi Cash Returns card was offering 5% cash back on all purchases made during the first three months. With this offer, you'd pocket 2.51% cash back, assuming you were charged the 2.49% convenience fee. Not bad, huh? However, if you don't pay the balance off right away, you'll incur interest charges based on a rate that varies from 9.99-17.99% (as of the printing of this book) on top of the convenience fee. Needless to say, your finance charges would be much higher than the cash back that you'd earn! (Please note that this 5% Citi offer has expired. Visit CardRatings.com to see the current "Credit Card Specials" from issuers.)

My opinion is that the ones who generally come out ahead with credit card tax payments are the IRS and the service providers. The IRS knows it's more likely to get paid if it offers card payment options, and this is a very lucrative business for the companies that accept card payments for the IRS.

A Better Choice for Paying Taxes

If you think you'll have trouble making your tax payment, consider the installment payment plan the IRS offers. You can spread out your tax payments, typically over five years or less. The IRS does charge a user fee to set up an installment agreement, which is $52 if you agree to have your payments deducted directly from your bank account and $105 if you'll be sending in checks.

You'll also pay a variable interest rate on the taxes you owe, which is currently 6%. (This interest rate, which is calculated each quarter, is the federal short-term rate plus 3%.) If you don't have the money to pay your taxes, why pay 2.49% and credit card interest rates when you can get such a great rate from Uncle Sam? Save your hard-earned money!

Not everyone can get an installment agreement, but your chances of getting one are very good if you owe less than $25,000. If you owe more than that, you could still qualify. If not, look into all your other financing options before you head down the pricey path of paying your taxes with a card. One possible exception to this rule would be a card that offered a 0% or very low introductory rate on purchases.

Steering Clear of Universal Default

Remember universal default, mentioned in previous chapters? It's a clause lenders bury in the fine print, the one that lets them raise your rate if you were late paying on another credit card (or maybe the electric bill), even if you have a perfect bill-paying record with that card issuer. Not only does the rate go up, but it can go sky-high.

Cardholders, consumer advocates, and policymakers have decried this practice. As a result, new legislation may outlaw the practice or place restrictions on it. Interestingly enough, some banks don't call it universal default anymore. Instead, they seem to be burying the fact that they periodically check credit scores and respond dramatically in even tinier fine print. Now many reserve the right to change your rate "at any time, for any reason." So if your credit score is lowered, even from a mistake on a credit report, many lenders still reserve the right to raise your rates to the max, regardless of your bill-paying record with them.

You might be wondering how the card issuers justify this practice, whatever they call it. As one exec put it in the groundbreaking PBS Frontline program *The Secret History of the Credit Card,* "The bank is not being unreasonable in raising rates when it has reason to believe that the risk of being repaid by the customer has increased." In other words, if you're behind on any debt, card issuers think you're more likely not to pay *their* bill. Therefore, they charge more to balance their perceived risk, which means higher interest rates for "high-risk" borrowers. Although this seems reasonable enough, one troubling aspect is that the rules determining "high-risk" status seem arbitrary and in some cases extreme. Case in point: It's hard to look at a 20% rate increase for one isolated late payment as anything other than an over-reaction.

Another serious problem is how unjust this policy is. The lender gets to change the terms on money that has already been borrowed—money it *chose* to lend at a lower rate. For example, say you charged something to a credit card that had an APR of 8.9%. Several months down the road, you're informed that the rate is now 27.99%. This new rate is *not* just applied to new purchases: It's also applied to the balance that you already carry on the card.

On the face of it, you might think this is clearly a breach of contract. Unfortunately, under current laws, because many card issuers have disclosed their ability and intent to change the terms of your cardholder agreement "at any time, for any reason" or for what critics perceive as being quite vague reasons, it is perfectly legal. Hopefully, lawmakers will pass legislation that outlaws universal default in any guise. (I discuss this and other important legislative changes that should be made later in this chapter.)

Ahead of the Pack

In the meantime, Citibank has raised the bar significantly by eliminating this unfair industry practice during the life of a card. The bank announced in 2007 that it won't increase rates at any time for any reason until a card expires and a new card is issued (typically two years). As of now, the only reason the rates will increase before the card expires is if a customer pays Citi late, exceeds the credit limit, or pays with a check that isn't honored.

When the time for renewal is up, Citi will take a look at the cardholder's credit profile and decide on the new rate. If the cardholder agrees to the new terms, fine. If not, the cardholder can pay off the balance at the old rate (charging privileges may be revoked).

Chase made a similar policy change that took effect on March 1, 2008. Chase says that it will raise the interest rate for customers' only if they violate the terms of the cardmember agreement by making a late payment, exceeding their credit limit, or paying with insufficient funds. One unique aspect of Chase's policy is that its cardholders can lower their interest rate through its "rate reset" option, assuming the rate increases for any of these reasons. All a customer has to do is sign up for automatic payments and make on-time payments for 12 consecutive months. Then Chase will reset the customer's rate to the lower, original nonpromotional rate.

Hopefully, other lenders will soon follow suit and at take similar steps in the right direction. But even if universal default is abolished or issuers totally stop practicing it on their own, they will likely continue to use risk-assessment models in some form. This is one reason why responsibly managing your credit is so important.

Prevention Is Key

Talking your way out of one of these rate hikes can be difficult after it has occurred (although it doesn't hurt to try), so it's important to avoid having it triggered.

Here's how you can protect yourself against universal default:

1. Always pay *all* your bills on time. If possible, pay bills when you receive them instead of when they're due.

    -   Online bill paying is becoming an increasingly popular option for many consumers.
    -   Also consider using automatic or electronic reminders to help organize your bill paying as well as automatic electronic monthly payments.
    -   If it will help, contact your various card companies and ask to have your due dates changed so that they fall at a time of the month that best coincides with your cash flow.

2. Avoid becoming what the banks consider a credit risk. Here are some reasons lenders might think that you're a credit risk:

    -   Late payments made to any creditor
    -   High debt-to-income ratio
    -   Lowered credit score
    -   Credit line exceeded
    -   Bounced check

3. Understand your card's terms. Make sure that your current balance is at as low a rate as possible. If your credit score is above 720, you should be able to qualify for the best rates. (Check the "Low Rate" section on CardRatings.com for the best current rates.)

4. Check your credit reports at each of the three credit bureaus at least once a year. Also regularly check your credit score. The sooner you find a mistake, the sooner you can get it corrected—hopefully, before universal default is triggered.

5. Read your mail. We've become so accustomed to receiving card offers in the mail that, many times, we send them straight to the shredder. From now on, give those envelopes a glance to make sure it's not one of your issuers relaying a change in terms. Although this won't prevent universal default from being activated, at least you'll be prepared for it and ready to strategize an action plan.

If you become a victim of universal default and have exhausted your options, consider using a nonprofit credit counseling service to help you deal with you debt situation. You can find out more information about such services and other related resources by visiting CardRatings.com/Book. Finally, consider posting a negative review about your card's universal default clause in our popular "Consumer Reviews" section. Hopefully, card issuers will consider changing their tactics if enough disgruntled consumers express their disgust. Power to the people!

What's Going on in Washington

As I mentioned, our elected officials have been discussing legislative and regulatory changes that would outlaw universal default. They're also considering many other consumer-friendly proposals, including reining in fees and requiring that increased rates apply only to future debts.

Congress is also considering proposals that require issuers to credit payments against the highest-interest debts first (before applying payments to lower-rate debt as is currently the rule), to solve controversial issues involving college students, to provide greater disclosure of any rate changes or fees, to use a "postmarked by" date when determining whether a payment is late, and to limit the amount of credit given to people who are under age 18. Here's hoping!

In addition, the Federal Reserve has introduced proposals for changing the rules that the card industry must follow. Until recently, its proposed changes primarily focused on how information is disclosed to us: how it should look, when we should receive it, and what we must be told. The Fed also recommends making interest rates and fees clearer and easier to comprehend. Issuers would have to give us more time—45 days' notice instead of the current 15—before they could make changes to the terms of card agreements. Lenders would have to show how much sending in only the required monthly minimum amounts will cost over the long run and how long it would take to get out from under paying only the minimums. Newer proposals from the Fed go much further, even calling for an end to universal default and double-cycle billing.

Although there's a decent chance of some new regulations coming from Washington, I don't think the fundamentals will change—even if they do away with universal default. Card issuers will always have their own very sophisticated risk models, and, believe me, they are very risk averse. In a way, I don't blame them: They're lending us "unsecured" money, without our homes or cars as collateral.

Should Rates Be Capped?

Some more extreme card reform proposals are promoting a federal cap on interest rates. Some politicians are proposing a 30% cap on rates. While I favor the vast majority of credit card reform measures, I am generally not supportive of capping rates. One reason is that I fear that 0% or low introductory rate offers will cease to exist if rates are capped. I guarantee you that card issuers are going to respond negatively in some form or fashion and some consumers are going to suffer. As a side note, interestingly enough, as of the printing of this book, I'm not aware of any rates above 30%. So, not sure how much a proposal would actually accomplish (sure sounds good on the campaign trail though!). ☺

But there's no excuse for the excesses we've been discussing. And issuers *do* hold a lot of power over us. They surely hold sway over our all-important credit reports and credit scores. Also, unless the bankruptcy laws are changed again, lenders are in a much better position to collect, even from those of us in the most dire of straits.

Lenders will also react to the state of the economy, the size of the deficit, the jobs outlook, and so on. As I write this, they're coming to terms with the effects of the sub-prime mortgage crisis, in which far too many people were given home loans they couldn't afford, many with unconscionable terms. More and more folks are facing fore-closure. Home prices are falling, yet relatively few are selling. Even the value of real estate that is not for sale has dropped.

This all means that, for many cardholders, the home equity loan safety net they relied on to get them out of card debt has disappeared. This is due to the fact that lenders are being much more selective in who they approve for loans. It also means that card issuers, some of which have made subprime loans, are being more cautious about who they give credit to and under what terms. Some are cutting back on lines of credit or raising rates, not wanting to take on what they see as too much risk.

Hopefully by the time you read this, the most consumer-unfriendly of the card industry's practices will no longer be allowed. Our country would be better off if the deck wasn't so stacked against cardholders, and I think it would be better for the issuers as well. After all, I've always maintained that disgruntled customers aren't usually good for business. ☺

Fortunately, having read this far, you know how to use cards to your financial advantage, even under these less than ideal circumstances. Next we take a look at what's coming our way from the card industry so you'll be poised to take advantage of new opportunities as they develop.

CHAPTER 12

Capitalize on Future Card Trends

In this final chapter, I let you in on some important issues and upcoming trends in the industry so you can continue to make sure you get the best deals. We discuss the following top trends:

- Cards will be accepted in new places.
- Smart cards will be smarter and safer.
- Issuers will keep finding new markets.
- Senior debt is a disturbing trend.
- New enticements will be trendy, targeted, and even practical.

Trend 1: Cards Will Be Accepted in New Places

New technologies have made it possible to use cards in places we never thought possible. Consider vending machines. Half the U.S. vending machines are expected to accept cards by 2009. They're already being used to sell all sorts of electronic equipment in department stores, to say nothing of soda. The USPS will remove all stamp vending machines that take cash by October 2008; the new equipment will accept only plastic.

According to various studies, consumers will spend between about 32% and 50% more when they can pay with a card (scary stuff, I know), so cashless vending is likely here to stay. This can be a great convenience, assuming that you're not a vending machine junkie or someone likely to be swayed by children "dying" for potato chips. And I'm sure we can all agree that it'd be great if quotations like this are soon a thing of the past:

> *Change is inevitable, except from vending machines.*
> —Source unknown

But this new market comes with new dangers, especially if you have children. You won't be able to end a discussion by saying, "Sorry, I don't have any more change." Certainly, the last thing college students need is another easy way to get themselves deeper in debt.

Children of all ages need to be warned not to overdo it at vending machines. Many students will likely be tempted by the new cashless vending machines in the cafeteria. The food for sale might be better for them than it was just a few years ago, but overspending *and* unhealthy food choices available at vending machines are important, timely subjects for family discussion.

Talk about the benefits of convenience versus the cost for the privilege—in terms of both your wallet and their waistlines! Point out that cashless vending is new and is designed to be very attractive to them—it's something we'll all have to learn to live with, *in moderation.* (However you define that is up to you.)

Let them know how high that cost might end up being if they use cards to buy soft drinks or snacks and don't pay off the bill as soon as it arrives. A vending machine that takes plastic presents a good opportunity to talk with your family about credit and finances in general.

If you're prone to impulse purchases, forewarned is forearmed: You might be sorely challenged by snazzy new cashless vending machines the next time you're in a department store. They'll be selling iPods, all sorts of other electronics gadgetry, and everything else they can. Keep the cards in your wallet and consider your budget before you toy with cashless vending!

Trend 2: Cards Will Be Even Smarter and Safer

Everyone wants to get through the line faster, and the latest in high-speed card transactions, "contactless cards," is reportedly 63% faster than paying in cash. With contactless cards, you don't have to swipe your card to make a payment. Instead, you simply wave your card near the card terminal. This definitely speeds things up when you're checking out at a register or paying at the drive-through at a fast food joint.

Artcubed, an IT consultant and member of CardRatings.com's forum, shares this report on his first time using the new technology:

> *It was significantly quicker than swiping, in my case. In the drug store where I first tried it, I normally have to swipe, press Credit and then OK, and then wait for approval; it usually takes about 45 seconds. Some guy was sort of in front of me but off to the side, so I decided to try making my contactless payment by tapping (similar to waving). Took about 5 seconds—no button pushing, just spit out a receipt, and I was done.*

Imagine how much time and aggravation you could save if, every time you got on the subway, went to the movies, or bought something, paying took less time and was easier and more convenient.

Say good-bye to swiping and hello to "tap and go" cards, technological marvels with names such as Chase Blink, AMEX ExpressPay, Visa Wave, and MasterCard PayPass.

These cards usually operate through radio frequency identification (RFID) tags, radio waves, antennae, integrated circuits, cryptography, and microprocessors. (Don't ask me to describe the technology in any more detail!)

Some large cities, such as New York City, have been negotiating with the major cards to come up with contactless solutions that work for commuters, government, and lenders. That will surely be a real plus to everyone who uses mass transit.

On the other hand, if it's so quick, easy, and convenient, too many of us will likely spend more, and not necessarily on things that are good for us! (My mouth waters just thinking of the donuts in the TV commercial advertising one quick pay card or another, where a man slows down the line even though he has his money out and is ready to pay!)

One department store reports that customers who used contactless cards spent 44% more. Businesses that appeal to young people, that do a big cash business, and that aggressively market rewards are also extremely pleased with sales on contactless cards. In other words, we have another subject to discuss with our young 'uns and the big spenders in the family!

Micro Transactions on the Rise

Card issuers are increasingly targeting small purchases under $10. For example, many fast food restaurants are increasingly accepting plastic. Expect this trend to continue since these small micro transactions, as they are sometimes called, can really add up quickly. Millions and millions of dollars of additional charge volume are quite enticing to issuers. Let's hope that our waistlines don't suffer in the process. ☺

Although I appreciate the convenience of being able to "blink" lunch, a movie, or some other purchase, I am uncomfortable with the fact that typically no signature is required to "wave" up to $25 at one time. It's too easy. I think it's preferable to take a minute to think about your budget and then sign for a purchase. I'm afraid contactless cards can make our charges seem less real—and distance us that much more from "owning" our debts and taking responsibility for them. (Call me old-fashioned if you'd like!)

Another negative is that identity theft and privacy experts have serious concerns about the RFID chips. They say it's too easy to steal our private information. The industry counters by saying it has state-of-the-art anti-fraud techniques in place. I say, where there's a will, there's a way. As a result, I'm personally steering clear of contactless cards for now. But given how beneficial the technology is to card issuers, I believe it will become much more foolproof in the near future. When that happens, I'll probably be waving from time to time, too. No one wants to wait!

Chase Spearheads the Move to Contactless Cards

Chase has been at the forefront of contactless payments and has aggressively promoted the technology for a few years now. In July, 2006, only one year after launching its contactless payment option, Chase had issued nearly seven million "blink" cards. Today, Chase boasts that it has over 10 million blink cards in circulation.

Trend 3: Issuers Will Keep Finding New Markets

Card issuers are increasingly eyeing both "underserved" and "unserved" markets (that is, markets with little or no competition from other creditors). Getting that first spot in someone's wallet is worth a lot in future business to lenders—more credit cards, car loans, mortgages, you name it!

Hispanic Americans are a good example of an underserved market. They're the fastest-growing demographic in our melting pot and are expected to have more than $1 trillion to spend in 2010, when they will account for nearly one-sixth of our population. To card issuers, they're ripe for specialized products and campaigns. I expect to see cards designed to specifically appeal to Spanish-speakers (there are already a few), both those who are already living the American Dream and those who are brand new to our financial institutions.

Similarly, market research shows that African Americans are underserved. They have fewer cards and use them less frequently than any other major group. Their buying power, which is estimated to be $981 billion in 2010, will be very attractive to lenders, who will be developing targeted appeals for these cardholders as well.

One of the latest unserved markets is high schoolers: Witness the offers for "prepaid teen cards" that have been popping up lately. This vast, largely untapped market is being sought after by card issuers and other entrepreneurs, who are well aware of the billions of dollars these youngsters spend—or get us to spend.

Although most teen cards are aimed at high schoolers, some are available for children as young as 13. Some have tools to help parents teach kids about money, along with cool bells and whistles to encourage kids to learn more. But many seem to be solely focused on making it easier for the precollege set to spend, spend, spend.

One key benefit is that these cards can dramatically cut down on the amount of cash that has to change hands between parents and teens. Avoiding a few visits to the bank or ATM machine can be a real time saver and a welcome convenience to many working parents.

Another benefit is that the prepaid cards expose parents—and kids—to far less liability than an open-ended credit card does. For example, if you put your child on your credit card and she or he spends a cash advance up to your credit limit, you'll be responsible for the bill, and it will be your credit score that takes the hit for increased utilization. With a prepaid card, your teen can spend only a certain amount.

Unfortunately, most of these cards come with lots of fees that really add up: activation fees, monthly fees, loading fees, over-the-limit fees, ATM fees, live customer service rep fees, paper statement fees, replacement card fees, and more. Yikes!

Don't be surprised if your teen pressures you to get one. Kids love the idea of having their own plastic, and the prepaid teen cards are marketed to them as cool status symbols. They certainly make it easier for youngsters to buy stuff.

Of course, we'd like to protect our kids for as long as we can and shelter them from the buying temptations at the mall or over the Internet, but that's virtually impossible in this day and age. So teach them about money and credit we must.

That brings me to another downside of the teen cards. Kids can learn only so much by using one of these prepaid cards: They aren't charged interest, won't get any bills, don't have to make any payments (unless you decide otherwise), and don't incur any debts or face any other consequences (for example, to their credit report) when they mess up.

Certainly, kids should go off to college with a clean slate. They'll have enough trouble keeping it that way once they get there! (For my advice on college kids and credit cards, see Chapter 7, "Start Out on the Right Foot—Credit Cards for Students and Savings for College.") I support giving kids some real experience with money management before they graduate from high school, but the current prepaid teen cards might not be the best tool for parents to use. Hopefully, better teen cards will be forthcoming.

While I'm on the subject, the other two reasonable card alternatives for teens—debit cards and secured credit cards—have their pros and cons as well. I've toyed with the notion of using all three with my teenager. But when it comes right down to it, I don't think most youngsters really understand that plastic in any form—prepaid, debit, secured, unsecured—is real money.

Although it's a little more inconvenient, for now I'm one of those who pays kids in cash or by check for jobs well done and for allowances. This makes spending and budgeting decisions much more concrete. When there's no more left, they're out of luck and it's time for Plan B—and that's a great time to sit them down and talk a bit more about money, credit, and budgeting!

Chores & Allowances Enter the Digital Age

PAYjr.com, a website that offers payment solutions for kids and teens, offers an innovative approach to tracking chores and allowances. The PAYjr Chore & Allowance System is an online system whereby kids are able to track their chores and be rewarded for completing them. The system has features such as a printable chore chart and online calendars.

Trend 4: Seniors and Debt— a Disturbing Trend

Unfortunately, far too many seniors are in no position to profit from their cards. Consider these five sad statistics:[1]

1. According to some studies, seniors are filing for bankruptcy at a faster pace than any other age group. The number of seniors declaring bankruptcy increased by more than 200% between 1992 and 2001.

2. Household debt among seniors age 75 and older increased by 160% from 1992 to 2004 according to the Employee Benefits Research Institute.

3. Sixty percent of households in the 55 to 64 age category had mortgages in 2001, a 46% increase from 1989.

4. From 1992 to 2001, the average card debt increased by about 50%. Seniors, though, had an 89% increase, with recent retirees (people in the 65–69 age group) having their average tab go up a whopping 217%![1]

5. Twenty percent of retirees with credit card debts spend more than 40% of their income on their debts.

The increase in senior indebtedness is the result of many factors, not the least of which is the astronomical cost of health care. The typical retirement age today is 62, three years before seniors can qualify for Medicare. Many early retirees find themselves without adequate health insurance, which means they're forced to use their cards to pay medical bills.

---

[1] "Retiring in the Red: The Growth of Debt Among Older Americans." demos-usa.org/pub101.cfm.

This problem is compounded by increases in the cost of living and decreases in the value of nest eggs for all but the richest retirees. The result, according to Liz Weston, author of *Deal with Your Debt* (Prentice Hall, 2005), is that seniors must often use cards to bridge the gap between their reduced fixed incomes and their increasing expenses. Sadly, today's seniors are going into debt to pay for necessities such as food, fuel, and taxes—not for the luxuries that younger folk might buy.

Reverse Mortgages: Watch Out!

With the economic outlook less than rosy, more seniors will likely be tempted by the hype of reverse mortgages: You get a loan against your home that you *never* have to pay back as long as you live there. Choose a lump-sum payment, a line of credit, or monthly checks.

Although a reverse mortgage might seem like the way to go, don't sign up for one until you get professional financial advice. I recommend against them for most people because they come with high fees and are quite complicated.

Credit Cards for Seniors

Although banks have well-established programs to attract seniors with free checks and safe deposit boxes, surprisingly, card issuers haven't really aggressively marketed directly to this age group. With retirees turning increasingly to cards, I expect to see more issuers going after them, but so far, senior cards have few unique benefits and appear to be more marketing ploys than anything else. Retirees are usually better off finding a "regular" card that meets their needs.

One notable exception is the AARP Rewards Platinum Visa currently being offered by Chase. It comes with a six-month 0% introductory rate on purchases *and* balance transfers (a balance transfer fee does apply), along with the typical one reward point for each dollar spent. Seniors who take advantage of this card and similar ones can cut expenses while they pay off debts at a lower rate. A unique feature of this card is that unlike almost all other cards offered by large issuers, this one doesn't have a binding arbitration clause (see Chapter 1, "It's Not Just Plastic—It's Money!"), which means that AARP cardholders have more legal rights and options than most cardholders.

Trend 5: New Enticements Will Be Trendy, Targeted, and Even Practical

With so many of us already having a pocketful of cards, lenders have to keep dangling carrots to tempt us into giving them a place in our wallets—or using their card when it's there. If we don't already happen to have it, why in the world would we want to bother to apply?

The card issuers who dangle the juiciest carrots are the ones that'll get the business of smart cardholders. Others will be taken in by sophisticated marketing that makes the carrots only *look* juicy.

Whatever is capturing the attention of a lot of people is a hot prospect for marketing new reward cards. Consider global warming and environmental concerns in general. Because they're becoming increasingly important to many people, some of the newest reward cards are "green." Most are being designed to attract people who were moved by the *March of the Penguins* movie (which includes me!) and

294 How You Can Profit from Credit Cards

are being promoted by major issuers, including Wells Fargo, Citibank, GE Money, and Bank of America. Their strategy is to market to as many of us as possible via our concerns about the environment, whatever they might be.

A carrot they're now dangling for these cards is a donation of a half a percent or so from every purchase to a well-known environmental group, such as the Sierra Club. They also might offer you discounts on ecofriendly goods.

Some cards even let you donate points to support complicated environmental projects. These are perfect examples of how targeted reward programs will evolve. A few major issuers are already publicizing sophisticated offerings to address complex issues, such as what you can do about greenhouse gases and how you can offset carbon emissions using your reward card! I guess the target market here must be the people who appreciated the details in Al Gore's movie.

All kidding aside, I'm glad to see the card industry take steps to support our environment. I'm sure we can all do more for the planet if we try a little harder. And as far as green cards go, lenders are right when they say these cards are an appealing, convenient, and painless way to support the environment. Some even have beautiful pictures of animals on them.

But the truth is, the way these cards currently work, you can usually do more for the planet—and for your wallet— if you use a plain ol' cash-back card. Compare the 1% or more you'd get on a cash-back card to the half a percent or so a charity would receive via a typical green card. My advice is to donate your cash-back money to your favorite environmental cause so it receives more than it would with the green card—often twice as much. Plus, it won't cost you a penny more. In fact, it might actually save you some money because you could get a tax deduction, to boot!

The cards offering eco-points raise some other issues, including the fact that you have to spend a lot to benefit

Mother Nature. Also factor in is this important caution about points from *USA Today*'s personal finance writer, Christine Dugas—which applies across the board to all cards offering them:

> *Rewards-card issuers can change their rules at any time, so in a year, your points could be less valuable. And there's no legal requirement for disclosing changes in points and benefits in advance. Only [some] changes in interest rates and penalties must come with a 15-day written notice.*

This is another reason why, based on the current green rewards, you are probably much better off with a cash-back card. Keep it simple, support environmental organizations with the cash you get back on the cards already in your wallet, *and don't litter!* ☺

New cards with perks geared to appeal to specific markets will be offered with increasing frequency. Competition is so fierce that I expect to see more cards that guarantee generous, unique, or practical rewards. If you own a home, for example, you might be attracted by cards that let you use points to pay down your mortgage. A few lenders have already introduced programs that let homeowners do just that. I must admit that using a card to pay down debt seems strange, but it can be an effective way to save money—as long as you're buying items you really need and you don't carry a balance on your cards.

Earn Rebates on Your Mortgage Payment!

American Express recently started allowing card-holders to charge their mortgage payments *and* earn reward points—after they pay $395 to sign up for the program. If you stick with it, you'll typically earn back the fee in few years or so. (The time frame largely depends on how much your monthly mortgage payments are and what type of card you have.) Then you can really rack up some nice rewards during the remaining years of your mortgage. Getting rebates on mortage payments has long been a dream of many ardent reward card users. Please note that the program is currently limited only to new mortgages or refinances offered through Indymac Bank; call 888-323-3656 for enrollment info. Hopefully, Amex will expand the program and will consider lowering the sign-up fee if the program is successful.

Watch For New Incentive Programs

Keep your eyes out for special bonuses in areas that are important to you. For example, you don't have to be a health nut to be attracted to the benefits of a "healthy living" card that Aetna and Bank of America have joined forces to offer. You earn three points for every dollar you spend on health-related purchases, including visits to doctors and dentists, hospitals, fitness and weight loss centers, and vitamin stores. Discounts also apply to purchases at sporting goods stores and drug stores, as well as for exercise equipment and medical supplies.

Also be on the lookout for other cards that benefit both the cardholder and the issuer. I think of these as win-win cards. The cardholder wins by getting cash back, rewards, or points, and the lender wins by increasing business. I'm hopeful that we'll also see more offerings with benefits that encourage people to manage their debts properly and use credit responsibly.

One such offering, Discover's Motiva card, introduced in 2007, is targeted to people who carry a balance and can use some extra motivation to pay their bills on time. When cardholders make six on-time payments in a row, they receive the seventh month's interest back in the form of a "Pay-On-Time Bonus."

If you send in that seventh payment promptly, it counts toward the next set of six timely payments, so you can get two bonuses a year. You can use the Pay-On-Time Bonuses, along with other Discover cash-back bonuses, to pay down your card bill.

On a related note, as mentioned in Chapter 7, Wells Fargo is giving incentives to college cardholders to learn how to manage credit. The bank sent a mailing to almost 78,000 randomly selected new college cardholders, offering a 60-minute phone card in exchange for completing an online credit education program. The students who completed the program used their cards more responsibly than the control group, so teaching people about credit early on seems to benefit both the students and the bank. Wells Fargo sees the possibilities in this win-win situation and is now offering online education to all new student accounts. I think that's great! These days, the incentive is a free matinee movie ticket from Fandango, which I hope will appeal more to college kids than the phone cards. I think they will—most already have phones, and anyway, which did you prefer way back when, phoning home or going to the movies?!?

The Rest Is Up to You

If you've gotten this far, you know my credit card mindset. May it brighten your financial future just as it has my own.

I truly hope you'll take full advantage of cards for your financial benefit. It's easy if you follow my advice:

- Make cards work *for you* instead of being a slave to them or totally avoiding them, as many people do.
- Look for opportunities to use low introductory rate cards to finance any and everything. And, in so doing, pay as little interest as possible—ideally, none!
- Maximize rewards and rebates to fit your lifestyle, interests, and needs.
- Utilize the free benefits that come with each card. While most cardholders are still in the dark, you can use your cards to save money on all sorts of things, ranging from car rentals to over-priced purchases.
- Use the cards you currently have and any that you get in the future to improve your credit score, not lower it.

You now know what to expect from card issuers, how they "think," and why it's so important to always read their fine print. If you play by the rules, the creative, out-of-the-box techniques I've discussed can add thousands of dollars to your bottom line through generous rewards and interest savings.

I can't stress enough that playing by the rules is crucial. You now know what they are, so abide by them. Keep your eyes on your credit reports and scores. Be sure to respond promptly if you see any errors or signs of identity theft. Finally, remember that you aren't married to your credit card! If you aren't happy with the terms and conditions of your current card, by all means, shop elsewhere for a better deal.

The rest is up to you. I sure hope you'll give my novel approach to cards a try. Let me know how you make out on CardRatings.com's forum, where you can share your tips and insights, as well as get some up-to-the-minute credit news and ideas. Maybe it's my Southern heritage, but I would like to think that we're friends now—see you on the Web, good buddy!

In closing, remember this: If you always pay your bills on time, don't spend more than your budget allows, view your cards as useful tools, stay on top of your credit picture, and always pay attention to the fine print, you'll be well on your way to a bright financial future. As I added the finishing touches to this book, I was listening to the radio and a line of a country song caught my attention. The song talked about how much the artist had learned in the later stages of his life. One of things he said he learned was that credit cards don't make you rich. I chuckled when I heard this! While I agree with this statement for this most part, I would argue that cards can indeed enhance your finances. So, go forth and profit from cards. You deserve it. Enjoy the ride—I know I am! ☺

Glossary

affinity credit card
A credit card typically offered through a partnership between a lending institution and a nonfinancial organization such as a school or a nonprofit. Generally, the organization receives a small percentage of each purchase made on the card. Additionally, cardholders might receive discounts or special deals from the organization.

amount due
Refers to the minimum amount due (usually about 2% of the entire balance).

annual fee
A yearly credit card usage charge billed directly to the consumer's credit card account. Annual fees usually range from $15 to $85.

annual percentage rate (APR)
A yearly interest rate used to determine finance charges. The APR must be disclosed for credit card purchases, cash advances, penalty rates, and so on.

authorized user
Anyone a cardholder legally permits to use his or her credit card. Authorized users are not legally responsible for charges made to a card, and their credit scores are unaffected by their ability to use the cards.

average daily balance
Daily totals of charges minus payments divided by the number of days in the billing cycle.

average daily balance billing method
For this method of calculating interest, the average daily balance is multiplied by the monthly periodic interest rate.

balance transfer
A balance transfer occurs when you move the amount you owe from one credit card to another, ideally to get a lower interest rate. Balance transfers have an annual percentage rate (APR) that is often different from the APR for purchases.

bankruptcy, Chapter 7
A type of bankruptcy that sells nonexempt property and then uses the proceeds to pay back creditors.

bankruptcy, Chapter 11
A bankruptcy plan that requires a company or debtor to go through the process of reorganization. Usually involves a corporation or partnership, but individuals and proprietors can also file a Chapter 11 bankruptcy.

bankruptcy, Chapter 13
A type of bankruptcy in which the debtor does not have to immediately forfeit property, but the debtor must have a steady source of income and a specific repayment plan. Individuals usually have three to five years to repay the debt.

cap
The maximum amount of an interest rate or a fee. An interest rate cap limits how much the charge for borrowing money can go up. A fee cap is the maximum amount you would have to pay— for a balance transfer, for example.

cash advance
The use of a credit card to get cash. Cardholders typically get cash advances from ATM machines, and issuers typically charge a much higher APR for cash advances than they do for purchases.

cash advance fee
A bank charge collected when a consumer uses a credit card to get cash. It is either a flat per-transaction fee or a percentage based on the amount of the cash advance. Some banks deduct the fee from the cash received; others charge the fee to the credit card account. Cash advance fees normally do not have a cap.

consumer credit counseling
Typically a paid service for consumers that helps them set up a budget and repayment plan with creditors. The counselor also usually tries to work with creditors to lower interest rates and fees. Reputable services will provide some free counseling.

credit bureau
A company that gathers information about consumers' credit habits and then sells it to third parties that have a legal and legitimate need for it, such as creditors and employers. The reports they sell generally have information on consumers' debt and payment history, available unused credit, and loan application history. Equifax, Experian, and TransUnion are the three major national credit bureaus. Also known as a credit reporting agency or a consumer reporting agency.

credit card
A plastic card used for purchases that is linked to the cardholder's revolving line of credit with a financial institution.

credit limit
The maximum amount of money available for use on a revolving line of credit such as a credit card. Most experts say you shouldn't exceed 10% of your credit line for credit scoring reasons.

credit line
The amount of credit available on a revolving debt. Also referred to as credit limit.

credit rating
A numerical ranking based on a consumer's financial information reported by credit bureaus. It judges a consumer's ability to repay debts based on income and credit history and is expressed in numerical form such as a FICO credit score.

credit report
The details of your personal and financial history collected by a credit reporting agency, which is also called a credit file. Included is information on your debts and payments, available unused credit, and loan application history. Lenders review your credit report in determining whether to approve your requests to borrow money—whether it's for a credit card, car loan, or mortgage. Landlords, employers, and insurers also view credit reports for decision-making purposes.

credit reporting agency
A company that gathers information about consumers' credit habits and then sells it to third parties that have a legal and legitimate need for it, such as creditors and employers. Equifax, Experian, and TransUnion are the three major national credit reporting agencies. Also known as a credit bureau or a consumer reporting agency.

credit score
A formula that assigns numerical values to certain credit-worthiness factors and then calculates the likelihood of a debtor repaying the debt. FICO credit scores, which most lenders turn to when making decisions about issuing credit, range from a low 300 up to 850.

debit card
A plastic card used for purchases that is linked directly to the cardholder's bank account, from which funds are taken for a purchase. PIN-based debit cards take the funds from the account almost immediately after a purchase. Signature-based credit cards take the funds from the account up to a few days later.

debt consolidation
Replacing multiple loans with a single loan. Debt consolidation usually results in a cheaper monthly payment but a longer term (or a longer length of the loan).

debt-to-income ratio
A financial percentage that compares the total amount paid toward debt to income. It is calculated by dividing your total monthly debt payments—including home, auto, student loans, and credit cards—by your monthly net income. Less than 30% is excellent, 30%–36% is good, 36%–40% is borderline, and 40% or higher is a red flag.

default
Failure to meet the requirements of a financial or legal obligation, such as not making payments or going over the credit limit. It is also a description used on credit reports for accounts that have not been paid according to the terms and conditions. A default is usually reported after several delinquencies and is a negative indicator for credit scoring.

default APR
Annual percentage rate charged if you fail to meet the terms on a credit card account, such as making a late payment, exceeding your credit limit, or if your payment to the card issuer is not honored (commonly called a bounced check).

encryption software
Software that websites use to protect customers' personal information, especially financial information. Encryption scrambles data so that only the person intended to receive the information can access it. It is important to ensure encryption software is being used before you send any type of personal information (such as a credit card information) for an online purchase.

extended fraud alert
A warning cardholders can ask the credit bureaus to place on their credit reports when they have been a victim of identity theft. In place for seven years, it requires that creditors contact you directly or meet you in person before they extend credit to you.

Federal Trade Commission (FTC)
A federal agency that works to protect consumers by enforcing consumer protection laws passed by Congress, including the Fair Credit Billing Act, Fair Credit Reporting Act, Equal Opportunity Act, Fair Debt Collection Practices Act, Truth-in-Lending Act, and Home Ownership and Equity Protection Act. The FTC also issues regulations that lenders must follow and offers consumer advice.

FICO score
The credit scoring system developed by Fair Isaac Corporation and used by most mortgage lenders and credit card issuers to determine the degree of risk potential borrowers pose. FICO scores range from 300-850. The higher your score, the better.

finance charge
Interest charged on outstanding credit card balances.

fixed rate
An interest rate that does not vary as much as a variable rate. Although some credit cards are advertised as having fixed rates, issuers can normally change a rate at any time as well as modify the terms and conditions.

floor
The lowest possible rate you can receive on a credit card or other revolving loan. For example, if the terms of a credit card read "prime + 4% with a floor of 9%," your interest rate will still remain at 9%, even if prime drops below 5%.

fraud alert
A warning you can add to your credit report that lets potential creditors know that you may be a victim of identity theft and requires that they take extra steps to verify your identity before issuing credit.

fresh start
The status of a debtor after bankruptcy.

gift card
A card with a built-in spending limit (e.g. $25) that has been issued by a store or a lender, usually in exchange for payment, but sometimes as a reward. Department store gift cards may be used only in that store, while gift cards with a Visa, MasterCard, Discover, or American Express logo can generally be used wherever the card is accepted.

grace period
The amount of time you have, typically after a billing period ends, to pay off your credit card balance before you're charged interest. Typically 20 to 25 days long, a grace period is in effect *only* when you are not carrying a balance.

hard inquiry
A request for a copy of your credit report in response to your application for credit, which will be factored in when your credit score is being calculated.

home equity
The portion of the current market value of a home that is not financed by a mortgage or other loan. Typically includes the amount of the homeowner's down payment, principal payments on loans, and appreciation.

home equity line of credit (HELOC)
A credit line where the amount that the borrower owns outright in a home is used as the collateral. A maximum dollar amount is set by the lender, and the homeowner can use some or all of the credit line during the time frame determined by the lender. Typically, borrowers have more flexibility with the repayment terms on HELOCs than on other home loans.

identity theft
Your personal information is stolen and used to obtain credit, goods, services, and/or cash.

index
A well-publicized interest rate that serves as the basis for making changes to the interest rate on credit cards and adjustable rate mortgages. A credit card's interest rate might fluctuate along with the prime rate listed in *The Wall Street Journal*. To determine the actual rate, lenders typically add a set number of percentage points to the index.

initial fraud alert
A 90-day warning that cardholders can ask the credit bureaus to place on their credit reports. If you have one added to your credit report, it will tell creditors that you *may* have been a victim of identity theft (for example, your wallet is missing). Before they give you credit, they must use "reasonable policies and procedures" to verify your identity.

inquiry
A look at your credit report by someone with a "permissible purpose." Lenders viewing your report in response to your requests for credit place hard inquiries on your report, which lower your credit score. When they look to decide whether to send you a card offer, it's called a soft inquiry and doesn't affect your score.

installment loan
A loan where a set number of regular payments are required over a specified term. Typically, the required payments are each for the same amount. Examples include fixed-rate mortgages and car loans.

interest
A percent of the amount of money you borrow that the lender charges for your use of the money. Also called a finance charge.

interest rate
The specific amount of interest charged. For example, a credit card might have an interest rate of 16.99% per year. Also called Annual Percentage Rate (APR).

introductory rate
Also known as a teaser rate, this is the low amount of interest that lenders charge for a few months up to a year or more, in the hope of getting us to apply for and use their cards. Typically, an introductory rate applies to purchases *or* balance transfers, which then rises to a higher APR after the introductory time has elapsed.

issuer
A bank or other lender that gives credit cards at varying interest rates and terms, based on its own definitions of creditworthiness and marketing strategies.

joint account
A credit card account shared by two (or more) people. Each person on the account is legally responsible for any debts that are incurred, and the account will show on each person's credit report.

judgment
A court decision that determines how much money you have to pay to satisfy a debt or as a penalty. Judgments remain on your reports for at least seven years and will lower your credit score significantly.

late charge
A fee assessed when a cardholder does not pay on time. Late fees can be as high as $39, as of this writing.

liability
Financial and legal debts that a borrower is responsible for repaying.

LIBOR
London Interbank Offered Rate. The interest rate banks are charged to borrow money from other banks in the London wholesale money market, which is usually lower than the prime interest rate used in the U.S. An index used for a few variable-rate credit cards issued in the U.S.

merged credit report
A combined summary of a consumer's credit history from the three major credit bureaus, Equifax, Experian, and TransUnion.

minimum payment
The smallest payment amount a creditor will accept on a credit card account in order to prevent the account from going into default. Typically, the minimum payment on credit cards is about 2% of the amount you owe (your balance).

monthly periodic rate
Monthly interest rate. Annual Percentage Rate (APR) divided by 12 (number of months in a year).

nondischargeable debt
In bankruptcy, a debt that cannot be absolved.

over-the-limit fee
A fee assessed when cardholders charge more than the allowed credit limit. Over limit fees can be up to $39, as of this writing.

penalty APR
Also known as default APR. The annual percentage rate charged if you default on the account, by making a late payment, exceeding your credit limit, having a bank not honor your payment, and so on.

periodic rate
The interest rate and how it relates to a period of time. The cost of debt per month is called the monthly periodic rate, and the cost of debt per day is called the daily periodic rate.

PIN
Personal identification number. A consumer-chosen, confidential code usually consisting of four to six digits that allows only the individual access to account information and use of a debit card at an ATM machine or with a merchant. Also, credit cards normally require PINs to withdraw cash from an ATM.

preapproved
Indication that a consumer has passed the initial credit screening requirements. Credit card companies can still deny credit or offer credit with higher interest rates if an applicant's credit rating doesn't meet their requirements. An example is a preapproved credit card offer that you get in the mail.

prime
The lowest interest rate banks charge their most creditworthy customers, usually corporations. The most common index used for variable-rate credit cards. Often, creditors use the prime rate as listed in *The Wall Street Journal* as the basis for their rates.

purchase APR
The annual percentage rate charged when you carry a balance month-to-month on any goods and services bought with your card.

rate
An amount expressed as a percentage that a consumer agrees to pay for borrowed money.

rebate card
A credit card that rewards customers with cash, merchandise, gift cards, or other services based on the amount charged to the card.

retroactive interest
Additional interest that lenders "go back" and charge. Card issuers using the two-cycle billing method charge retroactive interest on unpaid balances over a two-month period. Also refers to the interest lenders are currently able to charge on already existing balances when they raise the rate, even though the debt was incurred at a lower rate.

revolving credit
A type of credit line that does not have a specific repayment schedule, but requires a monthly minimum payment that pays interest and usually some principal on the debt. Credit cards have revolving credit lines.

same-as-cash
A way to purchase items such as furniture and electronics where the consumer has a certain amount of time to pay the bill, also known as "buy now, pay later, no interest"

loans. Typically, if full payment is made by the due date, which might be a year, no interest is charged. However, if even the smallest balance remains, interest is charged retroactively.

secured credit card
A credit card typically used by people with no credit or poor credit. In exchange for a card, they deposit funds into a savings account that the bank could use to pay the debt if the cardholder defaults. The deposited funds serve as a form of collateral.

secured debt
A debt that is backed by something that has monetary value, such as a house or a car, that the creditor can claim if the debtor fails to pay.

secured loan
A loan that is secured with collateral. For example, the collateral of an auto loan is the car that was purchased. If the borrower fails to repay the loan, the lender has the right to take the collateral.

security
Property that is used to secure a loan, also called collateral. If the individual fails to follow the terms and conditions, the bank can claim the property.

soft inquiry
A view of your credit report for reasons not having to do with an application from you for credit, and therefore, is not factored in to your credit score. For example, when a creditor utilizes your credit report for the purposes of offering you a preapproved credit card offer, it shows up as a soft inquiry.

spread
A set number of percentage points, also known as "basis points." To determine the rate on variable rate cards, lenders add the spread to the index. For a rate of "prime + 5%," you would add the prime rate of 5.25% (as of this writing) to the spread of 5%, which equals a rate of 10.25% on the card.

teaser rate
An introductory interest rate, usually well below the going market rate, used to attract new customers. A typical teaser rate would be a 0% rate on balance transfers for 6-12 months.

term
The amount of time, usually expressed in months or years, until a loan or debt is to be completely paid off.

two-cycle billing
A method for calculating interest based on the sum of the average daily balance for the previous and current billing cycles. Also known as double-cycle billing.

unsecured loan
A loan that is not backed by collateral. Credit cards are considered unsecured loans.

variable rate
An interest rate that changes according to the fluctuations of a specific index (for example, prime and LIBOR).

INDEX

A

AARP Rewards Platinum
Visa, 293
Accelerated Debt
Management, 110
account retention
department, 64
active-duty alerts, 215
Advanta Bank Corp., 73, 187
AFC (annualized finance
charge), 123
affinity cards, 199-203
airline reward cards, 43-45
bonus miles, 48-49
expiration dates, 46-47
fees, 45-46
losing rewards, 47-48
tips for frequent flyers, 49
American Express
Blue Cash card, 35
business cards, 187
Plum Card, 192
Private Payments, 152
American Express
Centurion, 204
annual fees, reward cards, 32
annual percentage rate. See APR
annualcreditreport.com, 211
annualized finance charge
(AFC), 123

App-O-Rama, 269-272
APR (annual percentate rate), 58
balance transfer APR, 58
default/penalty APR, 58
Introductory APR, 18
arbitration, mandatory
arbitration, 17
armed forces credit report rights,
active-duty alert, 215
automatic bill payments, 84
avoiding
credit card debt, 77
actively managing finances,
78-79
avoiding extra expenses,
81-82
cash advances, 85-86
getting support and save
money, 80
is a credit card right for
you?, 82
keeping perspective, 77-78
limiting cards, 85
paying balances in full, 82
paying early, 83
plan and save, 86-87
say no, 86
treat cards like cash, 84-85
default rates, 66

minimum payment trap,
  96-97
online fraud, 150-151
universal default, 277-278

B

BabyMint, 174
Baker, Gina, 186
balance transfer APR, 58
balance transfer fees, 13
balance transfer offers, 106-107
balance transfers, 69-73
balances, paying in full, 82
Bank of America, affinity
  cards, 200
bankruptcy, 116-118
  accounts handed to bill
    collectors, 225
  Chapter 7 bankruptcy,
    117, 225
  Chapter 13 bankruptcy,
    117, 225
  don'ts of working with
    collection agencies and
    creditors, 224
  protecting credit reports
    during, 223-227
  rebuilding credit, 227
Bilker, Scott, 61, 70, 72
billing cycles, 12
binding arbitration, 16
biweekly credit card payments,
  262-264
Black card, 204
Bland, Paul, 17
blank checks, 69-73
blink cards, Chase, 287
bonus miles, airline reward
  cards, 48-49

brand loyalty, college
  students, 156
budgets, 78
business cards, 186
  benefits of, 186-188
  choosing, 191-193
  credit criteria for, 188-189
  rebates, 189-191
Buxx card (Visa), 165
"Buy Now, Pay Later, No
  Interest" offers, 195

C

calculators, credit calculators, 99
Campbell, Dr. Mary Ann,
  31, 168
Capital One, 73
caps, reward cards, 37
card features, 19-21
card protection services, 251-253
card registration services,
  251-253
CardRatings.com, 8
Carpenter, Willard B., 148
Carte Blanche Card (Diners
  Club), 205-206
cash advances, 85-86
  fees, 122-123
  interest rates, 123-124
cash-back cards, 30-32
  529 college savings plans, 40
  caps, 37
  choosing, 32-33
  everyday purchases, 34
  mortgages, paying down,
    39-40
  receiving the money, 37
  saving rewards, 40
  tiered cards, 35-36

Castleman, Nancy, 66, 223
catalog cards, 130-131
CDW (collision damage
    waiver), 244
Center for Economic Justice,
    credit insurance, 256
changing terms, reward cards, 38
Chapter 7 bankruptcy, 117, 225
Chapter 13 bankruptcy, 117, 225
chargeback privileges, 5
Charles Schwab, 76
Chase, 55
    +1 card, 161
    billing cycles, 13
    contactless cards, 287
    Facebook, 161
    Freedom Card, 26
    universal default, 276
Chase Freedom Card, 29
check cards. *See* debit cards
ChoiceTrust, 212
choosing
    business cards, 191-193
    cash-back cards, 32-33
    credit cards, 6-8
        billing cycles, 12
        card features, 19-21
        fees, 13-14
        fine print, 14-19
        understanding terms and
            conditions, 9-11
Citi Chairman American Express
    Card, 251
Citi Diamond Preferred
    MasterCard, 247
Citi Dividend Platinum Select
    MasterCard, 34
Citi Home Rebate card, 39
Citi/AAdvantage card, 25

Citibank, 55
    MTVu card, 162
    secured cards, 184
    universal default, 276
Citibank Cash Returns Card, 36
CLUE (Comprehensive Loss
    Underwriting Exchange), 212
cobranded cards, 199-203
collection agencies
    complaints about, 226
    don'ts of working with, 224
college students
    credit cards and, 156-157,
        177-178
        advice from other students,
            169-172
        developing a new view
            about, 168-169
        marketing, 157-158
    debt, 159
    keeping your credit good, 168
    tips for credit card use,
        166-167
college tuition, saving for,
    172-173
    529 college savings plans, 173
    spending to invest, 173-176
collision coverage, 244-245
collision damage waiver
    (CDW), 244
comparing reward cards, 50
comparison shopping for lower
    interest rates, 61-63
complaints about collection
    agencies/creditors, 226
Comprehensive Loss
    Underwriting Exchange
    (CLUE), 212
consolidating debt, 104-105

Consumer Action, 54-55, 67,
124-126
consumer protection, 5-6
Consumer Reports, extended
warranties, 241
consumer rights, 127
contactless cards, 285-287
convenience checks, 124
correcting credit reports,
215-222
Craig, Jonathan, 76
credit
building/rebuilding with
secured cards, 185
rebuilding after
bankruptcy, 227
credit calculators, 99
credit card arbitrage, 265-269
App-O-Rama, 269-272
credit card companies, deals with
schools, 160-162
credit card debt. *See* debt
credit card payments, biweekly
payments, 262-264
credit card protection insurance,
254-256
credit card Russian Roulette, 90
credit cards
affinity cards, 199-203
basics of, 3
business cards. *See* business
cards
choosing, 6-8
billing cycles, 12
card features, 19-21
fees, 13-14
fine print, 14-19
terms and conditions, 9-11

college students, 156-157,
177-178
advice from other students,
169-172
developing a new view
about, 168-169
keeping your credit
good, 168
marketing, 157-158
tips for credit card use,
166-167
versus debit cards, 4
establishing credit, 6
making money with, 264-265
credit card arbitrage,
265-272
platinum cards, 203
power of, 1-3
prestige cards. *See* prestige
cards
secured cards. *See* secured
cards
for seniors, 292
store cards, 193-198
multiple accounts, 196-197
taxes, paying, 272-274
teens and, 164-166
credit counseling, 109-113
credit disability insurance, 254
credit discrimination, 127-129
credit education programs, Wells
Fargo, 297
credit freezing, 147
credit history, credit scores, 231
credit insurance, 254-256
credit involuntary unemployment
insurance, 254
credit life insurance, 254
credit lines, reallocating, 259-262

credit property insurance, 254
credit repair scams, 131-132
credit report rights, 214
credit reports, 213-214
  active-duty alerts, 215
  common errors, 216-217
  correcting, 215-222
  free annual reports, 210-212
  protecting during bankruptcy,
    223-227
  writing statements for, 222
credit scores, 6, 168
  FICO, 233. See also FICO
  finding, 234-235
  free credit scores, 228
  how they work, 229-230
    credit history, 231
    credit inquiries and new
      credit, 232
    mix of credit, 232
    payment history, 230
    utilization, 230-231
  improving, 227-228
  low-rate cards, 68-69
credit unions, interest rates, 62
CreditCardNation.com, 163, 169
creditors, complaints about, 226

D

daily periodic rates, 58
deadbeats, 2
debit cards
  basics of, 4
  versus credit cards, 4
  liability laws, 5
debt, 75
  avoiding, 77
    actively managing finances,
      78-79

    avoiding extra expenses,
      81-82
    cash advances, 85-86
    getting support and saving
      money, 80
    is a credit card right for
      you?, 82
    keeping perspective, 77-78
    limiting cards, 85
    paying balances in full, 82
    paying early, 83
    planning and saving, 86-87
    saying no, 86
    treating cards like cash,
      84-85
  bankruptcy, 116-118
    Chapter 7 bankruptcy, 117
    Chapter 13 bankruptcy, 117
  college students, 159
  depression and, 76
  diagnosing the problem,
    91-92
  fraud and, 132
  planning debt-defying
    strategies, 92
    avoiding minimum payment
      trap, 96-97
    finding extra cash, 94-96
    going cold turkey, 92-93
    living within your means, 93
  professional help, 109
    credit counseling, 109-113
  repayment plans
    asking credit card companies
      to work with you, 102-103
    balance transfer offers,
      106-107
    consolidation, 104-105
    facing your debt, 98-99

finding true cost of your debt, 99-102
home equity, 107-108
paying highest-rate card first, 103
paying lowest balance first, 104
revolving debt, 2
senior debt, 291-292
warning signs "you're-over-your-head-in-debt," 90-91
debt-defying strategies, 92
  avoiding minimum payment trap, 96-97
  finding extra cash, 94-96
  going cold turkey, 92-93
  living within your means, 93
debt settlement/negotiation, 114-115
default rates, 67
  avoiding, 66
default/penalty APR, 58
Demel, Heshan, 48, 73
department store cards, 193-198
  multiple accounts, 196-197
depression, debt and, 76
Detweiler, Gerri, 61, 90, 132, 188, 197
Diners Club card, 120
Diners Club Carte Blanche Card, 205-206
disadvantages of reward cards, 27-28
discounts
  international travel discounts, 249-251
  special merchandise discounts, 242-243
Discover Business Card, 190

Discover Business Miles Card, 190
Discover Card
  Motiva card, 297
  residual interest, 126
  reward cards, 25
  special merchandise discounts, 242
discrimination, credit discrimination, 127-129
DMP (debt management plan), 112-113
Ducks Unlimited, 203
Dvorkin, Howard, 84

E

Eisenson, Marc, 263
Enderle, Mark, 132, 216
environmental concerns, 293
errors on credit reports, 216-217
  correcting, 218-222
establishing credit, 6
everyday purchases, 34
expenses, avoiding extra expenses, 81-82
expiration dates, airline reward cards, 46-47
extended fraud alert, 143
extended warranties, 240-242

F

529 College Rewards American Express, 174
529 college savings plans, 172-173
  reward cards, 40
Facebook, Chase, 161
FACTA (Fair and Accurate Credit Transactions Act), 210

Fair Credit Billing Act
(FCBA), 239
FAKO, 233
family loans, 105
FCBA (Fair Credit Billing
Act), 239
fees, 13-14, 65-66
  airline reward cards, 45-46
  annual fees, reward cards, 32
  balance transfer fees, 13
  cash advance fees, 122-123
  for paying taxes with credit
    cards, 272
  secured cards, 182
FFP (frequent-flyer
  programs), 44
FICO, 228
  how they work, 230
    credit history, 231
    *credit inquiries and new
      credit,* 232
    mix of credit, 232
    payment history, 230
    utilization, 230-231
  users of, 233
FICO 08, 228
Fidelity, 529 College Rewards
  American Express
  card, 174
finance charges, 58
finding
  credit scores, 234-235
  secured cards, 182
fine print, 14-19
  secured cards, 183
Fish, Desiree, 204
fixed rates, 57-58
  versus variable rates, 53-57
floors, 54

Flur, Peter, 27
Foreman, Gary, 44
fraud, 130
  credit repair scams, 131-132
  debt and, 132
  fraud protection scams, 133
  online fraud, tips for
    avoiding, 150-151
  pay-first guaranteed loan
    scams, 130
  phishing, 135-138
  protecting yourself from, 149
  reporting, 135
  senior citizens, 133-134
  skimming, 138
  tips for avoiding, 153-154
fraud protection scams, 133
free credit reports, 210-212
frequent flyers, tips for, 49
frequent-flyer programs
  (FFPs), 43
Frequentflier.com, 44
future card trends
  cards accepted in new places,
    283-285
  issuers will keep finding new
    markets, 288-290
  new incentives to watch for,
    296-297
  new incentives will be trendy,
    targeted and practical,
    293-295
  senior debt, 291-292
  smarter cards, 285-287

G

gas rebate credit cards, 41-42
global warming, 293
Goodman, Jordan, 108

government intervention,
  universal default, 279
grace periods, 120-122
Grapevine, 27

H

Hammer, R. K., 13, 15
healthy living card, 296
HELOC (home equity line of
  credit), 107
Holmquist, Lars, 28
home equity, 107-108
home equity line of credit
  (HELOC), 107
Humane Society of the United
  States, affinity cards, 200
Hunt, David, 172

I

identities, ways thieves rob
  you, 139
identity theft, 130, 139-140
  actions to take if you know
    you are a victim, 142-146
  actions to take if you think
    you are a victim, 141-143
Identity Theft Affidavit, 145
identity theft insurance, 147
identity theft report, 143
improving credit scores, 227-228
InCharge Institute, 233
Indymac Bank, 296
inital fraud alert, 141
inquiries, credit scores, 232
installment payment plans,
  taxes, 274
insurance
  credit insurance, 254-256

identity theft insurance, 147
rental car insurance, 244-247
travel insurance, 243-244
interest charges, 58
interest (earned), secured
  cards, 183
interest rates, 52
  cash advances, 123-124
  fixed rates, 57-58
  fixed versus variable rates,
    53-57
  how rates are configured, 52
  lowering, 58-60
    comparison shopping, 61-63
  negotiating better rates, 63-65
  residual interest, 124-126
  secured cards, 183
international travel discounts,
  249-251
Introductory APR, 18
introductory offers, 69-73
  paying down loans, 74

J

JCPenney, 193
JumpStart Coalition for Personal
  Financial Literacy, 164

K

Killian, Mike, 83
Kuhlmann, Arkadi, 157

L

late payments, 69
Lawrence, Judy, 28
LDW (loss damage waiver), 244
lenders, universal default,
  280-281

liability coverage, 245
liability laws, 4-5
LIBOR (London Interbank
Offered Rate), 53
Lifelock, 148
live within your means, 93
loans
debt-consolidation loans, 104
family loans, 105
paying down with low-rate
credit cards, 74
London Interbank Offered Rate
(LIBOR), 53
losing rewards, airline reward
cards, 47-48
loss damage waiver (LDW), 244
lost luggage help, 249
low-rate cards, tips for using,
66-69
low-rate introductory offers,
69-73
paying down loans, 74
lowering interest rates, 58-60
comparison shopping, 61-63

M

Macy's Card, 194
mail solicitations, 8
reward cards, 25
managing finances, avoiding
credit card debt, 78-79
mandatory arbitration, 17
Manning, Robert, 156-157, 163,
169, 181
marketing credit cards to college
students, 157-158
markets, issuers will keep finding
new markets, 288-290

McAlister, Jevon, 65
means test, 225
Medical Information
Bureau, 212
merchants, qualifying merchants,
34-35
merged files, 217
micro transactions, 286
minimum payment trap,
avoiding, 96-97
Mintel Comperemedia, 26
money-management skills, teens,
162-164
Morris, Cindy, 92
mortgages
paying down with reward
cards, 39-40
rebates on mortgage
payments, 295
reverse mortgages, 292
Motiva card (Discover
Card), 297
moving credit limits from one
card to another, 259-262
Moyer, Sean, 159-160
MTVu card (Citibank), 162
multiple accounts, 196-197

N

National Foundation for Credit
Counseling (NFCC), 91
negotiating interest rates, 63-65
NellieMae.org, 159
The Net, 139
NFCC (National Foundation for
Credit Counseling), 91

O

O'Donnell, Janne M., 160
online fraud, tips for avoiding,
  150-151
online security, 151-152
  virtual numbers, 152-153

P

+1 card (Chase), 161
passwords, 141
pay-first guaranteed loan
  scams, 130
paying down loans with low-rate
  credit cards, 74
paying taxes with credit cards,
  272-274
payment history, credit
  scores, 230
payments, biweekly payments,
  262-264
perks
  card registration services,
    251-253
  credit card protection
    insurance, 254-256
  extended warranties, 240-242
  international travel discounts,
    249-251
  lost luggage help, 249
  price protection, 247-248
  purchase protection, 238-240
  rental car insurance, 244-247
  special merchandise discounts,
    242-243
  travel insurance, 243-244
perspective, avoiding credit card
  debt, 77-78
phishing, 135-138

PINs, 141
plan and save, avoiding debt,
  86-87
platinum cards, 203
Plum Card (American
  Express), 192
popularity of reward cards,
  25-27
power of credit cards, 1-3
preapproved offers, 7
prepaid teen cards, 288-290
prestige cards
  American Express
    Centurion, 204
  Diners Club Carte Blanche
    Card, 205-206
  keeping spending in check,
    206
price protection, 247-248
prime rates, 53
problems, diagnosing debt
  problems, 91-92
professional help for debt, 109
  credit counseling, 109-113
protecting
  credit reports during
    bankruptcy, 223-227
  yourself from fraud, 149
Pulaski Bank, 122
purchase acceleration, 28
purchase protection, 238-240
Putman, Steve, 200

Q

qualifying merchants, 34-35

R

Rachakonda, Sastry, 189
rate hikes, 54-56

reallocating credit lines, 259-262
rebates on mortgage
payments, 295
rebuilding credit after
bankruptcy, 227
Renick, Sam X., 163
rental car insurance, 244-247
repayment plans, 98
asking credit card companies
to work with you, 102-103
balance transfer offers,
106-107
consolidation, 104-105
facing your debt, 98-99
finding true cost of your debt,
99-102
home equity, 107-108
paying highest-rate card
first, 103
paying lowest balance first,
104
reporting fraud, 135
reports, other free reports you
may want to get, 212
residual interest, 124-126
retail cards, 193-198
multiple accounts, 196-197
reverse mortgages, 292
revolving debt, 2
reward cards, 20-24
529 college savings plans, 40
airline reward cards, 43-45
bonus miles, 48-49
expiration dates, 46-47
fees, 45-46
losing and using rewards,
47-48
tips for frequent flyers, 49

caps, 37
cash-back cards. *See*
cash-back cards
comparing, 50
disadvantages of, 27-28
Discover, 25
gas rebate credit cards, 41-42
history of, 25
popularity of, 25-27
spending levels, 28-29
terms, changing, 38
time limits, 36
years, 38
Rigg, Terry, 28

S

saving
cash-back rewards, 40
for college tuition, 172-173
529 college savings plans,
173
spending to invest, 173-176
money, 80
Savingforcollege.com, 173
scams, 133. *See also* fraud
schools, deals with credit card
companies, 158-162
Schumer Box, 10-11
Schumer, Senator Chuck, 10
secured cards, 180-181
benefits of, 181-182
building or rebuilding your
credit, 185
Citibank, 184
earned interest, 183
fees, 182
finding, 182
fine print, 183

interest rates, 183
what to do if you're
denied, 184
security, online security, 151-152
senior citizens, fraud, 133-134
senior debt, 291-292
Shell, gas rebate credit cards, 41
Sherry, Linda, 54, 125
skimming, 138
small businesses, rebate cards,
189-191
smarter cards, 285-287
special merchandise discounts,
242-243
spending levels, 28
reward cards, 28-29
spending to invest, saving for
college tuition, 173-176
split files, 216
spread, 53
Stoller, Ira, 7, 37, 136
Stretcher.com, 44
subprime cards, 65

T

tax savings, credit rebates, 176
taxes
installment payment
plans, 274
paying with credit cards,
272-274
teens
credit cards and, 164-166
money-management skills,
162-164
prepaid teen cards, 288-290
terms, reward cards
(changing), 38

terms and conditions,
understanding, 9-10
Schumer Box, 10-11
tiered cards, 35-36
time limits, reward cards, 36
TJX, 140
trailing interest, 124, 126
travel, international travel
discounts, 250-251
travel insurance, 243-244
trends, future card trends
cards will be accepted in new
places, 283-285
issuers will keep finding new
markets, 288-290
new incentives to watch for,
296-297
new incentives will be trendy,
target, and practical,
293-295
senior debt, 291-292
smarter cards, 285-287

U

universal default, 14-16, 274-276
avoiding, 277-278
Chase, 276
Citibank, 276
government intervention in,
279
lenders, 280-281
universities, deals with credit
card companies, 158-162
utilization, credit scores, 230-231

V

VantageScore, 234
variable rates, 58
versus fixed rates, 53-57

vending machines, 283-284
Ventura, John, 102, 131, 224
Verified by Visa, 152
verifying credit reports, 215-216
virtual cards, 152
virtual numbers, 152-153
Visa, Buxx card, 165
Visa Signature Cards, 205

W

warranties, extended warranties,
  240-242
Warranty Week, 241
Washington Mutual, free credit
  scores, 228
Watts, Craig, 231
Wells Fargo, credit education
  program, 297
Weston, Liz Pulliam, 116, 118,
  209, 235, 266, 292
Winship, Tim, 44, 47
World Master Cards, 205
writing statements for credit
  reports, 222

Y

Yapp, Carolyn, 41
year, reward cards, 38

Z

ZipDebt, 115

FT Press

FINANCIAL TIMES

In an increasingly competitive world, it is quality
of thinking that gives an edge—an idea that opens new
doors, a technique that solves a problem, or an insight
that simply helps make sense of it all.

We work with leading authors in the various arenas
of business and finance to bring cutting-edge thinking
and best-learning practices to a global market.

It is our goal to create world-class print publications
and electronic products that give readers
knowledge and understanding that can then be
applied, whether studying or at work.

To find out more about our business
products, you can visit us at www.ftpress.com.